O9-AIG-785

THE MIND AT NIGHT

THE MIND AT NIGHT

The New Science of How and Why We Dream

Andrea Rock

A Member of the Perseus Books Group
New York

Published by Basic Books,
A Member of the Perseus Books Group

Library of Congress Cataloging-in-Publication Data
Rock, Andrea.
The mind at night : the new science of how and why we dream / Andrea Rock.—1st ed.
p. cm.
Includes bibliographical references.
ISBN 0-7382-0755-1
1. Dreams—Physiological aspects—Popular works. I. Title.

QP426.R63 2004
154.6'3—dc22

2003022389

Text design by Reginald R. Thompson
Set in 11-point CG Elante by Perseus Books Group

First Edition
1 2 3 4 5 6 7 8 9 10—06 05 04

Contents

Preface

I'VE ALWAYS WONDERED WHY my brain doesn't simply rest at night, as my body does, but instead sets to work creating an artificial world that seems as real as waking life. I don't recall my dreams with any greater frequency than most people I know, but I'm intrigued by the ones I do remember and curious about what—if anything—they mean.

Often I awaken with no memory of dreaming at all, but sometimes, my experiences in that part of my life are so vivid that my mood for the day is colored by them. My dreams of flying come only two or three times a year but they are exhilarating. Making more frequent appearances in my night life, though, are the classic anxiety dreams in which I show up to take an exam for a course I've never attended or I arrive at a party and belatedly realize I'm missing vital pieces of clothing. Then there are the out-of-control dreams, in which I'm driving a car that loses its brakes or its steering just as I start down a steep, winding hill, or the pursuit dreams, where I'm being chased by some dangerous person or creature. The common thread is that all of the dreams feel utterly real, from the visual details down to the emotions they trigger.

In discussing dreams with friends, I have found that the themes in mine seem to be quite common, as is my curiosity about them. I was particularly intrigued when I came across an essay by the late physicist Richard Feynman in which he posed many of the same questions about dreaming that I had. Like Feynman, I was intensely curious about why images in dreams looked so real, but I also wondered how they could *feel* so much like waking life. My terror when I periodically dream of my children falling from a cliff or out a window is so physiologically real that I wake with my heart racing. Mulling over the mystery of what happens to our stream of consciousness when sleep descends, Feynman zeroed in on other fascinating questions: "What happens to your ideas? You're running along very well, you're thinking clearly and what happens? Do they suddenly stop, or do they go more and more slowly and stop, or exactly how do you turn off thought?"

As I discovered in the course of research for this book, you don't turn off thought. It just takes a different form. Feynman lamented the fact that he was unable to find answers to his questions about dreaming because there had been so little scientific investigation of the subject. But thanks to the dream research that has unfolded in the past two decades, many of those answers are now becoming available. I discovered surprising explanations about why dreams look and feel so real—fascinating in themselves but deeply revealing about how the mind works in waking consciousness. In fact, understanding more about what makes us tick during those other sixteen hours has been one of the most exciting aspects of my journey through the world of neuroscientific research.

When I began my reporting for this book, I quickly discovered that it's impossible for scientists to agree on something as seemingly simple as the definition of dreaming. Some define it narrowly as the creation of hallucinatory narratives complete with characters and a discernable plotline that occurs primarily during that period of rest known as rapid eye movement (REM) sleep—when, as the name suggests, you see a sleeper's eyes darting back and forth beneath closed lids. At the other end of the spectrum are researchers who classify any mental activity that occurs during any stage of sleep as dreaming, and some even argue that dreamlike mental processes during waking states, such as meditation, should also be included in the definition. After months spent interviewing scientists, serving in labs as a test subject myself, and digesting stacks of studies, dream reports, and other related material, it was clear to me that a definition of dreaming that edges toward the broader end of the spectrum best reflects the scope of knowledge that's emerged from dream research.

For the purpose of discussion in the chapters ahead, I define a dream as a mental experience during sleep that can be described during waking consciousness. Some dreams are relatively mundane, while others are hallucinatory masterpieces. Of course, we're likely to be able to provide a description only if we're awakened in the midst of a dream or immediately after it ends. But even though we don't recall the majority of our dreams, they're still being produced each night. And research demonstrates that they can affect the quality of our waking hours whether we remember them or not.

The mind at night is surprisingly active, I learned, and not just when it is churning out a scenario in which we're suddenly able to fly without an airplane. Using the same neural circuitry that permits us to navigate the world during the day, the brain on its night shift performs an impressive array of important cognitive tasks. For instance, when we're just drifting off to sleep, we experience dreamy but plotless imagery that is associated with one of the vital functions the brain performs at night: rerunning experience to extract what's important enough to be incorporated into long-term memory, thereby updating the internal model of the world that helps guide our daytime behavior. In the pages ahead, then, you'll discover how the mind concocts the vivid cinematic mental productions that we typically think of when the word *dream* comes to mind. But you'll also learn about the related and equally important, high-level mental activity that goes on each night entirely outside conscious awareness. Though you would not be able to describe that portion of what happens in your mind during sleep, it nevertheless has an enormous impact on who you are and how you make your way in the world.

FROM THE BEGINNING of recorded history, dreaming has captured the human imagination, as Robert Van de Castle amply demonstrates in his comprehensive history of dreaming, *Our Dreaming Mind*. The earliest records of dreams come from Mesopotamia, where clay tablets recounting the adventures of the legendary hero Gilgamesh included accounts of dreams and how to interpret their symbolic and metaphorical imagery. The tablets were found in the library of a king who ruled in the seventh century B.C., but oral versions of the dream-rich stories are believed to have circulated hundreds of years earlier. In both India and China by about 1000 B.C., texts had been written on how to decipher the meaning of dreams. These early conceptions of dreams revolved around the notion that they were messages from the gods that could foretell the future, and in many cultures, dreams still are believed to have that power.

The roots of *modern* scientific thought about dreams can also be found in ancient times. Aristotle proclaimed that, far from being a product of divine origin, "dreaming is thinking while asleep." The *Upanishads*, philosophical treatises written in India between 900 and 500 B.C., proposed that it is the dreamer himself who creates horses, chariots, and other objects appearing in the dream world and that dream objects were expressions of the dreamer's inner desires.

This notion was, of course, at the heart of Sigmund Freud's dream theory, which dominated both scientific and popular thought about dreams throughout most of the first half of the twentieth century. Freud described dream interpretation as "the royal road to understanding the unconscious activities of the mind." In his view, the unconscious consisted of both innate information that had never entered consciousness as well as experiences or thoughts that had been shunted off to the unconscious and remain repressed because they were memories, wishes, or fears that were unacceptable. The repressed desire to sleep with one's mother and kill one's father became perhaps the iconic example of Freudian theory.

Published in 1900, Freud's *The Interpretation of Dreams* argued that dreams spring from subconscious wishes (primarily sexual and aggressive desires, which Freud called libidinal drive) that the censoring ego normally suppressed in waking hours. To protect sleep from being disrupted, the mind then imagined these wishes being fulfilled by creating dreams—symbolic, disjointed tales that were filled with visual metaphors designed to disguise the desires and fears actually being expressed. These wishes sometimes arose from "day residue," meaning consciously remembered wishes that were aroused during the preceding day but were unfulfilled, or desires bubbling up from the unconscious once sleep relaxed the controlling grip of the mind's censor.

In Freud's view, dream symbols had to be translated—with the aid of a psychoanalyst—to uncover meaning. Analysts were taught to use Freud's technique of "free association"—instructing dreamers to say whatever comes into their minds about each element of the dream without censoring their thoughts. Using free association to decode a dream's seemingly bizarre, "manifest" content and reveal the uncomfortable hidden truth of its "latent" content was at the heart of Freudian psychoanalysis. A Freudian lexicon developed to explain what various symbols represented. The majority of symbols had sexual connotations, and these have permeated popular culture. It's difficult to divorce the image of a train entering a tunnel from its Freudian interpretation, a fact that Alfred Hitchcock used to his full advantage in the film *North by Northwest*, in which a seduction scene between Cary Grant and Eva Marie Saint in a train's sleeper car cuts abruptly to a shot of the train plunging into a tunnel.

In summarizing his view, Freud stated clearly that "the majority of the dreams of adults deal with sexual material and give expression to erotic wishes." He contended that "impressions from the earliest year of our life can appear in our dreams, which do not seem to be at the disposal of our memory when we are awake." In one of his best-known cases, for instance, Freud concluded that a patient's dream of seeing wolves sitting in a tree symbolized a traumatic early childhood memory of observing his parents having sex, as well as an underlying fear of castration.

Freud's insistence that most dream content reflected repressed sexual wishes was one of the major factors leading to the split that occurred between Freud and his one-time protégé, Carl Jung, whose dream theories also influenced popular thought on the subject throughout much of the past century. Unlike Freud, Jung did not believe dreams had to be decoded to decipher buried meaning. "The 'manifest' dream picture is the dream itself and contains the whole meaning of the dream," he wrote. Jung believed images in dreams could carry messages from the instinctive, emotional parts of the mind to its rational other half, but they weren't all disguised symbols representing repressed sexual urges. Often, in fact, dreams express positive desires for growth and development. He proposed analyzing dreams via a process called amplification, in which the personal meanings attached to the dream images are explored by the dreamer himself. If a central image in a dream were a ship, for instance, Jung would ask the dreamer to describe all of the characteristics of the ship as she would if she were speaking to someone who had never seen one before. That way, he could discover what the dreamer's specific associations to the image were, based on her culture and unique personal history.

In addition to meaning that could be extracted based on each individual's personal experience, Jung proposed that there was another level of meaning in dreams. In fact, he believed the most important dreams we have are the products of what he called the "collective unconscious," which reflects the inherited experiential record of the human species. As human anatomy bears telltale signs of its evolutionary past, such as vestiges of a tailbone in the human fetus, so Jung theorized that the mind "can no more be a product without history than is the body in which it exists." He argued that the collective unconscious was expressed through archetypes that appear not only in dreams but throughout history in the content of myths, fairy tales, and religious ceremony. Archetypal dreams are linked with strong emotions and occur more often around times of crisis or transitions in our lives, Jung contended.

The current revolution in thought about how and why we dream debunks some elements of the theories proposed by both Freud and Jung. But as you'll see, there are significant pieces of each of their theories that are now supported by scientific evidence. In the past decade, the revolution that began in a dank Chicago laboratory in the mid-1950s has accelerated, thanks to new technologies that allow us to actually see the brain at work even at the molecular level. In labs throughout North America and Europe, and from South Africa to Israel, researchers from fields as diverse as biochemistry, aeronautical engineering, microbiology, and robotics have joined neurophysiologists and psychologists in piecing together the puzzle of the dreaming mind.

The tale of discovery that unfolds in the chapters ahead explores how and why we dream, but it may also overturn your assumptions about how the brain does everything from the seemingly straightforward task of seeing a sunset (be it a sunset out there on the horizon or one that's part of your dreamscape) to more complex jobs such as learning, forming, and retrieving memories or dealing with difficult emotional issues. When your body is safely at rest and your brain therefore no longer needs to process information from the outside world, it is free to focus on other crucial tasks, including integrating new experiences into memory. What happens during this offline processing in turn helps guide your waking behavior.

It has also become clear that dream content can provide valuable information about our deepest preoccupations and feelings. "We have shown that 75 to 100 dreams from a person give us a very good psychological portrait of that individual," says Bill Domhoff, a psychologist and an expert on a system for quantifying and categorizing dream content that has been used for decades by researchers around the world. "Give us 1,000 dreams collected over a couple of decades and we can give you a psychological profile that is almost as individualized and accurate as fingerprinting." While some researchers insist that dreaming has no purpose, others argue that the dreaming process itself plays a role in regulating our moods.

If our brains are functioning normally, we do indeed dream each night, even though we recall only a fraction of those internal dramas. Researchers have devised simple methods that can help improve dream recall so that we can peer through this unique window on the mind more frequently. Scientists have also demonstrated that we can increase our ability to become aware that we're dreaming while a dream is still in progress and sometimes even deliberately control what happens next in the action—a remarkable phenomenon known as lucid dreaming.

During REM sleep, when the majority of dreaming occurs, the brain chemicals that are circulating in abundance are different from those that prevail during waking, as are the regions of the brain that are most active. This dramatically altered operating environment can allow us to make out-of-the-box mental connections that would be rejected by the logical information-processing centers of the brain in command during waking life. The free-form associations that give dreams their sometimes nonsensical quality may also explain why many artists and scientists claim to have come up with breakthrough concepts in dreams.

Ultimately, dream research may also help answer what many consider to be the most intriguing question of all: what is the source of the peculiar brand of self-reflective consciousness that appears to separate humans from other creatures—that nebulous quality that allows us to make intricate plans, fantasize, string memories together to create a personal history, or use abstractions such as language and art to represent our own mental processes? That quest for the roots of consciousness remains at the cutting edge of neuroscientific research today. The answers that are emerging already indicate that the line between dreaming consciousness and waking consciousness is not as rigidly defined as previously thought.

The significance of the new scientific field of dream research was eloquently summarized by Gay Gaer Luce in a U.S.-sponsored report on the state of sleep and dream research in 1965, when the field was first taking off. "For the first time, science is gaining a glimmer of the miraculous machinery of the mind at times when it is speaking only to itself," Luce said. "It is not oblivion that is studied in the exploration of sleep, but the entire realm of man's mental being."

1

Rockettes, EEGs, and Banana Cream Pie

We experience a dream as real because it is real. . . . The miracle is how, without any help from the sense organs, the brain replicates in the dream all the sensory information that creates the world we live in when we are awake.

—William Dement

BY THE TIME EUGENE ASERINSKY FOUND himself in a dungeonlike lab room at the University of Chicago in the fall of 1951, wiring his eight-year-old son, Armond, with electrodes to record his eye movements and brain waves as he slept, he was desperate. The experiment he was embarking upon absolutely had to work so that he could finally earn his degree and get a job. A perennial student at age thirty, with enough college course credits to qualify for the Guinness Book of World Records but no degree other than a high school diploma, Aserinsky was struggling to provide the basic necessities for his son and pregnant wife in an apartment so spartan that its only heat source was a potbellied kerosene stove. Hardly a candidate, it would seem, to make a discovery that would revolutionize scientific thought about the brain's activities during sleep and launch a research odyssey that would shed light on how the mind did everything from learning to regulating our moods.

But Aserinsky was hardly an ordinary student, and from early childhood on, he'd been living unconventionally, to say the least. After his mother died shortly following his birth, Eugene was brought up in Brooklyn solely by his father, a ne'er-do-well Russian immigrant who was a dentist by trade but whose true passion was separating people from their money in late-night card games. When Aserinsky was still in elementary school, it was already evident that he was extraordinarily bright, so his father recruited the boy as a card-sharking partner. Together, they developed a signaling system that fleeced countless unsuspecting chumps in pinochle games. Since the games usually went on until well after midnight, Eugene often skipped school so that he could sleep late. In fact, for about a third of the school year, his classroom seat was empty. In those Depression years, however, absences were often overlooked by school officials and his academic performance was so stellar that he skipped ahead a couple of grades. Enrolling in Brooklyn College at the age of fifteen, he soon transferred to the University of Maryland, where he managed to take courses in everything from Spanish to dentistry without ever getting a degree before dropping out to become a soldier when World War II began.

After he returned from England, where he'd served as a high explosives handler in the Army, friends persuaded him he was wasting his talent in the civil service job he'd taken in Baltimore to support his wife and two-year-old son, Armond. So he applied to the graduate program at the University of Chicago, which had a reputation for bending the rules to admit students who showed signs of brilliance. He apparently fit the bill. In later years, Aserinsky—a slightly built man with dark hair, a David Niven–style mustache, and a penchant for dressing formally in suit and tie even in the lab—loved to point out that he'd gone straight from a high school diploma to a Ph.D. without any degrees in between.

When he arrived in Chicago, however, he discovered that the only available adviser in the physiology department was Nathaniel Kleitman, the first and only scientist in the world who had devoted his entire career to the study of sleep. A Russian immigrant who lived to the age of 104, Kleitman was so devoted to his work that he'd spent a full month living in an underground chamber in a Kentucky cave to see whether the absence of environmental clues about time of day could shift the body's natural cycle to either a twenty-one-hour or a twenty-eight-hour day. (As he learned, the answer is no; our bodies have an internal clock that's naturally set to a sleep-wake cycle of twenty-four to twenty-five hours.) Later, he also served as a guinea pig in his own sleep deprivation experiment, staying awake for 180 hours straight, an experience that he concluded could be an effective form of torture.

Aserinsky loved physiology, but he had no intrinsic interest in sleep research. He became even less enthusiastic about his fate when he found that Kleitman—whom he described as "a man with a grey head, a grey complexion and a grey smock"—was usually tucked away out of sight behind his closed office door, responding with irritation whenever Eugene knocked. Kleitman may not have found him the best prospect for a graduate assistant, either, but as Aserinsky dryly observed, the primary criterion for selecting a graduate assistant "was that the candidate have a heartbeat." Since Aserinsky did qualify on that score, Kleitman immediately gave him a research task: observing sleeping infants to see whether blinking stopped gradually or suddenly as they fell asleep.

After several unproductive months pursuing Kleitman's goal, Aserinsky gathered his courage to knock on what he referred to as "the dreaded door" to propose a different project: studying eye movements of sleeping subjects throughout an entire night. He'd observed vigorous eye movements behind the closed lids of subjects who were sleeping, and he wondered whether those movements were haphazard or had some pattern and purpose. To his surprise, Kleitman agreed to the change, suggesting that Aserinsky pursue the project as a potential doctoral dissertation. He mentioned that there was an old polygraph machine stored in the basement of the physiology building that he might be able to use to record eye movements as well as brain waves and other physiological measurements on his test subjects. Well aware that he was taking a big risk—if the experiments produced no new data worthy of a doctoral dissertation, he would be continuing his pattern of collecting college credits without earning a degree—Aserinsky decided to proceed anyway.

"According to my anti-intellectual 'Golden Manure' theory of discovery, a painfully accurate, well-focused probe of any minutiae is almost certain to divulge a heretofore unknown nugget of science," he later said. "What lay ahead was a gamble—the odds being that since no one had really carefully examined the eyes of an adult through a full night's sleep, I would find something. Of course, the importance of that find would determine whether or not I would win the gamble."

Just as Eugene had been recruited into partnership with his father, Aserinsky enlisted the aid of his son, Armond, in his own brand of wagering. Starting in second grade, the boy began logging countless hours in the lab, first serving as a test subject himself and then helping his dad set up and calibrate the rickety recording equipment for other sleep subjects.

"The lab was horrendous—old and dark with stone walls—and the machine was ancient, so it was always breaking down," recalls Armond, who is now a clinical psychologist. "Getting prepped for the recording procedure was uncomfortable and I didn't like the all-night sessions, but I knew my dad needed help, and I was flattered that he talked over his findings with me and always took what I said very seriously."

The abandoned polygraph Aserinsky had rescued from the basement of Abbott Hall turned out to be one of the first machines of its kind. It picked up eye movements and brain waves through electrodes pasted on the subject's head and then translated those electrical signals into ink patterns scratched out by several pens onto long reams of paper. Recording a single night's sleep session consumed a stream of polygraph paper a half mile long.

This technique for recording electrical signals from the brain had been around since the early part of the twentieth century, when Hans Berger, a German neuropsychiatrist was able to record brain waves in subjects who were awake but relaxing with their eyes closed. He observed that these EEG (electroencephalogram) patterns showed consistent changes at sleep onset; subsequent studies in the 1930s at Harvard further classified differences in waking and sleeping brain wave patterns. But no one had tried all-night recordings of brain and eye movements as Aserinsky was doing, in large part because Kleitman and others mistakenly believed that sleep was a second-class state during which nothing important happened in the brain other than maintenance of basic body functions.

When Aserinsky hooked up Armond for a night's sleep session, he was startled to see that the pens periodically stopped tracing the patterns of slow, even waves that appeared in early stages of sleep and instead began wildly scratching out sharp peaks and valleys similar to patterns generated during waking hours. Since this finding contradicted the prevailing scientific view that the brain essentially shut down and remained in a passive state during sleep, Aserinsky at first assumed that the polygraph was simply malfunctioning. After consulting with engineering experts, including the man who'd designed the machine he was using, Aserinsky came up with a way to record movements from each eye independently and verify that the unusual patterns he was seeing were indeed real.

He repeated the experiment on adult sleepers and not only found the same spiky patterns he'd seen with Armond but confirmed that they occurred with clocklike regularity four or five times a night and coincided with rapid eye movements that were clearly visible beneath the sleeper's closed eyelids. Putting all of the evidence together, Aserinsky suspected that he might actually be seeing dreaming in action. His hunch was reinforced when he awakened a sleeping male subject who had begun crying out while experiencing wild eye movements that nearly unhinged the pens on the polygraph. The man reported that he had indeed been having a violent nightmare. As the study progressed, evidence mounted that when subjects were awakened in the midst of rapid eye movement periods, they almost always had vivid dream recall. But if they were awakened when no eye movements were present, they rarely remembered anything.

Kleitman was highly skeptical when Aserinsky first showed him the results he was getting on this strange sleep stage that he had begun to call the rapid eye movement (REM) period. Yet the consistency of the mounting body of evidence piqued the older man's interest, and he gradually became a believer, assigning another lab assistant to assist Aserinsky in making the REM recordings. But before presenting the new data publicly for the first time at a scientific meeting in 1953, Kleitman—who had a reputation as an extremely fastidious investigator—wanted to observe the experimental procedure first-hand with his own daughter as a test subject. When she experienced the same regular pattern of rapid eye movements throughout sleep, the case was sealed for Kleitman. The results of the REM experiments were published by the respected journal *Science* in 1953, and Kleitman granted his ultimate seal of approval: his name was listed behind Aserinsky's as joint author.

The landmark study forced scientists to completely rethink their assumptions about what happens during sleep. Far from merely idling all night, as they'd previously thought, the brain regularly revved up into a supercharged state akin to waking consciousness. Exactly what the brain was doing during these REM periods was a mystery, but dreaming unquestionably was an important part of the answer.

THE 1960S BECAME the golden age of dream research, as researchers from many disciplines rushed into the new field, exchanging ideas—some of them quite wild—and scientifically jamming like jazz musicians. But at the start, the crusade to answer the countless questions raised by the discovery of REM sleep was led almost singlehandedly by William Dement, who'd become fascinated by sleep research in his second year of medical school after attending a lecture by Nathaniel Kleitman.

When an enthusiastic Dement knocked on the infamous closed door to Kleitman's office in 1952 to see if he could become an assistant in his lab, Kleitman peered out, asked if Dement knew anything about sleep, and when the young med student replied honestly that he didn't, the taciturn Kleitman simply said "Read my book" and closed the door with a force just short of a slam. Dement quickly caught up on his reading and went to work in Kleitman's lab, where he helped Eugene Aserinsky complete REM sleep recording sessions for the study that finally earned him his long-awaited degree.

It wasn't long until Dement was on his own, however, because Aserinsky wasted no time clearing out of Chicago when he finished the REM experiments. Though his discovery had caused an initial flurry of public excitement, it certainly didn't bring him fame and fortune. Feeling increasing pressure to bring home a paycheck that would support his family, he took the first job he was offered in the summer of 1953—at the Bureau of Fisheries in Seattle. There, he conducted experiments to see whether the movements of salmon could be controlled by running electric currents through water. Though it was a far cry from sleep research, a job was a job, after all, and Aserinsky was happy for the moment to put the arduous demands of all-night sleep recording sessions behind him.

Dement was thrilled to be taking the lead in dream research at the Chicago lab. Unlike Kleitman and Aserinsky, he was a great believer in Sigmund Freud's theory that dream interpretation was the "royal road" to understanding the unconscious activities of the mind. "Freudian psychoanalysis seemed to permeate every nook and cranny of society in the 1950s and I was an ardent disciple," Dement wrote in *The Sleepwatchers*, an account of his early days in dream research. Since Freud had theorized that psychosis could erupt in the waking state if we didn't have dreams as an outlet to discharge the energy of the libido, Dement eagerly set about doing REM studies on schizophrenics in a state hospital, to see whether their mental illness might spring from an inability to dream. The theory didn't pan out—the EEG results showed they experienced normal REM cycles, and they reported having dreams.

But Dement was undaunted—he had so many other theories and unanswered questions to explore. During his final years of medical school, he spent two nights a week running sleep studies in Kleitman's lab to more precisely define the characteristics of REM and other sleep stages. Combining those sleepless nights with the other demands of life as a medical student meant that he frequently fell asleep in the back of the classroom the following day—a problem that landed him in the dean's office at one point—but the end result was well worth his troubles.

The paper that he and Kleitman published in 1957, describing the characteristics of REM and other sleep stages, laid the foundation for information about sleep and dreaming in most medical textbooks for decades to come, and Dement's infectious enthusiasm for dream research helped launch similar investigations in other labs around the United States and in Europe.

By meticulously charting nightlong EEG recordings, Dement found that healthy adults pass through predictable sleep phases, which have since been divided into five standard stages of sleep. In the relaxed presleep period, we begin to tune out noise and other external influences, and our brain generates the regular rhythm of alpha waves—the same kind of pattern displayed by the mind in meditation, a serene state devoid of purposeful thought. We then enter stage I sleep, also known as sleep onset, when we may experience what's known as hypnagogic imagery—brief, dreamlike visual imagery that often is drawn from that day's experience. Next comes stage II, a period of light sleep lasting from ten to thirty minutes, as the brain downshifts into the large, slow delta waves that characterize the deep sleep of the third and fourth stages, known as slow-wave sleep. While we may talk in our sleep at any point during the night, it is in these deepest sleep stages that sleepwalking typically occurs.

After fifteen to thirty minutes in this deep sleep, we move back up through the first two stages and enter the first of our REM periods, when our brain waves shift to the short, rapid patterns that resemble waking brain activity. When we're in REM, our muscles completely relax, and though our eyes move and hands or feet may occasionally twitch, we are essentially paralyzed so that we can't physically act out our dreams. Nevertheless we're highly aroused physiologically: our breathing becomes irregular, our heart rate increases, and genitals become engorged in both males and females. The initial cycle from waking to REM normally takes between fifty and seventy minutes, and thereafter REM returns about every ninety minutes. During the first half of the night, slow-wave sleep predominates and REM periods may be as brief as ten minutes, but as the night progresses, non-REM sleep grows lighter and REM periods last longer, stretching from twenty minutes to as much as an hour as morning approaches. All told, adults spend about a quarter of the night's sleep in REM, another quarter in deep sleep, and the remainder in stage II light sleep.

Perhaps most significantly, the early REM experiments by Dement, Kleitman, and Aserinsky showed that dreams were far more likely to be recalled when subjects were awakened from REM: dreams were reported on 74 percent of REM awakenings as compared to less than 10 percent in non-REM. These initial results led Dement and other researchers to conclude that dreaming occurs exclusively in REM sleep, while the minimal reports of dream recall they found in non-REM could be written off as fragments of dreams recalled from earlier REM periods.

The widely accepted assumption that REM sleep equaled dreaming brought the new field of dream research to life, and Dement was quite effective at spreading the gospel that for the first time it was possible to actually pinpoint when a dream was in progress. Having earned both his medical degree and his doctorate in physiology, Dement left Chicago in 1957 for New York City, where he conducted dream research at night while completing his internship and residency at Mount Sinai Hospital. In order to run his dream experiments without having to spend nights away from his wife, he converted part of his apartment to a sleep lab, running local ads to recruit test subjects. A member of the Rockettes happened to see the ad, and she spread the word among other members of the Radio City dance troupe that they could earn money for simply sleeping in Dement's lab—an idea with great appeal to many of the young women. Though the research was entirely aboveboard, the routine that ensued made Dement quite the object of curiosity in his apartment building as a steady parade of women came straight from the chorus line to do their nightly stint in the lab.

"A lovely woman, still in theatrical makeup, would arrive at the apartment building and ask the doorman for my room," Dement recalls. "In the morning, she would reappear, sometimes with one of my unshaven and exhausted male colleagues who had spent the night monitoring the EEG. One day, the doorman could finally stand it no longer. 'Dr. Dement,' he demanded, 'exactly what goes on in your apartment?' I just smiled."

Exactly what was going on in his apartment and in a growing number of other labs was an exciting new foray into uncharted territory, as Dement and others used all kinds of creative experiments to try to understand how dreams are created and how they are connected to our waking life. Since the Soviets had beaten the United States into space with the launch of the satellite *Sputnik*, government funding for basic research of all kinds was suddenly free-flowing as the 1960s dawned, and dream research was one of the beneficiaries. In 1964 alone, the National Institute of Mental Health funded more than sixty studies on sleep or dreaming. From New York to Boston, Washington to

Cincinnati and on campuses in Virginia, Texas, and Oregon, researchers were drawn to this hot new field, where so little was known that they were likely to come up with something new no matter what they chose to investigate.

There were countless intriguing questions to be answered and no limits to the creative methods researchers invented to get results. Could dream content be manipulated? Dement was the first to try this by ringing a bell while subjects were in REM sleep, but out of 204 attempts, only 20 dreams actually incorporated the sound of the bell as part of the dream plot. Researchers have had limited success in affecting dream content by spraying dreamers with water and—more recently—squeezing sleepers' arms with blood pressure cuffs while in REM, but the majority of dreamers ignored these manipulations too. On those occasions when real-world stimuli do make it through our sensory barriers, they are quickly and ingeniously woven into the ongoing plot of the dream. For instance, a sleeping test subject sprayed with water may report a sudden rain shower in the background of his dream, but there's no dramatic change in the dream's course.

Nor was there any significant effect on dream content from presleep experiences, such as serving sleepers banana cream pie or pepperoni pizza right before bedtime, depriving them of fluids to see whether they had persistent dreams of being thirsty, or showing them violent or erotic films. Dreaming brains appeared to be fiercely independent directors, relying on some yet-to-be-deciphered criteria for selecting characters, setting, and plot in their nightly internal dramas.

Other experimenters proved that even those who claim not to dream do in fact concoct dream scenarios throughout the night. If awakened while REM is still in progress, subjects remember their dreams, but if they are awakened several minutes after REM has ended, the memory of the dream typically vanishes. Yet another study probed whether dreams are different at different points in the night and found that dreams early in the night revolved around current events in the dreamer's life while, as the night progressed, dreams incorporated more events and characters from the past.

Did the jerky eye movements of REM sleep indicate sleepers were following the action in the dream as they would images on a movie screen? Early experiments by Dement suggested this was the case, but subsequent studies by other investigators found that eye movements did not in fact directly correspond to dream content.

One of the biggest preoccupations of the early researchers was understanding how visual imagery in dreams was produced, since the strongest sensory perception while dreaming is unquestionably visual. Investigations of dream content from the 1890s on consistently showed that nearly every dream contains visual imagery, while slightly more than half contain some auditory component. Among other sensations, touch or feelings of movement are present in less than 15 percent of dreams, while taste or smell rarely figure into dream experience at all.

One of the best-known experiments to test the source of visual imagery in dreams took place back where it had all begun, at the University of Chicago. After sleep research pioneer Nathaniel Kleitman retired, psychologist Allan Rechtschaffen used the lab before forming his own makeshift dream lab in an old gray-stone building around the corner from Abbott Hall. He ran cables from an EEG machine in his office to subjects who slept on foldout beds set up each night in other offices up and down the hallway after their occupants went home for the evening. Rechtschaffen created a lively atmosphere that encouraged rigorous but creative scientific thinking among the young researchers in his group. His wide-ranging curiosity and commitment to the highest scientific standards made him one of the most respected figures in the field. He was considered a tough reviewer for grant proposals or scientific papers, which made winning his approval all the more valuable. In the early days at his lab, young researchers often would come up with a new hypothesis about dreaming in the afternoon and test it that very night on the housewives and students who were paid to sleep while being recorded and periodically awakened—a process that went more smoothly with some than others.

"We once had a subject who was complaining about everything as we hooked him up to the EEG—he didn't like the surroundings, the electrodes, the smell of the acetone," recalls Rechtschaffen. After the problematic student finally was prepped for the EEG and tucked into bed, Rechtschaffen and his assistant returned to the office where they monitored the EEG recordings. The assistant wryly speculated that after all the trouble the subject had put them through, he probably wouldn't fall asleep. Unaware that the intercom to the sleeper's room was switched on so that the young man in bed could hear every word they said, Rechtschaffen replied, "If he doesn't fall asleep within two minutes, I'm going to electrocute him." With startling speed, the chronic complainer slid into stage I sleep.

Rechtschaffen came up with a novel way to test whether signals transmitted from the retina (the gateway for visual information from the outside world to the brain in waking) played a role in creating dream imagery. Amazingly he succeeded in getting test subjects to go to sleep with their eyelids taped halfway open. Once the sleeper entered REM, Rechtschaffen would sneak into the bedroom with a small light to illuminate objects such as a comb, book, or coffeepot that he would hold up in front of the sleeper's taped-open eyes. Then he would exit, and his research colleague David Foulkes would awaken the subjects via intercom and ask what they had been dreaming about. None of the dreamer's reports included images of the objects that had been dangled in front of their eyes. Clearly dream imagery was generated internally, though it wasn't yet clear how.

Additional experiments indicated that except for some decrease in the clarity of background detail and intensity of color, the quality of visual images we see in our dreams is nearly on a par with what we see when we're awake. Most dreams are also clearly experienced in color, though for some unknown reason, between 20 and 30 percent play out in black and white. While reports on dreams all the way back to Aristotle included references to color, from the 1930s to 1960, the prevailing opinion among research psychologists as well as among the general public was that we dream in black and white. Not coincidentally, this period was also when photographs and film images were primarily black-and-white. Though color photography was invented in the 1860s, it did not become readily available for public consumption until the 1940s. Similarly, Technicolor made a big splash beginning in the late 1930s with a few movies such as *The Wizard of Oz*, but full-color films didn't become common until the 1950s.

During this period, when psychologists asked their subjects if they dreamed in color, the majority said no: a 1942 survey of college students found only 10 percent claimed to frequently dream in color, and only 9 percent reported dreaming in color in a 1958 study at Washington University in St. Louis. But when sleepers in a 1962 study were actually awakened during REM sleep and asked directly about the appearance of color while their dreams were in progress, 83 percent reported color in their dreams. "It is surely not chance that this flourishing of black and white media coincided with the flourishing of the opinion that dreams are a black and white phenomenon," says Eric Schwitzgebel, a University of California at Berkeley professor who studied this curious trend and concluded that it wasn't the content of dreams that had changed during that period but public perception—or more accurately misperception—of dream imagery. In short, it was another example of the pervasive power of suggestion that can make eyewitness accounts in criminal investigations so unreliable.

While many investigators were focusing on unraveling the secrets of dreaming per se, others examined the underlying state in which it occurs, trying to understand why we need sleep at all. In addition to working on developing standards used today for classifying different stages of sleep, Allan Rechtschaffen and his students investigated what happened when animals were deprived of sleep. They conducted sleep deprivation experiments in rats and found that those deprived of all sleep died after two to three weeks. The sleep-deprived rats became extremely debilitated and had difficulty regulating body temperature, but the cause of death could not be isolated.

Less extreme studies in humans showed that when deprived of REM sleep, subjects automatically compensated by entering REM sooner and staying in it longer the next time they went to sleep. A similar rebound effect was seen for the deeper slow-wave sleep, so obviously both types are essential. In fact, nature itself provides evidence suggesting that total sleep deprivation can eventually cause death in humans. A rare genetic disease called fatal familial insomnia (FFI) was first identified in 1986 as the cause of death of thirty members of an aristocratic Italian family. Since then, the disorder has been identified in thirty other families around the world. Those suffering from the genetic disorder typically lose their ability to sleep when they reach middle age, though some have been struck in their teens. After weeks without sleep, FFI victims' pulse and blood pressure rise and they sweat heavily. They then have difficulty maintaining their balance, walking, and/or speaking and in the final phase—usually after several months without sleep—they fall into a state akin to a coma and die. The disease severely damages a portion of the brain called the thalamus (the sensory gateway to the cortex). Further research is needed to determine whether the insomnia or the thalamic damage directly causes death.

As Nathaniel Kleitman had established through his sleep experiments in underground caves, our biological clock (the specific location of which has been identified as a cluster of cells located in the brain where the optic nerves intersect) determines the body's rhythms for rising and falling body temperature, hormone secretion, and onset of drowsiness, which occurs not only at day's end but also typically between 2 and 4 P.M. While that internal clock generally runs through its repetitive rhythms "about every twenty-five hours" even when there are no environmental stimuli, such as the sun rising or setting to cue wake and sleep cycles, it does seem to go through some adjustments at different stages in life. During adolescence, not only does the need for sleep increase from eight hours to ten or more hours nightly, but drowsiness sets in later than usual, as well, leading to the desire to sleep later in the morning—which is why teenagers suddenly can sleep until noon. And in later stages of life, sleep becomes fragmented, with even healthy elderly people typically awakening for a few seconds scores of times during the night, though they may not recall doing so because the arousals are often so brief as to be detectable only on EEG recordings. Interrupted sleep in turn leads to increased daytime sleepiness and the stereotypical image of grandpa nodding off in midsentence.

Another crucial question that was answered in the early days of dream research was whether REM sleep was exclusively a human phenomenon. Dement did initial work on the sleep cycle of cats, which had been favored subjects for brain studies since the 1930s. Not only were their brain structures similar to humans', but their size and cost made them convenient research animals. After French neurobiologist Michel Jouvet demonstrated in 1960 that EEG patterns in sleeping cats were similar to the human REM pattern, other investigators probed how widespread the phenomenon was in the animal kingdom. Subsequent research has shown that reptiles don't experience REM sleep, but mammals do, and so do the few species of birds that have been studied. REM sleep duration varies from as few as forty minutes a day in cattle to as many as seven hours a day in opossums. Predatory carnivores spend a greater proportion of time in all stages of sleep, and domestic cats, freed of the need to hunt for food, can spend more than two hundred minutes a day in REM. Researchers still have not come to a consensus on whether these variations are significant.

In humans, REM sleep begins in the womb and changes as we age. It has been detected as early as twenty-six weeks in the life of the fetus and appears to go on for twenty-four hours a day. Among newborns, REM accounts for about 50 percent of total sleep and declines steadily until a child reaches the age of four, when it stabilizes at the normal adult level of 20 to 25 percent of total sleep time. When we reach middle age, REM begins to decline, dropping to less than 15 percent of sleep time in our later years.

What purpose REM serves was a mystery to these pioneering scientists, but early clues were provided in a novel experiment conducted by Jouvet's group in Lyon. Jouvet surgically disconnected the portion of the cat's brain that normally paralyzes its muscles during REM and found that the cats, though still deeply asleep, would rise and appear to be stalking imaginary prey or attacking invisible enemies when they entered REM. Jouvet found that acting out pursuit behavior sometimes continued for as long as three minutes while the cat was fully asleep. As a result, he theorized that this stage of sleep in mature animals provided an opportunity for them to mentally rehearse behaviors essential for survival, so that the necessary neural circuitry could be maintained in peak condition even if that particular survival skill—say, defending against an enemy—wasn't actually required on a daily basis in waking life. When deprived of REM sleep for more than three weeks, cats subsequently fell directly into REM sleep from waking and spent 60 percent of their time in that stage. Cats deprived of REM for periods of thirty to seventy days also experienced changes in waking behavior, becoming abnormally hungry, restless, and hypersexual.

Jouvet's work so electrified American investigators that in 1962 Rechtschaffen invited the French scientist to speak in Chicago at the second meeting of the professional association he and Dement had formed in 1960 for the rapidly growing multidisciplinary specialty of sleep and dream research. A year later, the group met in New York, and at that meeting, a figure who'd long been missing from the field wandered through the crowd, attracting little attention until a young researcher happened to spot his name tag and realized he'd just bumped into the man who discovered REM. The young man blurted out "You're Eugene Aserinsky? I thought you were dead!" Most scientists thought Aserinsky had dropped out because he'd simply lost interest, but the reality was that his career had been derailed by family tragedy. His wife suffered a mental breakdown after the birth of their second child while Aserinsky was still conducting the REM experiments in Chicago, and after being institutionalized several times, she committed suicide. Sadly, though he attempted a comeback, he died in a car accident in 1998 after retiring from a rather lackluster college teaching career.

But the field he'd launched continued to grow exponentially as researchers exchanged ideas in meetings such as those organized by Rechtschaffen and Dement. "At the meetings everyone tried to keep up with everything, no matter how seemingly remote it might be from their own workaday interests," recalled David Foulkes. "The group, despite the gradually increasing disparity of its interests, both worked and played well together."

In keeping with that inquisitive, anything-goes spirit, dream researchers were quick to go wherever the action was. In the early 1960s, that was Lyon, France, where Jouvet was conducting his innovative experiments with sleeping cats. Among those who made the pilgrimage was an ambitious young psychiatrist from Harvard Medical School. Brilliant and opinionated, alternately charming and abrasive, he was about to change the face of dream research.

2

The Anti-Freud

Those dreams that on the silent night intrude,
And with false flitting shapes our minds delude,
Jove never sends us downward from the skies,
Nor do they from infernal mansions rise;
But all are mere productions of the brain.
And fools consult interpreters in vain.
—Jonathan Swift, "On Dreams"

J. ALLAN HOBSON VIVIDLY REMEMBERS sitting on the shore of a lake in Maine on a starry summer night as his teenage buddies marveled at the immensity of the universe and the mysteries that other galaxies might hold. "It seemed so silly to focus wonder exclusively on the universe when there was so much behind our eyes that we didn't understand," he recalls. "What intrigued me was how our minds had the capacity both to construct that image of the cosmos and to generate these romantic feelings about it." At the time, Hobson was a counselor at a summer camp for dyslexic students run by his mentor, an educational psychologist named Page Sharp. Sharp gave the young man from Hartford, Connecticut, advice that became the underlying theme of his career: to comprehend the mind and all its mysteries, you must study the brain.

When he arrived at Harvard in 1955 to study psychiatry and neuroscience, Hobson was a Freud devotee, having avidly devoured *The Interpretation of Dreams* and everything else Freud had written. Even his undergraduate thesis in English focused on Freud and Dostoyevsky. But by the time Hobson began his residency a few years later, he was becoming skeptical of Freud and disillusioned with psychiatry in general because neither seemed solidly grounded in anything he'd learned about how the brain worked.

"In our training as residents, we were treated as if we were psychoanalytic patients—as if any question we asked were motivated by some neurotic conflict. That was abusive to patients and abusive to us," Hobson explains on a warm autumn afternoon in the sun-drenched study of his lovely Victorian home, just a short drive away from his lab at Massachusetts Mental Health Center. As an example, he recounts an incident that occurred during a seminar for first-year residents. Jack Ewalt, then head of Harvard's psychiatric department, remarked that Hobson seemed to believe that neuroscience would actually be able to explain how consciousness was created by the brain—a prospect Ewalt considered iffy at best. When Hobson said that he didn't just believe it but knew it, Ewalt gave him a psychoanalytic response: "You're talking to me as if I were your father." The young resident's reply was classic Hobson: "No, my father would never make a stupid comment like that."

When Hobson was only one year into his residency, he left Harvard for a stint at the National Institutes of Health (NIH), where he became intrigued by sleep research upon meeting Frederick Snyder, a senior scientist and early dream researcher who was doing REM recordings at night in the neurology lab. When Snyder told Hobson he could actually tell when people were dreaming, Hobson—never one to take anything on faith—said he wouldn't believe it until he saw it for himself. "When I watched the brain waves changing in a sleeping subject, I was hooked in one night," Hobson recalls.

He was thrilled to get a year-long fellowship in Lyon in 1963 with Michel Jouvet, whose work on the sleep cycle of cats seemed just the sort of hard scientific exploration he was craving. Jouvet referred to

REM as paradoxical sleep, and dreaming as "a third state of the brain, which was as different from sleep as sleep is from wakefulness."

Hobson was particularly interested in Jouvet's experiments with cats that still experienced REM sleep even though their forebrains had been surgically removed. Jouvet's work indicated that REM sleep itself was triggered by a knob-shaped area called the pons at the base of the brainstem, and Hobson believed that it would be possible to discover exactly how this happened by probing a cat's brainstem with microelectrodes, tiny devices that could detect the firing of individual brain cells. He says Jouvet saw no merit in his plan, so Hobson decided to return to Harvard before the year was up. He got permission to do his animal research part-time while he finished his psychiatric residency at nearby Massachusetts Mental Health Center, where he set up his neurophysiology lab in 1968.

One of his fellow psychiatric residents was Eric Kandel, who later received the Nobel Prize for research demonstrating that the neurochemical serotonin played a crucial role in learning. Kandel, who had done his experiments with snails, advised Hobson to start his research on the mechanics of REM sleep in the simplest animal possible. But REM was difficult to detect in animals other than mammals, so Hobson ultimately decided to stick with cats. He teamed up with Robert McCarley, a medical resident who was fascinated by neurobiology but was also talented in computer programming and quantitative analysis.

Hobson, a self-described carpenter-tinkerer, built his own microelectrodes to work in the brainstem, an area of the brain that had never previously been probed in a living animal. The two men combined their respective strengths and found a way to insert the microelectrodes in the brainstems of cats, identify which individual nerve cells were firing, and then send those electrical signals through an audiovisual system so they could both see and hear cells firing as the cat went through its normal sleep cycles. "McCarley and I would trade off, one manning the fort and the other running home for a while, but we often both stayed up all night recording this dramatic activity from the brainstem. We were wild, our research was on the edge, but we knew we were on the verge of finding something no one thought we'd find," says Hobson.

Among those who thought Hobson was pursuing a dead end was David Hubel, a Harvard neuroscientist, who was also using microelectrode recordings to study the visual cortex in cats to try to gain a better understanding of how the brain sees. Hubel and his collaborator Torstein Wiesel won the Nobel Prize in 1981 for that work, which explained how visual images are formed via communication between the retina and the visual cortex. "Hubel originally had worked on sleep, but he switched to studying vision because he represented the widely held view that neural activity would cease in sleep," Hobson says. "He was convinced that when we stuck a microelectrode in the brainstem we'd get nothing but silence, and of course it was the exact opposite."

What Hobson and McCarley eventually found and published in 1977 was a controversial neurophysiological explanation of dreaming that effectively kicked the legs out from under Freudian theory and most other existing psychological approaches to interpreting dream content. Based on the brain cell firing patterns they saw, Hobson and McCarley concluded that REM sleep turned on when brainstem neurons in essence flipped a switch that completely altered the brain's balance of neuromodulators—those crucial brain chemicals that act as messengers from one neuron to another and cause chemical changes inside the receiving neurons, activating or deactivating whole sections of the brain.

When we're awake, our brain is bathed in two key neuromodulators that are essential to alert, waking consciousness: norepinephrine (which helps direct and focus our attention) and serotonin. Though serotonin now is probably best known for its effect on regulating mood (Prozac and similar antidepressants work by increasing the amount of serotonin circulating in the brain), it also plays an important role in judgment, learning, and memory. After we first fall asleep, as the brain's overall level of activity falls, these two brain chemicals stop circulating and are replaced instead by another neuromodulator, called acetylcholine, that excites the visual, motor, and emotional centers of the brain and transmits signals that trigger rapid eye movements and visual imagery in dreams.

The acetylcholine-soaked brain operates under entirely different rules from its waking state: motor impulses are blocked so that we're

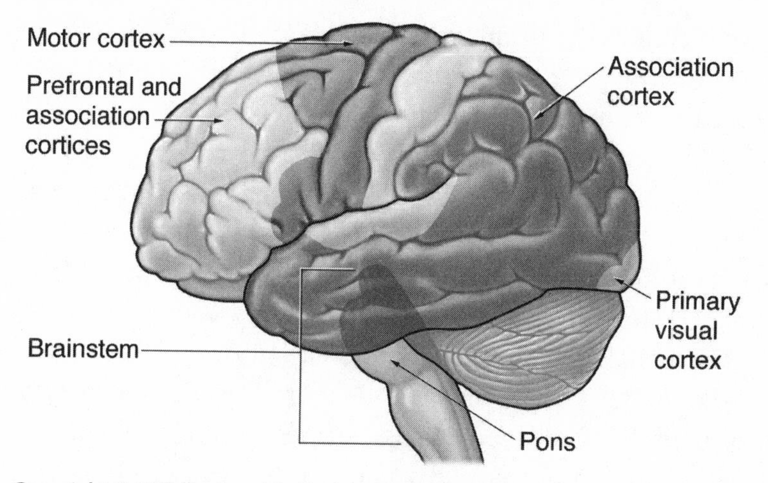

FIGURE 2.1 The pons area of the brainstem is involved in triggering the stage of sleep when vivid dreaming most often occurs. The prefrontal cortex is the seat of logical thinking; the primary visual cortex is a receiving station for signals from the retina during waking hours, and the motor cortex transforms intention into actual movements, such as running or throwing a ball. Associative cortices piece together information from the senses and memory to create the visual imagery we see whether we're awake or dreaming.

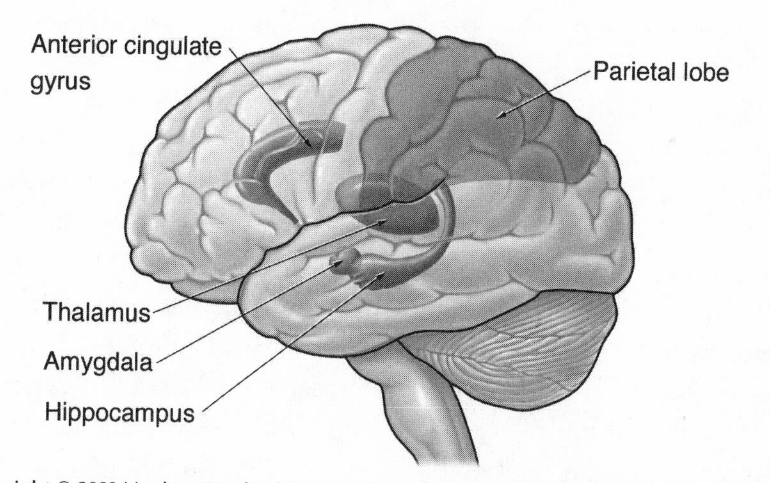

FIGURE 2.2 Brain structures or regions that play a significant role in the creation of dreams. The thalamus is a gateway for sensory information and helps direct our attention; the amygdala is at the core of our emotional system, directing the fight-or-flight response; and the hippocampus is essential in memory formation. The parietal lobe specializes in spatial orientation and forming mental imagery, while there is some evidence suggesting that the anterior cingulate gyrus may be where our sense of conscious self-awareness originates.

essentially paralyzed—in our dreams, we can't steer that speeding car down the hill or slam on the brake, no matter how hard we try. Incoming sensory information is also shut off, so the brain proceeds to interpret all of its internally generated images and sensations as if they were real. In this altered state, Hobson says, the brain does its best to spin a dream plot to match brainstem signals that may randomly stimulate an intense feeling of fear one minute or a sensation of freefalling the next. Hobson and McCarley's landmark study maintained that since the signals that initiated the creation of dream imagery came from the primitive brainstem and the more highly evolved cognitive areas of the forebrain were just passively responding to them, the dream process had "no primary ideational, volitional, or emotional content." The resulting dream was the product of the forebrain "making the best of a bad job in producing even partially coherent dream imagery" in response to chaotic signals from the brainstem.

They argued that the sense of judgment we need to recognize that we're dreaming and the ability to remember exactly what we dreamed are limited because the two neuromodulators needed for those functions are in short supply until we awaken. Therefore, we forget most of our dreams simply because we lack the neurochemicals needed to imprint them on memory, not because we have a Freudian censor in our mind furiously working to repress their taboo content.

Like a tide ebbing, acetylcholine gradually recedes and the REM period ends, only to be unleashed again roughly ninety minutes later. Hobson and McCarley said it was this consistent chemical dance led by the brainstem that generated dreams. By insisting that dreams contain no hidden message and that the dreaming process itself is triggered by an electrochemical process as automatic and devoid of thought as a heart beating or lungs breathing, Hobson was eviscerating Freudian dream theory. As for Freud's former disciple Carl Jung, Hobson dismissed his notion of the collective unconscious and archetypal symbols as a form of religion—something for which he had no patience—but he agreed with Jung that dreaming was a creative process in the brain and any meaning that resulted was absolutely transparent.

Hobson was not arguing that dreams were meaningless; in fact, he himself considers dreaming simply another form of consciousness and records significant dreams right along with highlights of his waking experience in personal journals that's he kept since 1973, now totaling more than 120 volumes. But he insisted that every single characteristic of a dream could be traced to the underlying physiology of the brain during REM: "Dreams are bizarre because the brain has stopped secreting the chemical guidance systems we have in place when we're awake, and this is the result: you can't think your way out of a paper bag, you hallucinate, you make all these errors in judgment, emotion runs wild—with anxiety, elation, and anger predominating—and you can't remember much of it."

In his view, the settings and characters our brain dredges up from our personal memories or imagination as it scrambles to form a plot to respond to this chaotic electrochemical state may reflect our emotional preoccupations, and reflecting on those preoccupations can provide insight. But the plot fits the emotions, and we can easily infer meaning without having to decode symbols in dreams to find forbidden wishes or repressed memories.

Armed with his physiological evidence that Freudian theory was based on outmoded biology, Hobson delighted in Freud bashing, especially when he spoke at professional meetings filled with psychotherapists, some of whom he debated on stage. "We pulled out all the stops, we were almost gloating, and as a result we made enemies for life," says Hobson now, acknowledging that he "created heat where light may have been more useful."

He has no regrets, however, about his efforts to repackage his dream research for mass consumption through a novel science-as-art exhibit that opened in Boston the year his landmark study was published. Titled *Dreamstage: A Multi-Media Portrait of the Sleeping Brain,* the exhibit's main attraction was a volunteer who could be seen through a one-way mirror sleeping while hooked up to an EEG that monitored brain waves, eye movements, and muscle tone. Instead of the electrical signals being scratched out in ink on reams of paper as they would be in a sleep lab, every brain-wave change, every eye movement and muscle twitch was converted into waves of laser lights rippling on the walls—brain waves in green and eye movements shimmering in blue. The signals also were represented in audio form as changing musical tones beamed from a synthesizer, the brain's version of a little night music. To emphasize the feeling of going into a bedroom environment, visitors were asked to remove their shoes before entering the carpeted, darkened exhibit rooms. "The only people who objected to taking off their shoes before coming in were some psychiatrists. They accused me of having a foot fetish," Hobson says.

Crowds flocked to the exhibit, which was featured on the cover of the *New York Times Sunday Magazine*. Its popularity led to a traveling version of *Dreamstage* the next year, when the exhibit made a six-city tour across the United States, starting in San Francisco. Federico Fellini, whose films Hobson had admired for their dreamlike quality, was so taken with the concept of *Dreamstage* that he told Hobson he'd be happy to serve as the volunteer sleeping behind the mirror if the exhibit ever came to Rome. Hobson's scientific peers, however, were less enthusiastic, grumbling that the extravaganza wasn't real science but simply egotistical grandstanding intended to publicize his theories and advance his career.

"You get publicity and everyone says you're narcissistic, which is true, but your arguments get popularized and understood when you immerse people in science this way rather than just telling them about it," Hobson says. "It was the high point of my life because I'd always wanted to be in the circus. *Dreamstage* was my circus."

When *Dreamstage* ended, Hobson recycled some of the equipment from the exhibit to set up a sleep lab in the Neurophysiology Department at Massachusetts Mental Health Center, where a series of photos of a sleeping volunteer from the show still adorns the entrance to his group's offices. But Hobson also wanted to study dreams in a more natural setting, so once again, he put his tinkering talents to work and developed a device called the Nightcap that would allow dream reports to be collected while subjects slept at home. The Nightcap was simply a bandana containing sensors that recorded eye and head movements in order to detect the beginning and end of REM sleep and transferred the information to a pocket-size recorder. Recruiting sleep study subjects instantly became easier and less costly. Tie the bandanna around your head pirate style, smooth the adhesive-backed eye movement sensor onto one eyelid, and you were ready to report dreaming data from the comfort of your own bed rather than traipsing down for a night in a sleep lab. The equipment also could be set up to automatically awaken subjects to report dreams when the sensors indicated they had entered REM.

Though all of his prior work had been done with animals, collecting dream reports had become a top priority for Hobson. Convinced that he and McCarley had figured out what triggered dreaming, he wanted to identify the formal features that characterized dreams: What were the predominant emotions and types of mental activity being experienced? How did they correspond to the physical state of the brain in REM? And how did they differ from waking cognition? In his view, the hallmarks of dreaming—hallucinatory images, disjointed narratives, wild emotions, and lack of judgment or reflective self-awareness—occurred during waking only in people whose minds were deranged. Like his nemesis Freud, he hoped that understanding how dreaming worked would shed light on the mechanics of mental illness too.

Above all, though, he hoped dream research would lead him to his Holy Grail: unraveling the secrets of consciousness, often termed the "mind-body" problem. He believes that every state of the mind—from dreaming to all forms of waking consciousness—can be explained entirely by the type of brain cell activity occurring at a given point in time. There is no "mind" over matter. Rather, mind *is* matter. Self, free will, and other such lofty concepts all boil down to a particular firing pattern among neurons. Obviously, this viewpoint disturbs anyone who believes in the concept of a soul that is separate from the body. It is hard to swallow even for the nonreligious, because it is at odds with the notion of a higher self within us that is somehow separate from the brain—the "I" who is aware of being aware.

Hobson is messianic himself in proclaiming that our emotions, memories, and thoughts are simply reflections of the Morse code of the brain's electrical and chemical activity. Nowhere is that made more clear, he argues, than in the transitions between sleep and waking, when physical changes in the brain unquestionably lead to shifts in the nature of thought and perception.

"People who object to what I say do so with that part of themselves which thinks that self is something separate and qualitatively different from the body. Yes, it's hard to imagine how consciousness arises from the brain, but it's much harder to imagine it arising without reference to anything, unless you believe in a God that controls spirits and deals them out. Accepting that the mind and brain are one severely challenges religion, but it needn't diminish the wonder of life," he says.

FORTUNATELY FOR HOBSON, such meaty questions were also of great interest to two other well-known scientists who were just forming a novel program in the 1980s to fund exactly this kind of research. The Mind-Body Network was the brainchild of Jonas Salk, famed for his polio vaccine development, and Nobel Prize–winning physicist Murray Gell-Man. Both served on the board of the MacArthur Foundation, which was in the process of providing long-term funding for cutting-edge multidisciplinary research. Hobson was one of the first three scientists chosen to participate in the group, whose members met four or five times a year to brainstorm and exchange information about their respective research projects. "I think Gell-Man and Salk felt if they had successfully tackled the problems of particle physics and infectious disease, surely our group could figure out the mind-body question," says Hobson. "I remember sitting across the table from Murray in Chicago when I explained the kind of research I wanted to do and he agreed that's exactly what they wanted, too."

For a full decade beginning in the late 1980s, the MacArthur network funded research in Hobson's lab aimed at identifying characteristics of dreaming consciousness and tracing their source to specific physiological conditions in the dreaming brain. If you dream that you're trying to run but your feet are mired in quicksand, it's simply because, according to Hobson's research, your brain's motor activity circuits have been activated by random brainstem signals. Those circuits in turn are issuing orders for your body to run, but since the brainstem is preventing those signals from reaching your leg muscles, the perception carried through into the dream is that you're trying to run but you're stuck, so you weave that into the dream's plot.

Clearly, many dreams were accompanied by strong emotions, so Hobson's group also collected data on emotions in subjects' dream reports and found that just three emotions accounted for 70 percent of the feelings dreamers said they experienced: anxiety was the most common, followed by elation and then anger. Other emotions, such as affectionate or erotic feelings, shame, and guilt, were rare in dreams, each accounting for less than 5 percent of reported emotions. This too was consistent with Hobson's theory because the chemical changes triggered by the brainstem during REM were known to stimulate the brain's emotional circuits, particularly an almond-shaped structure called the amygdala, which is the seat of the body's flight-or-fight response. If you're feeling anxious, terrified, or overcome by road rage in your waking hours, you can bet your amygdala is blasting at full volume, just as it would be when you're dreaming of being chased or of showing up totally unprepared for a final exam.

Hobson also zeroed in on what he considered another defining feature of dreams: their bizarre quality. Why does your dream start off in a hotel room in Paris, then suddenly shift to an underground cave that somehow also resembles your college dorm room? Why are you fruitlessly searching for a photo album in your bedroom and then, without any transition whatever, traveling on the space shuttle with a friend from kindergarten? According to Hobson, dreams are inherently bizarre because the portion of the brain that focuses attention, runs reality checks, and makes logical connections in waking consciousness is unhinged during dreaming. Therefore dreaming was by definition bizarre, a kind of madness.

"What we saw and looked for was shaped by what was in our minds, and we were more or less convinced that dreaming correlated with REM," Hobson says.

While REM clearly was the most favorable state for producing vivid, detailed dream narratives, other researchers had found evidence that the brain also concocts dreams in other stages of sleep. Scientists who had explored non-REM dreaming concluded that rather than dreaming only two hours out of eight per night during REM, nearly all of our sleeping hours are filled with some form of mentation, which sometimes resembles daytime thought and other times becomes more hallucinatory. Hallucinatory dreamlike thought may even briefly intrude in waking hours when our attention to external sights and sounds is relaxed. In short, they proposed that the more highly evolved, thought-producing parts of the brain were actively involved in dream creation and that the line between waking and dreaming could actually become rather fuzzy.

Hobson supported his contention that dreaming is by its very nature hallucinatory with results from his own group's experiment designed to clarify the differences between waking and dreaming mentation. They equipped test subjects with beepers so that researchers could periodically and without warning check in to sample the nature of their thinking throughout the day while they were sitting on the subway or working at their desks. At night they used the Nightcap to collect dream reports from sleep onset through non-REM and REM stages. This sampling produced eighteen hundred usable reports, which were then given to judges who scored them based on various characteristics, including degree of emotion, quality of thinking, and bizarreness. From a quiet waking state through sleep onset and on into REM, the frequency of thoughts decreased fourfold while the frequency of hallucinations rose tenfold.

MORE THAN A DECADE before Hobson and McCarley's influential theory was published, psychologist David Foulkes also had demonstrated in studies at the University of Chicago that dreaming did indeed take place outside REM. His first study showing these results became the basis for his doctoral dissertation, which he completed in 1960. Foulkes at first accepted the widely held belief that dreaming occurred only in REM, but he wanted to find out how early in the REM cycle dreams began. To be absolutely thorough, he tried waking subjects before EEG patterns signaled the beginning of REM to ask them what, if anything, was going through their minds. To his surprise, he found that more than 50 percent of the reports subjects gave on awakening indicated that dreaming was occurring even before they entered their first REM period. In later studies the percentage of REM-like dream reports at sleep onset was shown to be as high as 70 percent. "I gave up trying to find out how and where REM dreaming began, because I could find no point at which dreaming ceased," says Foulkes.

Of course, the question of how you define "dreaming" was at the heart of objections raised by those who argued that dreams occur only during REM. Hobson's definition of a dream in the attention-getting 1977 paper outlining his new theory in the *American Journal of Psychiatry* was "a mental experience, occurring in sleep, which is characterized by hallucinoid imagery, predominantly visual and often vivid; by bizarre elements; . . . and by a delusional acceptance of these phenomena as 'real' at the time that they occur." In contrast, Foulkes included as dreaming any report of mental content, including what others might call thinking. Critics argued that non-REM dream reports were less vivid and hallucinatory than REM dreams—much more like waking thought processes—and therefore not worthy of being labeled dreams.

But additional evidence that dreaming wasn't solely a feature of REM came from John Antrobus, a cognitive psychologist at the City University of New York. He found that when people sleep later than usual in the morning, they tend to have unusually vivid, memorable dreams, the "superdreams" that they often describe to others. This is the time of day when the body's internal clock shifts as we approach waking and causes widespread brain activation. Dream reports during this time frame contained visual images that were brighter and clearer than in the typical dream, and they also were unusually detailed and long, regardless of whether they occurred during REM or non-REM sleep. "If dreams were uniquely correlated with REM sleep, this wouldn't have been the case," Antrobus says.

Certainly, the typical REM dream report tends to be longer and more detailed than the average non-REM account, as shown by the following two dream reports collected in a 1963 study by Allan Rechtschaffen and Gerald Vogel. Awakened during slow-wave, non-REM sleep, a subject gave this dream description:

> I had been dreaming about getting ready to take some kind of an exam. It had been a very short dream. That's just about all that it contained. I don't think I was worried about it.

The same sleeper was awakened during REM later in the night. Even though the subject matter of the dream described below is similar to that of the earlier one, there are obvious differences in the length and degree of detail in the reports:

> I was dreaming about exams. In the early part of the dream, I was dreaming that I had just finished taking an exam and it was a very sunny day outside. I was walking with a boy who was in some of my classes with me. There was sort of a break, and someone mentioned

a grade they had gotten in a social science exam, and I asked them if the social science marks had come in. They said yes. I didn't get mine because I had been away for a day.

While REM dreams typically were longer as well as more emotionally charged and colorful than their non-REM counterparts, Foulkes found—as Antrobus did—that as the night progressed, dreams from non-REM sleep were often indistinguishable from REM dreams. The following dream report from a subject awakened twenty-five minutes after the last REM period of the night is a prime example:

> I was with my mother in a public library. I wanted her to steal something for me. I've got to try and remember what it was, because it was something extraordinary, something like a buffalo head that was in this museum. I had told my mother previously that I wanted this head and she said, all right, you know, we'll see what we can do about it. And she met me in the library, part of which was a museum. And I remember telling my mother to please lower her voice and she insisted on talking even more loudly. And I said, if you don't, of course, you'll never be able to take the buffalo head. Everyone will turn around and look at you. Well, when we got to the place where the buffalo head was, it was surrounded by other strange things. There was a little sort of smock that little boys used to wear at the beginning of the century. And one of the women who worked at the library came up to me and said, dear, I haven't been able to sell this smock. And I remember saying to her, well, why don't you wear it then? For some reason or other I had to leave my mother alone, and she had to continue with the buffalo head project all by herself. Then I left the library and went outside, and there were groups of people just sitting on the grass listening to music.

While a roomful of psychologists could argue endlessly about how to interpret that dream, there's no disputing that it would be hard to distinguish it from the typical REM dream. Subsequent studies have indicated that at least 5 to 10 percent of awakenings outside REM produce dream reports that are identical to those in REM, though there is no question that the majority of vivid, storylike dreams do occur when our brains are in the highly activated REM phase of sleep.

Like Hobson, Foulkes put no stock in Freudian dream analysis or other forms of dream interpretation. He believed that dreaming as we experience it is the accidental by-product of two separate evolutionary developments: the emergence of REM sleep and the development of consciousness in humans, which created the urge to make narratives out of any available data the brain receives. Whenever the story-spinning portions of the brain were activated, as they regularly were in REM, they couldn't help but churn out a dream.

The conclusions Foulkes reached about the basic nature of dreams, however, were different from Hobson's. First, he concurred with John Antrobus that dreams were not inherently bizarre. He suggested that the perception of all dreams being wild, hallucinatory sagas springs from the fact that most of the dreams we remember are so emotionally charged or odd that they wake us. We sleep through the blander, more realistic ones that fill the bulk of our hours, and thus don't recall them.

He based his views on evidence from his own work in the sleep lab, which he considered the best setting for collecting dream reports. When researchers monitored subjects' EEG patterns in a sleep laboratory and awakened them in the midst of both REM and non-REM episodes, many of the dream reports they collected indeed lacked the bizarre flights of fancy and sudden shifts of setting we associate with dreaming. Just as a witness's report taken at the scene of a car accident would be more accurate than her recollection of details hours later, immediate reports of nighttime dream content were more reliable than accounts based on memories of dreams after awaking in the morning, Foulkes argued. A truly representative sampling of a night's worth of dream reports collected in the lab contained for the most part relatively coherent images strung together in a plausible way.

Foulkes also concluded that the creation of dreams as we know them is a high-level cognitive process that develops much later than most people assume. His conclusions emerged from meticulous, extended studies of children's dreaming, which provided fascinating insights on how human consciousness develops. As he explained in his book *Children's Dreaming and the Development of Consciousness*, "To dream, it isn't enough to be able to see. You have to be able to think in a certain way. You have to be able to simulate at first momentarily, and later in more extended episodes, a conscious reality that is not supported by current sense data and that you've never experienced before."

Foulkes's groundbreaking studies of children's dreams came about almost by accident. In a variation on the University of Chicago studies he'd done exploring whether adult subjects' dream content could be manipulated by viewing violent films at bedtime, he began an experiment to see whether children's dreams would be affected by presleep viewing of violent and nonviolent episodes of the television show *Daniel Boone*. Though he found the TV episodes had no significant impact on kids' dream content, he realized that he'd hit upon a far more interesting research angle to pursue. "I had a slowly dawning realization of what a dope I'd been in trying to see how these silly films would change dreams when in fact we didn't even understand what the baseline properties of children's dreams were—no one had done an objective study describing what they were like," says Foulkes.

When he took a research position at the University of Wyoming at Laramie, Foulkes set up a sleep lab to study a group of children he recruited through newspaper ads for what ranked as the most extensive sleep lab project ever conducted on human dreams in either adults or children. The study was launched in 1968 with fourteen children between the ages of three and four and another group of sixteen kids who were between nine and eleven years old. With the exception of four children in the older group who moved out of town, all of the children remained in the study for five years. For nine nights a year, they came into the sleep lab, where they were awakened three times nightly, primarily during REM sleep.

The sleeping rooms were made homey with toys and posters. Parents of younger children sometimes stayed to see them off to sleep, but Foulkes also frequently served as surrogate parent, reading them bedtime stories and fetching drinks of water before it was time for lights out. Though other lab personnel often were present, Foulkes was the one who consistently awakened children to ask them the crucial question: what was happening just now? Asking if they'd been dreaming might be suggesting that he expected a positive answer and also demanded a degree of introspection that could be beyond younger children's ability. He simply wanted them to report objectively, as if they were describing what they had just seen through a car window as they were traveling down a road.

Foulkes also tested the children's waking cognitive skills in daytime sessions several times a year. To gather this information for the younger children, he ran a two-week-long nursery school during the first three summers in order to closely observe children's play behavior and interaction with other people. "We wanted to include every waking observation that might have something to do with dreaming and in effect compare the daytime child with the nighttime child," he says.

His findings were startling, for they contradicted assumptions commonly held by both scientists and parents about the nature of children's dreams. Foulkes's data showed that children's dreams didn't become similar to adults' in either form or frequency until they were between nine and eleven years old. When he awakened children in the sleep lab, the rate of any dream recall at all during REM sleep was no more than 30 percent until children passed that critical ninth birthday, after which dream reporting rates reached the adult level of around 80 percent. Even more significantly, the dream content the children described differed dramatically from adults' and evolved over time in a consistent pattern among the children studied.

The dreams of children under age five consisted primarily of brief, bland, static images in which they frequently saw animals or were thinking about daytime activities such as sleeping or eating. Typical are these dream reports from one of the children in the study—a four-year-old boy named Dean:

> I was asleep and in the bathtub.
>
> I was sleeping at a co-co stand, where you get Coke from.

Between ages five and eight, children's dream reports became more complex, with action sequences and interactions between characters, but the child himself didn't regularly appear as an active character in the dreams until age seven or eight. When awakened at age six, for instance, Dean gave the following report, which characterizes dreaming ability at this stage of mental development:

A cabin at Barbara Lake. It was little and I looked in it. Freddie and I were playing around, with a few toys and things.

By age eight, Dean's dreams developed longer narratives in which he was featured as a more active player:

My family—my sisters and my mom—and I were going on a trip skiing. We were flying there. I could see the airplane and the people and things at an airport. And when I turned around, I took the wrong plane, and I went to the Olympics instead. I got worried when I went to the Olympics because I missed the plane. I could see the people at the Olympics, they had a torch, and people skiing and stuff.

A dream reported by Dean's sister Emily at age twelve reflects the further evolution that Foulkes pinpointed as occurring after children reached eleven, when their dreams, like adults', reflect personal concerns and emotional preoccupations:

I was in a car with two friends of mine, and another girl and her mother, who was French, was driving us home. She had a French accent and was talking to us. And there was something in the street that was mine and I told them that that was my choker out there in the street. And so we stopped and one friend got out to get it. And this other guy, her father, he was in the car too, he just drove off and left her there, standing out in the middle of the street. And we were all just looking at each other in the car, wondering. At the end of the dream I was kind of excited because he left her out there in the street all alone, and kind of angry toward him.

Critics who rejected Foulkes's conclusions have argued that collecting dreams in the sleep lab rather than a home setting biased the results. A team of researchers at Hobson's neurophysiology lab conducted a home-based study in which parents collected eighty-eight dream reports from fourteen children from age four to ten. Parents were told the study's purpose was to determine the nature and frequency of children's dreams and that they shouldn't pressure children into reporting dreams, though on five of the nights, children were instructed to repeat to themselves "I will remember my dreams" prior to going to sleep. Over a period of thirteen consecutive nights, parents collected dream reports using a microcassette recorder when they awakened children in the morning and sometimes also during the middle of the night. The results of the Harvard study showed children were able to give detailed reports of dreams that were similar to adults' in length, number of characters, settings, and bizarre qualities. Children as young as four and five years old reported dreams and said they themselves were active characters in most of them. The researchers concluded: "Because this wide range of dream mentation is only revealed to trusted confidants in a familiar and comfortable environment, an important implication is that the sleep laboratory may not be the best source of naturalistic dream data."

In response, Foulkes says that what the parents—mainly professional couples from the Boston–Cape Cod area—knew about the study influenced the results. "One can imagine not only the general cultural pressure that contemporary Cambridge-area doctors and lawyers would feel to see to it that their children perform 'well' in any test of imaginativeness," he argues, "but also specific pressure from an investigative team whose theory also specifies that children's dream reports must be imaginative." Foulkes had done studies himself showing that when the same method was used to collect children's dreams at home and in the lab, there was no significant difference in content or recall.

Other critics who doubted Foulkes's findings about children's dreams argued that the paucity and mundane content of dream reports in younger children was due to immature language and recall skills—in other words, an inability to accurately describe what they were dreaming. But Foulkes's daytime tests of the children's cognitive abilities actually showed that children who most often reported dreams did not have better memories, vocabularies, or descriptive skills than their counterparts who reported fewer dreams. Instead, the children with the most frequent dream reports were those who scored well on tests that measure visual-spatial skills, such as a standard test in which they are shown a picture of a colored pattern that they had to reconstruct with blocks. Foulkes concluded that visual imagination abilities develop gradually and are a crucial prerequisite for dreaming.

His point was supported by unexpected results among two children in the study. Two boys in the eleven-to-thirteen age group seldom reported dreams during REM awakenings. Though they had average memory and verbal skills and were adequate students in school, the boys scored abnormally low on the block design test, with results in the same range as five-to-seven-year-olds. "In their case, even more clearly than for the five-to-seven-year-olds, it can't be that the children are having dreams but simply not remembering or describing them very well. It seems much more likely that they were simply not having dreams or not having very memorable dreams," argues Foulkes.

Foulkes's argument that children younger than five lack some of the cognitive visuospatial skills essential for dreaming is also supported by studies of dreaming among the blind, some of which have been conducted by his wife, cognitive psychologist Nancy Kerr. Children who become blind before the age of five rarely experience visual imagery in dreams. Those who lose sight between the ages of five and seven sometimes retain visual imagery, while those blinded after age seven are able to dream much as sighted people do and to form visual imagery in waking consciousness, such as conjuring up a mental picture of people they've met since losing their sight. Since Foulkes found the span between ages five and seven to be the critical period in the development of dreaming, he contends that it is during this period that the brain becomes capable of creating visual images without relying on direct perceptual experience. "Dreaming is related not to how we see but to how we are able to think about persons, objects, and events when they are not physically there," says Foulkes.

That thought process, of course, is also what allows the blind to have visual experiences even though they no longer get input from their eyes. Raymond Rainville, a psychologist who lost his sight at the age of twenty-five and has since studied the phenomenon of dreaming among the blind, says that when he was newly blinded, the visual images in his dreams had the same clarity and quality of what he used to see before losing sight. "Being able to see in my dreams was the first step in my conscious recognition that sight and vision were different phenomena. Vision is a way of thinking from my point of view," he says.

But after more than three decades without sight, Rainville says that in the majority of his dreams now, he is a blind person, and most of the images in the dream are in the same category as the visual imagery he creates during waking hours. "I can create visual images of things or people I've never seen based on information I get from other senses. I've never seen my own children, but I'm very sure I know what they look like, and when I dream of them, I see them," he says. But when he dreams about the home where he grew up and experiences that occurred before he was blind, those visual images are qualitatively different—he sees them with the same clarity and confidence as he did when his eyes were available as tools for conveying information from the outside world. "Most of the imagery in dreams is memory dependant, and as you get older, more and more of memory stored is blind memory," he notes. These vivid dreams evoking preblind times occur for Rainville just a couple of times a year, and usually only when he's out of his normal routine or has experienced an emotionally provocative event in waking hours.

He recounts one dream in which he is a boy of eleven or twelve walking to the beach as he often did with his grandfather. He sees vivid images of the panorama of people passing by, particularly one alluring woman wearing a blue bathing suit and shiny black earrings. He and his grandfather stop for pizza, and as they're waiting for it to cool, his grandfather excitedly tells him to look up to see who's coming. "I am sure he means somebody from our place, family, but as I look up the scene turns into a still life. Then it is a postcard and then I know it is a dream," Rainville recalls. He says such preblind dream narratives are filled with happy imagery, but they always create powerful feelings of sadness upon awakening to the reality of being blind. "Nevertheless, remembering what it was to see plays a very important and stimulating role in maintaining the psychological capacity to visualize realistically. It is also reassuring to know that the neurological underpinnings are still there," he adds.

He says dreams also play a crucial role in his ability to navigate new surroundings and to imprint visual imagery. If he has to learn the route to his dentist's new office, he eventually has what he calls a consolidation dream, in which all of the auditory and sensory data he's absorbed on the first couple of trips is pulled together to give him a mental picture of the new place or route. Only after he's "seen" his way in the consolidation dream can he negotiate the route as if he were in his own home, where he navigates with the same confidence as a sighted person. Such dreams also help consolidate other kinds of new visual imagery. "When my daughter gets her hair cut short, I will Braille it, appreciate it, comment on it. However, the next time she crosses my path or I think about her, in my spontaneous waking image she will still be wearing long hair. Once I dream of her in her new hairdo, that is, once I have seen it, she will appear to me in it pretty much consistently from that time on." He says others who were blinded at some point after early childhood have reported similar dream experiences.

Foulkes was intrigued by the data from children's dreaming studies showing how this visualization capacity relied upon by the blind gradually and naturally emerges in children, but he was most surprised by how long it took for children's dreams to include images of themselves as active, on-the-scene actors in their own dreams. He found it particularly significant because neuropsychological evidence showed that if we couldn't generate a given category of imagery in dreaming, we couldn't do it in waking either. This suggested the startling possibility that until they are at least seven years old, children don't have a conscious self-identity. The tests psychologists use to gauge whether children have developed this sense include asking a child whether she is the same person she was when she was a baby, or whether she would be the same person if she had a different name. "In telling us about their dreams, children are telling us about operations they can and cannot perform in their mind's eye," he says. "And best of all they are telling us this without even realizing it."

In the mid-1980s, Foulkes ran another dreaming study with children between the ages of five and eight in Atlanta, where he was on the faculty at Emory University and was running a sleep lab at a state mental health institute. He wanted to see if he could replicate the first study's results on the development of conscious self-identity. He did.

Summarizing what he believes children's dreaming tells us, Foulkes says, "Consciousness is not a luxury afforded full-blown to creatures born as immature as we are and facing as much to learn as we do. Consciousness emerges slowly, and its eventual scope is not even approached until the early grade-school years. With the emergence of active self-representation, of autobiographical memory, and of a sensed self that lends continuity to experience, the human person emerges. We dream because we have achieved consciousness."

Though Foulkes intended to do further experiments using analysis of children's dreaming to identify when other key features of consciousness emerge, his hopes were dashed when his funding for dream research was eliminated in 1991 at the state facility where he operated his lab. Unable to find other backing for his research, Foulkes's career abruptly came to an end, and he retired in Oregon—a development that dream and sleep research pioneer Allan Rechtschaffen considers an unfortunate loss. "David is the most careful, considerate experimenter I've ever seen, and his work should have had more of an impact," he says. Foulkes chalks up his fate to the politics of funding meted out by government agencies. "The decision to retire was thrust upon me, and there's a sense in which I can accept responsibility because if you don't bend to the current twist of the wind in neuroscience, then you're going to drop out of favor," he says, noting that the major wind he'd resisted was the neurophysiological explanation of dreaming as the brain simply doing its best to make sense of random signals from the brainstem. "Within the field of sleep and dream research there was less and less support for basic psychology," Foulkes says.

Other researchers interested in dream content or the psychological aspect of dreams echoed Foulkes's view of how Hobson's well-publicized theories have affected the course of dream research. Observes Bill Domhoff, a dream researcher at the University of California at Santa Cruz: "Hobson comes out with his theory and becomes the anti-Freud. It vaulted him to celebrity but it was very polarizing. He becomes Mr. Science, and the other side is seen as nonscience, wiping people like Foulkes out of the picture. Hobson got the stage and the money and that shapes a field mightily."

In response to such criticisms, Hobson says being the anti-Freud certainly got him attention but he doesn't believe it helped him get funding for his work. In fact, federal funding for dream research in general began to dry up in the 1980s, with research for sleep disorders taking priority among those controlling the purse strings. "What they were really mad about is their labs got closed and they lost grants. I didn't do that. The NIH did," he says. He also denies that he dismissed the importance of psychology in the study of dreams, noting that he is in fact a great believer in psychotherapy, as long as it's the right kind—that is, in his view, not psychoanalysis. Indeed, his 1977 paper that created such a stir in the psychotherapy community clearly stated that while the primary motivating force for dreaming was physiological rather than psychological, that did not imply that dreams "are without psychological meaning or function."

Providing a broader perspective, cognitive psychologist John Antrobus says that even though Hobson and McCarley's theory still doesn't explain how a dream actually is created, he does give Hobson enormous credit for recording neuronal activity in the brainstem to confirm its role in accounting for the alternation of REM and NREM (non-REM) sleep stages, especially at a time when little attention was given to structures underlying the brain's surface. "Here was this brain that looks like it's wide awake 20 percent of the night—the EEG looks like a waking EEG," says Antrobus. "How do you account for that? We didn't know the brainstem was doing this. It was Hobson and McCarley who pointed out what was activating the brain to give it the superficial characteristics of waking. That was the big contribution of Hobson's work."

But did the brainstem really turn on dreaming? That assumption was about to be challenged by an inquisitive young man named Mark Solms, who—like Hobson—was a determined researcher with no qualms about questioning authority on a scientific point. And to make the debate even more interesting, he was a psychoanalyst and staunch defender of Freud. His findings, along with research using technology that captured the dreaming brain in action as never before, would help bridge the divide between the Freudians and the neurophysiologists and uncover further surprises about what was happening in the mind at night.

3

Experiments of Nature

Perhaps it is simply the ghost of Freud that is getting in the way.
—*Allen Braun*

GROWING UP IN A TINY VILLAGE in a remote corner of Africa that is now part of Namibia, Mark Solms and his brother, Lee, were inseparable, in part because they were among the only English-speaking children in town. They had settled in this former German colony in southwest Africa because it was home to a rich diamond deposit and their father was an executive with the diamond giant DeBeers. But when Lee slipped off a rooftop he'd scrambled onto while playing and suffered a brain injury at the age of six, not only was he himself forever changed, but he indirectly sent his younger brother Mark on a quest that would shape his life.

"In retrospect, I believe my brother's accident led me to study neuroscience in the particular way I did, because I wanted to understand how people are organized by their brain function. Not just the brain's cognitive aspects, such as how we learn to speak or read, but rather how the brain gives us our personality and sense of self," says Solms. "How can it be that a person comes from this lump of tissue, and how could my brother as a person be changed entirely because of damage to portions of that lump of tissue?" Studying exactly how damage to specific areas of the brain affects behavior was in fact what led Mark Solms to discoveries that uncovered surprising and vital new pieces of the dreaming puzzle.

Though he's now based in South Africa, Solms travels regularly to New York in connection with his work at the New York Psychoanalytic Center, which encourages the exchange of information and research among neuroscientists and psychoanalysts. Over breakfast in an Upper East Side hotel dining room with a decidedly British ambience, Solms's earnest passion for his work is apparent as he explains how he came to focus on dreaming as a window into the workings of the mind.

As a student of neuroscience in Johannesburg in the early 1980s, Solms found that he was being taught much about superficial brain mechanisms but next to nothing about the larger questions that interested him. Nothing, that is, until he was persuaded by friends to take a seminar on Freudian dream theory taught, not by a scientist, but by a professor of comparative literature. The focus of the seminar was a manuscript Freud had written in the late 1800s speculating about what brain mechanisms might underlie the dreaming process. "Most of my friends were in the arts, history, and philosophy and I was the odd man out, studying the brain, so they were excited to find a seminar for me in their world," he recalls. "I was fascinated listening to these speculations about the brain functions underlying dreaming—wishful thoughts, coping with strong emotions—all the meaty stuff about lived lives that I wasn't hearing about in neuroscience."

As a result, for his doctoral dissertation, Solms decided to update Freud, whose speculations about the neurological basis of dreaming relied on a body of knowledge about how the brain works that had changed significantly since his theories on the subject were published in 1895 as "Project for a Scientific Psychology." For starters, Solms closely read Hobson's studies showing that signals from the brainstem during REM sleep triggered dreaming and that the more highly evolved forebrain simply did its best to make sense of the randomly generated chaotic signals it was receiving by producing hallucinatory dream imagery. Though Solms says he thought Hobson's 1977 paper was "unnecessarily destructive, stacking the cards in ways that made the Freudian effort look more ridiculous than it really was," he maintains that he never set out to disprove Hobson's model. "Hobson's view was *the* view of how the brain generated dreams. It dominated the field and I was just a student, so I had no reason to doubt its fundamentals. All I intended to do was elucidate in greater detail what the forebrain actually does with those dream-activating impulses coming from the brainstem," Solms says.

Solms—who already was on his way to becoming a Freudian scholar and leader in the psychoanalytic field—suspected that dreams were created in a more complex way than Hobson's theory indicated. If Solms could pinpoint exactly how the more highly evolved parts of the brain participated in creating dreams, he might be able to prove that Freud was correct in proposing that dreams draw on our memories from early childhood to the present and symbolically express the strong emotions that drive our inner life.

The young researcher began his quest by doing classic neuroanatomical detective work. Working in the neurosurgery department, first at a hospital in Johannesburg and then in London, Solms had an opportunity to study every patient who had any type of brain damage (known as lesions), whether due to stroke, tumors, or traumatic injuries like his brother's. He questioned each patient about what effect, if any, the illness or injury had on his or her dreaming. His method of inquiry paid off almost immediately: one of the first patients he examined claimed to have ceased dreaming entirely. That patient had a lesion in the parietal lobe, which is the portion of the brain that combines various forms of sensory information to create our sense of spatial orientation and mental imagery. It's what allows us to conjure up a scene of relaxing on a South Pacific beach when we're daydreaming, to envision the route we'll take to stop by the bank, or to imagine how we'll reconfigure the counter space to remodel a kitchen.

As he came across increasing numbers of patients with damage to this region—all of whom claimed to have stopped dreaming as a result—Solms searched the medical literature and found that there had been previous scattered case reports all pointing to that same conclusion. This all made sense to Solms, and there was nothing in it to contradict Hobson's theory: EEG recordings showed that the patients still experienced REM sleep, so Solms assumed that the signals from the brainstem that switched on REM were being transmitted as usual but dreaming didn't occur, simply because the picture-making machinery that received them in the forebrain was broken.

But Solms was truly startled by two other patterns that emerged among the patients he encountered. While most people with injuries to the brainstem do not retain sufficient consciousness to be able to report whether or not they dream, he had a few such patients who said they still continued to dream—something that should have been impossible under Hobson's theory about how dreams were triggered. "I started to worry about why I was seeing all of these patients with parietal lesions who had stopped dreaming but none who'd stopped as a result of damage to the brainstem," he says. So Solms again searched the medical literature, assuming that even if he hadn't found such patients himself, surely he'd find other published reports of them. He couldn't find a single one. "I was absolutely dumbfounded," Solms recalls. "If you're going to claim a certain brain structure performs a certain function, then you have to be able to show that damage to that structure leads to loss of that function."

At that point, everything about the prevailing theory on dreaming became open to question. As Solms reviewed earlier work, he read the studies by David Foulkes and Gerald Vogel showing that subjects reported dreams in the majority of awakenings at sleep onset before the first REM period of the night, as well as John Antrobus's research showing vivid dream reports during non-REM at the other end of the cycle, in the morning before awakening. "When I saw that the connection between REM sleep and dreaming wasn't watertight after all, I started to think that maybe the whole process was driven by the forebrain rather than the brainstem." He speculated that REM sleep indeed was switched on when the brainstem was flooded with the neurotransmitter acetylcholine, as Hobson had shown, but that dreaming itself was an entirely separate process that could occur only when specific mechanisms in the higher portions of the brain were also activated.

If this turnabout in thinking proved true, it would establish a physiological basis for viewing dreaming as a mental process driven by more complex brain structures, rather than simply a chaotic response to the brainstem's random electrical signals. Not only could the age-old fascination with dream content be justified scientifically, but in Solms's view, this new direction for research would prove that the obituaries that had been written for Freudian dream theory were premature. If dreaming and REM sleep were two distinct processes, each with its own on/off switches, then it was possible that dreams could be driven by the motivational regions of the brain, in keeping with Freud's notion that dreams expressed our deepest wishes and fears. And if regions of the forebrain that are strongly linked to memory formation also proved to be involved in dream creation, that would support Freud's suggestion that the characters, settings, and actions in dreams were drawn from the vast stores of the dreamer's personal experiences, including early childhood ones that were outside the realm of conscious recall.

Solms's speculation that dreaming and REM sleep were separate processes controlled by different brain mechanisms soon waxed to conviction when he saw a second unexpected pattern. He discovered reports of dreaming ceasing altogether in yet another group of patients—those with damage to both the right and left sides of a section deep in the middle of the brain's frontal lobe. The tissue in this area is called white matter because it is rich in neural pathways that are coated in a glistening white fatty sheath that enables neuronal signals to travel quickly over long distances. One patient suffered damage in this area from a knife wound in the eye that penetrated both sides of the brain's midsection, while others had lesions in this area due to a specific type of tumor called a butterfly glioma that projects down into the white matter like a pair of wings. All told, Solms had only nine of these patients, which he feared wasn't enough to support any valid scientific conclusions. Damage to this well-protected area due to injury or natural causes was uncommon, but when Solms decided to go back through decades of medical reports to see if other such cases had been described, he struck scientific gold.

Throughout the 1950s and into the 1960s, one of the treatments for schizophrenics and other delusional patients was a modified version of prefrontal lobotomy, the surgical procedure used to tame McMurphy, the hero in Ken Kesey's *One Flew over the Cuckoo's Nest.*

In the gentler version, known as a prefrontal leukotomy, surgeons found that they could cure their patients' hallucinations by cutting into exactly that area of the brain that had been injured in the nine patients who reported to Solms that they no longer dreamed. So although nature itself doesn't often create damage to that crucial section of white matter, surgeons had done so in vast numbers of people for years, and Solms found that an overwhelming majority of them said they had stopped dreaming. "It was there in black and white to see for decades, and no one noticed," he says.

Prefrontal leukotomies also provided information about the function of the area of white matter, known as the ventromesial forebrain, that lies in the lower and middle portions of the brain's frontal lobes. Both the people who'd had the procedure and the group of nine patients with injuries whom Solms had found experienced similar behavior changes afterward. They became completely apathetic, displaying little spontaneity or curiosity about the world. This wasn't surprising, because the same brain area—sometimes called the seeking system—had been well studied in animals and was known to shift into high gear when an animal was motivated to meet its basic needs or seek pleasure, from foraging for food to pursuing a mate. In humans it was also the area that lights up in brain-imaging studies when an addict is merely shown slides of drug paraphernalia or when a smoker is desperately scavenging for a cigarette. In short, the ventromesial forebrain is the brain's "I want it" system, and Solms was convinced that it—not the primitive brainstem—was the crucial structure needed to generate dreams.

But what was it about this particular brain region that could make it so crucial to dreaming? Solms agreed with Hobson that acetylcholine was the key to turning on REM sleep, but he hypothesized that it was a different brain chemical—dopamine—that switched on dreaming itself. Dopamine levels surge when the brain's reward system is activated in waking by activities an individual finds exciting or pleasurable—from taking drugs such as cocaine or alcohol, to sex, to gambling or thrill-inducing activities like bungee jumping. A plunge in dopamine transmission is associated with a feeling of complete boredom. Though the white matter deep in this midsection of the brain is rich with fibers that transmit both of those neuromodulators,

Solms suspected that dopamine was the one that really triggered dreaming, because medications used to treat schizophrenia worked to eliminate hallucinations in a simple way: they blocked dopamine transmission in that portion of the brain.

If his suspicion were correct, an increase in dopamine transmission should somehow intensify dreaming. In fact, dopamine's ability to do just that had been demonstrated in a 1980 experiment by Tufts University psychiatrist and dream researcher Ernest Hartmann. Hartmann found that giving test subjects drugs that increased dopamine transmission in the brain greatly jazzed up their dreams. Though subjects who had been given the drug had the same number and duration of REM cycles as subjects who were given placebo, the people who'd had the drug reported dreams that were substantially longer, more bizarre, vivid, and emotionally intense than those of the control subjects.

Solms became more convinced that the brainstem alone did not trigger dreaming when he encountered another fascinating group of brain lesion patients: those who couldn't stop dreaming, even when they were awake. These patients suffered damage to a specific group of cells in the base of the forebrain that played a crucial role in Hobson's view of how dreams are created. Hobson contended that the brainstem's dream-generating signals projected onto these cells (called basal forebrain nuclei) and that they in turn activated the forebrain structures needed to create visual images and the other stuff of which dreams are made. If Hobson's theory were correct, then damaging those cells should result in a loss of dreaming, but Solms found just the opposite was true. Damage to those cells and closely related brain structures instead created patients whose nighttime dreams were unusually vivid and frequent and who had difficulty distinguishing between dreams and waking experience during the day. The reality-testing system that goes off-line when we dream—allowing us to fully believe that we're back at the high school prom wearing nothing but our underwear—normally comes back online when we awaken. Not so for patients with damage to these clusters of cells.

For instance, one of Solms' patients was a thirty-two-year-old man who'd suffered a head injury during an auto accident that damaged his basal forebrain nuclei. Not only did his dreams become more vivid, but frequently he would wake up from a frightening dream only to find that the dream seemed to continue while he was awake. He said the experience was "terrifyingly real," ending only when his wife would awaken and convince him that his visions of ghosts or small animals crawling around the room were merely hallucinations.

Another of Solms's patients was a forty-four-year-old widow who suffered damage to this area due to an aneurysm, which led her to have much more vivid dreaming at night, as well as daytime experiences in which she says her "thoughts just turned into reality." She was lying in bed one morning thinking of her late husband, when he suddenly appeared in the room with her. After they'd spoken together for a while, he helped her to bathe. Then, in an instant, she realized she was still in bed and totally alone in the room. It was difficult to believe that nothing she'd imagined had actually happened. The woman explained that she wasn't asleep and hadn't been dreaming then or during similar daytime dreamlike experiences she'd had: "It wasn't just seeing things. It was as if it was real—as if it was really happening—and many times I couldn't make out what did happen from what didn't."

Commenting on her case, Solms says, "It's the same feeling we all get occasionally when we awaken from a particularly vivid dream and it takes a while to realize that the events occurred only in the dream. Instead of just thinking wouldn't it be nice if my husband were here, her thoughts turned into what she perceived as a real experience. That is, in essence, what dreaming is."

Looking at the sum of the evidence, Solms now firmly believed he had the makings of a new theory of dream creation. The fact that most dreams occur during REM sleep was actually a misleading coincidence, he argued. REM sleep and dreaming were in fact two separate processes with different off/on switches and probably different biological purposes. As earlier studies by Antrobus, Foulkes, and others had shown, REM was the sleep phase most conducive to dreaming, but dreaming also occurred outside REM, especially when we were first falling asleep and again in the morning as our bodies were preparing to wake. What all three states had in common was an elevated state of brain activation, which was only the first step needed to create dreaming. "The three periods of sleep during which you are most likely to experience a dream, therefore, are characterized not by the unique physiology of the REM state (which characterizes only one of the three periods) but by various types of arousal. This suggests that a certain amount rather than a certain type of arousal is a necessary precondition for dreaming," Solms says.

The high level of activation needed to dream occurred most frequently during REM, as demonstrated in studies by various researchers from the 1960s on in which 80 percent of awakenings during REM produced dream reports. But several studies also showed that dreams were reported in 5 to 20 percent of awakenings from non-REM sleep, and Solms argued that dreaming itself could not occur even during REM unless the elevated level of brain activation in turn switched on the seeking system in the forebrain. That system, driven by dopamine, would then activate the more complex structures needed to construct dream imagery and plot. As a physiological underpinning for Freud's theory that dreams have their roots in subconscious wishes, this dream-generating system was the perfect fit. "It was fascinating to see that the part of the brain that appeared to be crucial for switching dreams on is exactly the part of the brain that you would have predicted on the basis of Freud's most unlikely theory," concluded Solms.

ENTIRELY BY COINCIDENCE, just a few months after Solms's new theory and supporting evidence appeared in print in 1997, two American researchers using sophisticated brain-imaging technology to map the dreaming brain in action published their own groundbreaking findings, which provided the most detailed view yet of what happened in the brain as it moved from waking to dreaming consciousness and back again.

Tom Balkin was conducting sleep deprivation experiments in 1989 when he first met Allen R. Braun, a neurologist at the National Institutes of Health who specialized in Parkinson's disease and other movement disorders. At the time, Balkin was chief of the department of behavioral biology at the Walter Reed Army Institute of Research, and both he and Braun were fascinated by the many unanswered questions about the brain during sleep. When EEG recordings were the only way to view changing brain activity, scientists assumed that the entire brain became charged up during REM, but Braun suspected that only selected areas were zooming into action and that discovering which areas those were would provide greater understanding of what the brain really was up to. "It seemed to me this was one last great mystery, but to solve it, you'd have to get a total picture of changes occurring simultaneously in all parts of the brain from sleep to waking," says Braun. So in 1991, by which time neuroimaging technology had advanced to provide the level of detail he and Balkin would need to achieve their goal, the two began collaborating on studies that yielded a series of fascinating three-dimensional portraits of the brain at work.

They used a technique called PET (positron-emission tomography) scanning, which measures blood flow to indicate which regions of the brain are most active at a specific point in time. The PET scan produces an image of the brain that can be displayed on a computer screen, with areas of greater and lesser activity coded in different shades of vibrant color. Over a period of two and a half years, Braun and Balkin met regularly in all-night sessions at the NIH lab in Bethesda, Maryland, to scan subjects before they went to sleep, during REM and non-REM sleep stages, and then again after awakening in the morning.

What they saw opened a new window on exactly what happens in specific regions of the brain during our nightly internal odysseys. As we move into the deepest stages of non-REM sleep, activity in nearly all parts of the brain decreases, but the areas that take the first and steepest plunge (activation levels drop by about 25 percent) are the prefrontal cortical regions that we use for the highest order of information processing, such as planning, logical thinking, and problem solving. "These areas are the first to fall asleep and the last to come back online," says Balkin.

Deactivation of these areas is accompanied by sharp drops in levels of serotonin and norepinephrine, which help us focus attention and solve problem when we're awake. Then a surge of the neuromodulator acetylcholine (which fosters free-wheeling associations) turns on REM sleep. As that happens, remarkable changes visible in the PET scan images occur, and Braun believes that they explain much of the phenomenology of dreaming. All of the areas that were geared down during slow-wave sleep charge back up again except for one: that logical, reasoning portion of the prefrontal cortex that is humankind's latest evolutionary acquisition. Its inactivity would explain why time and space orientation often are jumbled and why we have no reality testing: we don't question the fact that our dead grandfather is dressed in knight's armor and driving a taxicab.

Because the portions of the brain that normally order our thinking are off-line, what we're experiencing as reality in a dream sometimes can be a hallucinatory world, much like what a schizophrenic experiences in waking consciousness. In fact, subsequent brain-imaging studies show that the functional anatomy of dreaming is almost identical to that of schizophrenic psychosis, with the major difference being that for dreamers, the visuospatial system is most highly charged, while for schizophrenics, the audioverbal system is activated. It's no wonder delusional patients often claim to hear voices that dictate their behavior.

Most surprising, though, Braun and Balkin's PET scans revealed that selected portions of the brain are much more active during REM than they are in waking consciousness. The primary visual cortex, which is our portal of visual information from the outside world, is shut down, which is why sleeping subjects whose eyes were taped open in early dream experiments never incorporated into their dreams any images of objects that were flashed before their eyes. But the visual association areas involved in creating mental images and recognizing faces are wildly active, above normal waking levels, making dream imagery richly visual. Braun and Balkin also saw increased activity in an area of the prefrontal cortex that would light up when waking subjects were creating a story based on a series of events from memory. Braun speculates that activation of this area in dreaming reflects the brain's attempt to assemble the visual images into a narrative form.

The area of the brain that allows us to put memories in sequential order and to temporarily store ongoing events in short-term or working memory remains off-line during REM. But the brain structures involved in long-term memory formation and retrieval are actually more active than when we're awake, he says, which creates ideal conditions for REM to play a critical role in long-term memory processing. "REM may provide a situation in which long-term memory traces can be processed off-line, either consolidated or pruned, while the brain is not actively processing information generated during REM itself," Braun says.

This paradoxical situation in which long-term memory processing centers are firing wildly, while the areas needed for storing current experience (the dream itself) in working memory for later retrieval are not, helps explain why we can easily remember what we had for breakfast at 8 A.M. but not what we were dreaming at 4 A.M. Braun maintains that dream content actually is encoded in the brain, as demonstrated by the fact that we can spontaneously remember fragments of a dream if we see or feel something during the day that is associated with what we dreamed the night before. Our poor dream recall really reflects an impairment in our ability to retrieve that memory.

Perhaps most significant, Braun and Balkin found that the structures in the brain that light up when we are feeling strong emotions or craving the object of our desires also are more supercharged during REM than in waking. Operating full tilt is the limbic system, which is the brain's long-term emotional memory center. When we're dreaming, emotions appear to be behind the steering wheel while the brain's attention-directing, decision-making machinery is snoozing in the passenger seat. Similar results were seen in brain-imaging studies by Pierre Maquet and his research group at the Universite de Liege in Belgium. Maquet concluded that the patterns of activation in the amygdala (which generates the body's fight-or-flight response and other intense emotional reactions) and other cortical areas provided a biological basis for the processing of memory during REM, particularly emotionally influenced memories.

As for the question of what actually triggers the dreaming process, the PET scans could provide no clear answer. The pons area of the brainstem, the key to dream generation in Hobson's model, was significantly activated during REM, but so was the motivational area of the forebrain that played a crucial role in Solms's model.

Allan Hobson responded to the flood of new data from the PET scans by applauding the technological advances in brain imaging that made it possible to describe the activation pattern of the brain in REM. He acknowledged that the consistent results of the various brain-imaging studies required a rethinking of his model, noting that "dream emotion may be a primary shaper of dream plots rather than playing the secondary role in dream plot instigation," as he had originally proposed. He suggested that although the focus of a dream's plot shifts from the dreamer feeling lost, to missing a train, to not having proper credentials or suitable clothing, they all satisfy the driving emotion—in this case, most likely anxiety. And he also observed that evidence was fast accumulating to indicate that both non-REM and REM sleep benefit learning and memory, a feature that had not been part of his model.

He seized upon the imaging studies' evidence that quite different mechanisms underlie waking and dreaming consciousness to support his quest for the Holy Grail: proof that brain and mind are one, that our state of consciousness is nothing more than a reflection of the particular mix of brain chemicals and neural connections that happen to be active at any given moment. "The initial loss of contact with the outside world at sleep onset, with its flurry of fleeting hypnagogic images, the deeply unconscious oblivion of sleep early in the night, and the gripping hallucinoid scenarios of late-night dreams, all have such strong and meaningful underpinnings in brain physiology as to make all but certain the idea that our conscious experience is the brain-mind's awareness of its own physiological states," he said.

He even came up with a new model explaining our periodically shifting states of consciousness, saying that just as it was no longer acceptable to equate REM sleep with dreaming, it was no longer possible to regard waking as a single state. The narrow categories into which consciousness had been categorized previously—REM sleep, non-REM sleep, and waking—weren't adequate to describe the many variations that humans actually experience, ranging from focused thought needed to perform mathematical calculations to waking hallucinations experienced by schizophrenics or people tripping on LSD. In Hobson's new model, there were three variables that determine our state of mind at any given point in time. The first was the overall activation level of the brain (based on EEG measures of brain waves). The second was the specific mix of neuromodulators that are predominant in any given state. And the third was whether the brain is processing information generated in the outside world (as it would in alert, waking consciousness) or internally generated information (as it would when dreaming or meditating in silence with closed eyes).

As for Solms's studies, Hobson praised the contribution the neuropsychologist had made using "experiments of nature in the form of strokes" to correlate the locale of brain lesions with changes in the dreaming process and to shed light on how the forebrain participated in constructing dreams. He invited Solms to Harvard to present a paper to his research group. Impressed by Hobson and his colleagues, Solms in turn invited Hobson to appear with him to speak about dreaming at the New York Psychoanalytic Center. Shortly thereafter, Solms received a message from Hobson saying that he was happy to accept Solms's evidence from the brain lesion studies, but if Solms intended to use that research to try to support Freudian dream theories, "that's where we have to part company."

Says Solms, "Prior to that I'd been pleasantly surprised by how scientifically correct in his attitude he was. I don't know why he's got such a bee in his bonnet about psychoanalysis, but it is really like Lucifer to him: if you mention Freud, he gets out his cross. It's unfortunate because it creates a black spot in his vision." Critics contend, though, that Solms has his own pro-Freudian bee-in-the-bonnet, given that he is an active voice in the psychoanalytic community and has served as editor and translator for collections of Freud's complete works.

In any case, Solms was encouraged that Braun's work validated many of his findings. "If you look at the PET images, you see that when we're most likely to be dreaming, the parts of the brain that have to do with memory, visuospatial image generation, motivation, and all of the structures that have everything to do with the emotional life of a mammal are lit up like a Christmas tree. If you put that together with my lesion studies and had to guess what's going on here, you'd say here's a type of cognition that's intensely motivated and emotional. It has to do with memory and is not guided by the self-reflecting structures that normally give our behavior its rational and civilized veneer," he says.

While the new scientific evidence didn't prove Freud right, Solms maintains, it was at least compatible with many of Freud's ideas.

Thus ensued a persistent war of words between Hobson and Solms over Freud and their own conflicting theories of how dreams are triggered. It was in essence the culmination of the battle that had brewed for decades between neurophysiologists on one side of the divide and psychologists and psychiatrists on the other whose interest in dream content and dream analysis as a psychotherapy tool had come to be viewed as misguided by many. For decades, neuroscientists regarded psychotherapy as unscientific, while therapists viewed most neuroscience as simplistic because it excluded the psyche. Neuroscientists were interested in *how* we dream, while psychologists were preoccupied with *why* we dream.

Solms argued that since the new evidence was forcing Hobson to revise the dreaming model that he'd used for years to publicly demolish Freudian theory, he now should be willing to admit that Freud may have been at least partly right. Hobson had made adjustments to his theory to account for the more active role of complex brain structures in dreaming, but he still contended that neither Solms's data nor the brain-imaging studies could provide "the faintest modicum of support" for Freud's ideas that the meaning of dreams was disguised or censored or that dreaming provided some special access to unconscious motives via the technique of free association to bizarre dream material. Nor could he tolerate Solms's linking the role of the brain's seeking system in dream creation to Freud's idea that dreams equaled wish fulfillment. "In dreams I'm running away from things half the time. Is that wish fulfillment? Freud is very hard to kill. It is part of our culture now to think this way," Hobson says.

He insisted that the pons area of the brainstem was the generator of both REM sleep and dreaming but that dreaming in fact might be merely an accidental by-product of REM sleep, which he suggested had its own functions, such as regulating body temperature, maintaining the immune system, and performing a crucial balancing act with serotonin and other crucial neuromodulators. If dreaming is indeed simply a by-product of the brain's need to enter a state intended to serve these other purely physiological functions, "dream content might be quite irrelevant, telling us only what a subject's mental state might be like if he or she were to become delirious," said Hobson in an article he wrote in 1999 for a journal edited by Solms that was read primarily by psychoanalysts. In a statement that couldn't help but push every button imaginable for a Freudian, he concluded: "In this sense, the interpretation of dreams in terms of unconscious motives would make about as much sense as interpreting the ravings of an alcoholic in the throes of delirium tremens."

Perhaps the most objective insight on the matter came in a commentary by Allen Braun published in the same journal. Braun agreed with Solms that the imaging map of the dreaming brain was compatible with psychoanalytic theory in some important ways. The fact that the emotional and long-term memory systems were supercharged while the centers for rational thought were dozing could be viewed in Freudian terms as the "ego" relinquishing its command and giving the unconscious freedom to romp freely. And the activity in the motivational region could support Freud's idea that dreams were powered by our most basic drives and wishes. But Braun sided with Hobson when he argued that since the symbol-creating portion of the brain (the prefrontal cortex) was off-line, dream content could not possibly reflect unconscious desires that were censored and disguised via symbols requiring elaborate decoding and interpretation. "I think you can use dream content on the face of it, what Freud called the manifest content—for self-therapy or psychotherapy," he says, "but there's no interpretation needed, because nothing is disguised."

Neatly summing up his view of the Hobson-Solms debate, Braun wrote in his commentary: "Stepping back a short distance, this is what I see: Hobson, a consummate biological psychiatrist, now argues against reductionism and passionately advocates the study of subjective conscious experience. Solms, a psychoanalyst, is attempting to recast dynamic psychology in neurochemical terms. It sounds to me like these gentlemen are approaching common ground. Perhaps it is simply the ghost of Freud that is getting in the way."

JUST TWO YEARS LATER, in one of those truth-is-stranger-than-fiction twists of fate, Hobson himself became one of the "experiments of nature" upon which Solms's neuroanatomical dreaming study was based. While traveling with his wife in the south of France in February 2001, Hobson suffered a stroke. Ironically, it affected only the brainstem—the portion of the brain that had been the focus of much of his life's work. His wife, Lia, a neurologist, recognized his sudden difficulty in swallowing and other initial symptoms as signs of a stroke and quickly got him to the emergency room of the Princess Grace Hospital in Monaco, where he remained for ten days before being transferred by air ambulance to Brigham & Women's Hospital, in Boston, just a block away from his neurophysiology lab.

Ever the curious scientist, Hobson became an observer of his own condition while hospitalized, dictating his perceptions for journal entries that chronicled what often became a waking nightmare. Because the stroke was confined to the brainstem, he suffered no lasting cognitive impairments. But among the most striking immediate results of his brainstem lesion was that for the entire ten days he was hospitalized in Monaco, he was unable to sleep at all.

"The worst time is the night because I am alone, usually from 7 P.M. to 7 A.M., and because I cannot sleep a wink. I'm just awake, my mind working actively in the dark all night long," he dictated in notes on day six of his insomnia. Of course, dreaming also ceased. Instead, when he closed his eyes even momentarily he would see a vault over his body upon which he would view projected images of hallucinations of geologic forms, inanimate sculptures, and disconnected human body parts. He also had horrific hallucinatory experiences in which he felt that he was being catapulted through space, as he described in his journal: "The illusion that I was actually moving at very high speed for at least 100 meters through space was so completely convincing and so terrifying that I said to myself, 'So this is what death is like.'"

Hobson did not have what he terms a vivid, sustained dream until thirty-eight days following the stroke. In that dream, he was traveling with his wife abroad and discovered she had given another man a drill bit from a treasured tool Hobson kept at their weekend home, a farm in Vermont. Describing the dream in his journal, Hobson said: "It seemed to me odd that she would give a stranger one of my most precious tools without asking me. I was feeling very vexed and apprehensive." In the dream, his wife confides to him that she needs to have a secret life, and for much of the rest of the dream, he is wandering alone, unable to find her.

Though the dream contains elements that obviously are tailor-made for Freudian analysis, Hobson observes: "I didn't need the dream to tell me that I was worried about my ability to maintain my relationship with my wife as an impaired person. It is a strong emotion and it creates the whole scenario. Emotion is running the dream show." He argues that those who say he proclaimed that dreams are meaningless misunderstood him. "Dreams are dripping with meaning, but they don't have to be interpreted. Dreaming is the way it is, probably for some reasons that are more like Freudian ideas than it might first appear. There must be some kind of reworking of memory going on, but it isn't buried stuff you can't manage. It's probably just the opposite: in dreaming we're trying to integrate and come to terms with the difficulties of having emotions."

Drawing conclusions from his stroke experience, Hobson says Solms's "findings have reopened debate about the relative importance of brainstem and forebrain structures in the neurogenesis of dreaming." As for the correlation between REM sleep and dreaming, Hobson already had acknowledged in 1988 that at least 5 percent of non-REM dreams were indistinguishable from dreams in REM, and today he summarizes his stance by saying, "Dreamlike mentation occurs in all states, but REM is the best state to study dreaming."

In the end, however, Hobson comes back to his own bedrock position on how dreams are generated: "Once recovery began and my brain stem had recovered its ability to support sensorimotor functions, my dreaming recovered, too. I have no doubt that normal dreaming requires a normal forebrain and that severe damage to the forebrain leads to a loss of dreaming, which may even be permanent. But based on my experience, I also have no doubt that a normal forebrain cannot sustain normal dreaming as long as the brainstem is dysfunctional."

For his part, Solms concedes that Freud may have been wrong about the meaning of dreams being disguised and censored, noting that the bizarreness of dreams may simply be due to the fact that the frontal lobes of the brain aren't performing their usual executive decision-making functions. But he is convinced that it's the motivational circuits of the forebrain—not the brainstem—that trigger the dreaming process. Certainly it's clear from study after study conducted by researchers around the world that the overwhelming majority of dreams—particularly the vivid memorable ones we recall and recount to others—occur during REM sleep, probably because it provides the high level of overall brain activation that is a prerequisite for dream creation. But it's also indisputable that such dreams also can occur during other sleep phases, albeit less frequently. Solms has begun brain-imaging studies aimed at identifying what brain regions are activated during these non-REM dreams, and that kind of evidence may eventually answer the question of what really triggers dreaming.

While the Freudian Wars may be drawing to a close, another long-standing unresolved question about dreaming continues to be a subject of hot debate among researchers. Does dreaming serve any biological purpose at all? Many scientists who wouldn't agree on much else about dreaming—such as Hobson and David Foulkes—maintain that dreams are merely an accidental by-product of other evolutionary developments, without any specific function of their own. We happen to periodically experience high levels of brain activation, and when that happens, our neuronal networks can't help but process information and spin narratives, because that's what they're designed to do. Researchers such as Tom Balkin argue further that these periods of activation during which dreams occur actually serve only one simple biological purpose: to keep the neural networks tuned so that the brain is prepared to return to fully alert, waking mode when the need arises.

But there's another scientific camp contending that REM sleep evolved for reasons that were crucial to mammalian survival and that, as a result, dreaming itself has come to serve a variety of important biological functions. Mounting evidence from recent studies indicates that clues to support this viewpoint actually are right before our eyes—in the content of our dreams.

4

The Lesson of the Spiny Anteater

Dreams were never designed to be remembered, but they are keys to who we are.

—Jonathan Winson

WITH HIS GLEAMING SHAVED HEAD, Bill Domhoff is easy to spot in a crowd. The denim-clad, laid-back psychologist is at a New England conference on dream research, giving a presentation on using his statistical programs and search engines, available through the Internet, as tools for collecting and analyzing dream reports for research purposes. The Web site he established, DreamBank.net, contains more than 11,000 reports, including dream journals from a few individuals that span decades, as well as dreams from teenagers, children, and blind men and women.

A psychologist at the University of California at Santa Cruz, Domhoff specializes in content analysis, which is a scientific method for tackling a basic but essential task: accurately describing what it is we actually dream about. Examining what dreams look like, how they might change over time, and what similarities and differences exist in dream content in various cultures around the world provides fascinating clues that help answer questions about how dreaming evolved. Gaining more information about dreaming's evolutionary history in turn provides insight into what purpose—if any—it serves.

A wealth of information has been provided through content analysis, which was pioneered by Domhoff's mentor, Calvin Hall. An innovative scientist, Hall first began collecting dream reports in the 1940s from college students at Case Western Reserve University, where he was head of the Psychology Department. Rather than analyzing dreams and trying to interpret what they meant, he focused on simply quantitatively describing what it is we dream about and which emotions most often accompany dreams. Over the next three decades, Hall expanded his efforts, gathering dream reports from children and adults, including dreams collected by anthropologists from people living in remote traditional cultures throughout the world. When he died in 1985, Hall had amassed the world's largest and most systematic body of findings on dream content, drawn from his collection of 50,000 dream reports. The quantitative coding system he developed with collaborator Robert Van de Castle to categorize dream content has been used by researchers from North America and Europe to India and Japan to compare how dreams differ from culture to culture and to see how women's dreams compare to men's or how a single individual's dreams change as he or she ages.

Thanks to Domhoff's efforts, much of Hall's data on comparisons of dreams across cultures became available publicly for the first time in the mid-1990s. The results show that there are more similarities than differences in dream content among all people regardless of where or how they live. Throughout the world, women's dreams contain an equal number of male and female characters, but in men's dreams, nearly 70 percent of characters are other men. Both sexes have dreams that feature more misfortune than good fortune, more negative than positive emotion, and more aggression than friendliness, but men generally have more physical aggression in their dreams than do women. Children's dreams contain little aggression, but that element begins to increase during teenage years.

People in small tribal societies tend to have the greatest proportion of physical aggression in their dreams, with the highest reports among the Yir Yiront, an Australian Aboriginal group for whom 92 percent of dream interactions were aggressive—defined to include everything from aggressive feelings to nasty remarks to physical attacks on possessions. Among industrialized societies studied, however, Americans ranked highest for aggression in dreams, with scores of 50 percent for U.S. males (34 percent for females) versus 29 percent for Swiss men and 32 percent for Dutch men. "The physical aggression reflected in Americans' dreams certainly fits in with the fact that in our society we kill each other more frequently than do the Swiss or the Dutch," says Domhoff.

The chief character in our nightly dramas is nearly always the dreamer, but about 95 percent of our dreams involve other characters too. The rest of the cast consists of people, animals, and mythical figures, with adults dreaming mostly of other adults. Animals feature more prominently in the dreams of children and people living in more primitive societies. Homes or other buildings are the most common dream settings, and automobiles or other conveyances also frequently pop up as scenes for dream action. The majority of dreams during REM sleep are filled with motion, especially walking or running, while dreams in other phases of sleep are less action oriented.

The popular idea that dreams are chock-full of sexual experiences—stemming in part from Freud's views that all dreams were fulfillments of wishes, usually sexual in nature—is in large measure wishful wakeful thinking. The Hall–Van de Castle content analysis data indicates sexual activity crops up in no more than 10 percent of dreams, while other studies have shown no more than a third of dreams contain explicitly sexual content, with men more likely to dream of sex with strangers while women tend to dream of partners that they know. Perhaps not surprising, sex seems to loom larger in both waking fantasy and reports about dream life among college students. When veteran dream researcher William Dement asked a group of college students what they would most like to dream about if they could control content, 95 percent of males said they'd opt to be having sex (ironically, that answer was given by only 5 percent of female students, who preferred adventure and romance as main attractions). And in a 2002 survey of Canadian college students, asking what they most frequently dreamed about, sexual experiences ranked second in prevalence only to being chased, with 77 percent of students reporting it as a frequent theme.

The Hall–Van de Castle content analysis system essentially treats a dream report as a story or play in which there are several categories to be tracked, including characters, settings, objects, types of social interactions, activities, successes or failures, misfortunes or good fortune, and elements from the past. The method measures how often various elements appear in a dream report, based on the assumption that the frequency of occurrence reveals the intensity of a person's interest or concern regarding a specific character, activity, or interaction. To detect any statistically significant differences, the results of this quantitative analysis of the elements in an individual's dream or dreams of a specific group of people are then compared to the norms that Hall established by coding thousands of dreams. For instance, in a study comparing dreams of male schizophrenics to those of healthy males, schizophrenics' dreams had a significantly higher proportion of characters who were aggressors, while the percentage of dreams incorporating success or at least one friendly interaction was well below the norm.

Content analysis also reveals that there is remarkable consistency in what an individual dreams about over time. It suggests too that our dream plots have striking continuities with our waking lives. The dream lives of American college students remained relatively unchanged throughout the second half of the twentieth century, despite major cultural upheavals during that period. Examining dream journals kept by individual subjects over many years further indicates that there is remarkable continuity in what we dream about over time. For instance, a woman Hall called Dorothea (to guard privacy, those who volunteered dream reports were always given pseudonyms) provided more than five hundred dreams in a dream journal she'd begun at the age of twenty-five in 1912 and continued through the age of seventy-six. Using content analysis to examine the dreams, he found that six elements appeared with the same frequency throughout that fifty-year time span. For instance, one of every six dreams involved loss of an object, usually her purse; being in a small or messy room or a room that was being invaded by others featured in 10 percent of the dreams; and another 10 percent focused on interactions between the dreamer and her mother. Being late or missing a bus or train was a theme in one of every sixteen dreams. As she grew older, being left out or ignored was the only theme that significantly increased in frequency for Dorothea, a schoolteacher who remained single throughout her life. Other studies of dreaming among the elderly living in nursing homes revealed a similar theme—primarily a preoccupation with loss of control and resources.

Sometimes features of a dream plot pop up recurrently because they contextualize an emotion. For instance, a common dream theme is showing up for an exam without ever having attended a class or read a textbook in the subject. Variations on this might be finding yourself on stage in a play for which you've never been given a script, or at a podium about to give a speech without any notes or ideas of what you are to say. The common thread in all of these situations is of course the emotion driving the dream: anxiety about being unprepared. Our own experiences in waking life will tailor what the details of plot will be—for an actor it will be a dramatic scene and, for an academic or politician, perhaps the podium.

Using the content analysis method to compare one person's series of dream reports to the norms and detect any changes in patterns over time also sheds light on Domhoff's claim that a sufficient sampling of dreams can provide an accurate reflection of a dreamer's concerns and relationships in waking life without resorting to interpreting symbols or looking at any other material outside the dream report itself. Among the cases he describes in his book *The Scientific Study of Dreams* is that of a young man he calls Mark who recorded forty of his dreams in the summer after he graduated high school, another twenty during his junior year in college, and then another fifty in the year after he finished college. Mark's series of dreams had a very low proportion of male to female characters: 38 percent male versus 62 percent female, which is almost a complete reversal of the male norm of 67 percent male versus 33 percent female characters. The dreams contained a higher-than-normal percentage of familiar characters versus strangers and a below-the-norm amount of aggression.

As it turns out, the unusual characteristics of his dreams do fit with the circumstances of Mark's waking life, says Domhoff. Mark's father died when he was very young, and his only close family members are his mother and grandmother. He spends most of his time with a few close friends, nearly all of whom are women, and he is a very low-key, nonaggressive person. "Mark was of particular interest to us because our coding system picked up on the ways in which he is an atypical male," notes Domhoff.

Domhoff concurs with Calvin Hall's conclusion that dreaming is essentially the form thought takes when the brain is operating under the physiological conditions of sleep. As Hall put it, "Although images are the only means by which ideas find sensible expression in dreams, other media such as words, numbers, gestures, and pictures are employed in waking life for making one's thoughts known." He viewed a dream as "a highly private showing of the dreamer's thoughts" and said the importance of dreams lies in their ability to illuminate "the basic predicaments of a person's life as that person sees them," in a form that is less distorted and superficial than what the dreamer would say about those issues in waking life.

In a study of both dreams and waking fantasies of boys and girls between the ages of nine and fifteen, Swiss dream researcher Inge Strauch used the Hall–Van de Castle system to examine content and found an interesting difference between waking fantasies and dreams that supports Hall's point. In fantasies, children took an active role in both aggressive and friendly interactions, while in dreams, they more often tended to be victims of aggression and passive recipients of friendliness. Strauch concluded that "children in our study portrayed themselves in their dreams as they conceive of themselves in everyday life, while in their waking fantasies they imagined themselves as they would like to be." Another significant difference: three out of four dreams contained some bizarre element, while fantasies were more reality based, with less than one-third having a bizarre quality.

The seemingly bizarre elements in dreams may stem from the brain's tendency to use figurative thought, however. Taking advantage of the same metaphor-making abilities we use in daily thinking, the brain creates visual images and actions in dreams to express our emotions and preoccupations. Cognitive scientists studying waking thought now see figurative language not just as a colorful embellishment of speech but as a crucial part of our basic thinking process, vital to forming conceptions about ourselves and the world. From childhood on, we incorporate conceptual metaphors that use concrete elements from our experiences to express more abstract concepts. George Lakoff, a leading linguist and cognitive neuroscientist at the University of California at Berkeley contends that we have an extensive system of metaphor that is part of our everyday conceptual systems, helping to structure our waking thought. To illustrate his point, he cites the variety of journey metaphors we use to describe relationships: "We've hit a dead end, look how far we've come, we may have to go our separate ways, we're spinning our wheels, or we're at a crossroads."

The abundance of this kind of figurative processing of information may explain some of the unusual features of dreams that distinguish what happens in dream experience from life in the "real" world. Consider a couple of the more memorable dream scenarios that most people experience at one time or another. Dreams of being able to fly under one's own power were reported by more than half of participants in two surveys of college students that Domhoff conducted. These flying dreams, typically reported as being pleasant, may be the brain's way of metaphorically conceptualizing happiness, since similar metaphors are used in our waking thought to express elation—we're high as a kite, walking on air, floating on cloud nine. Another common dream scenario reported by about half of participants is appearing naked or inappropriately dressed in public—a theme that usually first emerges when we are in our teenage years. "Caught with your pants down" is just one of the corresponding metaphors that crop up in our thoughts and speech in daily life to express feelings of embarrassment or anxiety reflected in those dreams.

Many of these kinds of dreams fall into a category popularly known as universal dreams—common themes reported by subjects regardless of where or when they live. In analyzing results of a 2002 survey of the most frequent dream themes reported by nearly twelve hundred college students in three different Canadian cities, Tore Nielsen and Antonio Zadra, of the Sleep Research Center at Hopital de Sacre-Coeur in Montreal, found that several themes surfaced as the most common, not only among the current crop of young men and women but also among a similar group surveyed in the 1950s, despite forty years of social and cultural change. In the Canadian survey, the four most prevalent themes over time were dreams of being chased, falling, being involved in a school situation, or having a sexual experience. The most common dreams recalled from childhood in the survey were, again, dreams of being chased, followed by scenes in which the dreamer is trying again and again to do some task—certainly a characteristic feature of waking life for children as they assimilate new knowledge and skills daily. Dreams of flying and falling also were in the top four. Some dream themes, though not the most frequent, were considered by dreamers to be of equal importance to dreams they most often experienced. For instance, dreams about someone who has died being alive again or about someone in the dreamer's life being dead, while not the most prevalent, were ranked as extremely important personally. Nielsen cautions that what we claim to recall dreaming about may not accurately reflect what we actually dream about most often, so future studies using daily sampling of dream content would be helpful in gaining a greater understanding of what kinds of dreams are most typical and which might qualify as universal.

While dreams of being naked, falling, or flying may be especially memorable, both content analysis and surveys such as Nielsen's consistently reveal that being pursued by someone or something is the most frequently viewed nightly drama we experience. The fact that this theme is the most common among dreamers regardless of when or where they live may in fact be connected with how dreaming evolved.

A growing amount of evidence supports a fascinating theory about the evolution of human dreaming that was proposed in the 1980s by Jonathan Winson, an aeronautical engineer who switched to neuroscience because he came to view unraveling the mysteries of the brain as the ultimate engineering challenge. Winson was intrigued by the fact that when animals were involved in any activity essential to their survival during waking hours—such as a cat stalking prey or a rabbit becoming hyperalert in the presence of a predator—brain cells in the hippocampus (a structure that is crucial in memory formation) began firing regularly at six bursts per second, a unique pattern known as theta rhythm that he studied extensively in his lab at Rockefeller University. Since the only other time theta rhythm appeared was during REM sleep, Winson hypothesized that this stage of sleep was vital to processing information from the day that is critical to an animal's survival. He believed that understanding how REM had evolved would also shed light on the dreaming process in humans.

Looking for evolutionary clues, he found that an unusual mammal known as the spiny anteater has a unique sleep pattern—it does not experience a typical REM sleep cycle with theta rhythm. In more recent investigations, Jerome Siegel at the University of California at Los Angeles found that the sleep state in the spiny anteater "appeared intermediate between REM and non-REM sleep." In fact, the spiny anteater is an oddity in many ways: it is a modern-day reminder of primitive times because it is an egg-laying mammal known as a monotreme, the first category of mammals to evolve from reptiles. Because the more common forms of mammals we see today branched off from the monotreme line about 140 million years ago, Winson theorized that REM sleep as it exists in most animals also emerged at about the time that split occurred. That development would mark the appearance of the world's first dream.

Winson contends that, prior to the development of REM, primitive mammals had to do on-the-spot processing of newly acquired survival-related information, such as the location of food sources or routes to take to avoid predators. This new information would have to be integrated with previously stored memories in the prefrontal cortex, the brain's planning and decision-making system, which then would make any necessary adjustments in the brain's models for future behavior. For instance, if eating red berries on the bush by the pond made an animal sick on a given day, that information would have to be encoded in memory and the mental blueprint for behavior amended so that the animal would avoid those berries in the future.

But consolidating memory and making corresponding adjustments in neural networks governing future behavior while remaining alert and taking actions to respond to changing conditions in the external world is a less efficient mode of operation, as is evident in the disparity between the primitive behavior of the spiny anteater as compared to the more highly evolved behavior of cats, monkeys, or even rats—all of which appear to dream.

Winson believes that REM sleep developed as a way for this critical memory processing to occur off-line. In effect, it allowed the prefrontal cortex to develop more advanced perceptual and cognitive abilities than are seen in reptiles or primitive mammals such as the spiny anteater. As further evidence, he points to an anatomical difference between the brains of mammals that have typical REM sleep and the spiny anteater, whose convoluted prefrontal cortex is much larger in relation to the rest of its brain than any other mammal's, including humans. If REM sleep had not emerged as nature's innovative off-line means of integrating new experience with prior memory, higher cognitive abilities in species ranging from cats to apes to humans could not have developed because the prefrontal cortex would have had to expand beyond the skull's capacity to contain it. As Winson puts it, had the organization of man's brain remained similar to the spiny anteater's, "he might have needed a wheelbarrow to carry it around."

Another biological function of REM sleep that meshes with Winson's theory about when dreaming evolved was suggested by the French dream-research pioneer Michel Jouvet. He proposed that this dream-rich sleep stage facilitates the establishment of genetically encoded behaviors that increase an organism's odds of survival. Interestingly, non-REM sleep emerged only when mammals evolved from reptiles. Warm-blooded creatures' new ability to maintain their own constant internal temperature also required that they conserve energy, which appears to be one of the functions of sleep in general. Without sleep, temperature regulation can't be maintained. But during dreaming, the brain uses more energy than in waking and the body is paralyzed, thus increasing a sleeping mammal's vulnerability to predators. So REM sleep also had to have some clear adaptive advantage. Egg-hatched reptiles come into the world sufficiently developed to survive on their own, while most live-born mammals face a steep learning curve to arrive at self-sufficiency. Dreaming sleep provided a way to speed that process along and boost mammals' odds of survival. That would explain why human fetuses spend nearly all of their time in REM and newborns spend about half of their sixteen hours or more of daily sleep in REM, which speeds the maturation of their nervous systems. And it fits with the fact that mammals whose offspring are born in a relatively self-sufficient state, such as dolphins, have the least amount of REM, while it is highest in creatures whose young are born in a relatively immature, helpless state, such as opossums. A study of infants born prematurely showed that the REM stage accounted for 80 percent of total sleep for a baby born ten weeks prematurely, while a baby born only two to four weeks early spent 58 percent of sleep in REM. Stephen LaBerge, a dream researcher who started his career in the lab at Stanford University, suggests that when newborns smile in their sleep, you may be seeing this brain wiring process in action. Unwittingly they are establishing a skill that will serve them well in future social interactions—including securing a mate—and doing so well before they manifest the behavior in waking hours.

Piecing together all of the evidence, many researchers have concluded that part of what's going on during REM in both animals and humans is that the brain is literally being wired. The intense neural activity of REM sleep may be required to establish neural circuitry and pass along genetically encoded information crucial to survival—instructions for hunting, mating, and other vital behavior. This proposed purpose for REM sleep is one of the few that is supported by evidence across species.

In short, dreaming in humans evolved from a mechanism inherited from lower species in which both genetically encoded, survival-related data and crucial information drawn from daily experience are processed in the brain during REM sleep. Dreaming is consistent with its early mammalian origins because its content is predominantly sensory, and especially visual, rather than verbal. "In man, dreams are a window on the neural process whereby, from early childhood on, strategies for behavior are being set down, modified, or consulted," according to Jonathan Winson.

Of course, human dreaming is more sophisticated than animal dreaming because our neural networks have a complexity that allows us to become acutely aware of our emotions and to create narratives, using language and drawing on a personal history that gives us a sense of continuity. Nonetheless, dreaming's roots in that basic animal model can be seen in the worldwide human propensity to have frequent dreams of being chased or confronting other frightening situations, according to Antti Revonsuo, a cognitive neuroscientist at the University of Turku in Finland. In keeping with Winson's theory, Revonsuo argues that dreaming in humans evolved as a means of simulating threatening events in a safe, virtual reality created by the brain during sleep. He points out that in the prehistoric environment in which humans and their ancestors lived as hunter-gatherers for hundreds of thousands of years—in fact, for 99 percent of human evolutionary history—life was filled with survival threats so severe that most humans didn't live past the age of twenty-five.

To be among the select few who lived to reproduce in those conditions, an individual would have to be skilled at perceiving and coping with survival threats of that time—from animal predators, to aggressive strangers, to environmental dangers, to social rejection by the tribe. The off-line rehearsal of survival skills that Winson describes developed in early mammals with the emergence of REM sleep and became further refined in humans. Those who were most adept at this nocturnal rehearsal of threat avoidance skills were most likely to survive dangers in waking life, says Revonsuo. Good dreamers, in short, lived to pass on their abilities to the next generation.

For Revonsuo's theory to hold water, the brain systems responsible for the fight-or-flight response would have to be operating at full speed during dreaming, and as brain-imaging studies repeatedly have demonstrated, that is indeed the case. But how could mere mental rehearsal of survival skills be effective in improving those skills if they are just imagined, not physically carried out? The answer is that the brain is fooled into believing that its motor commands in dream plots actually *have* been followed. For instance, when we are being chased by a tiger or a threatening stranger in a dream and our brain issues the command to run or climb a tree to safety, the unique physiological conditions that prevail during sleep paralyze our muscles, preventing us from carrying out the command, but the brain nonetheless produces the experience of movement by sending copies of those motor commands to our sensory systems.

"The brain thus receives internally generated information about issued motor commands and computes the expected consequences of those commands," Revonsuo explains. "The sensory system is not informed that these commands were not in actual fact carried out by the muscles, and therefore the illusion of movement comes about." For the forebrain and specifically the motor areas of the cortex, dreaming about escaping by running or climbing a tree is identical to the real experience of carrying out those actions during waking. "Dreamed action is experientially and neurophysiologically real," says Revonsuo.

Accordingly, these survival-behavior rehearsals that occur in dreams can be thoroughly effective whether we recall the dream or not. In fact, Winson and Revonsuo's views of dreaming's evolutionary roots and original function would also help explain why the brain's physiological conditions during dreaming appear to be designed to discourage dream recall.

As Hobson discovered, the predominant neuromodulator circulating through the brain during REM dreams is acetylcholine, which creates optimal conditions for brain cells to forge and strengthen connections in order to encode memory and reshape our mental model of the world. At the same time, levels of serotonin and norepinephrine—neuromodulators that are essential for learning and focusing attention—plummet, impairing our ability to actually recall the dream itself unless we awaken before it's ended and immediately direct our attention to recalling it. Also, the crucial area of the prefrontal cortex that allows us to place events in a time sequence—connecting what happens now to what happened a minute ago or last week—is essentially off-line, a situation that Allen Braun believes contributes to our amnesia for dream content.

As Jonathan Winson argued, dreams were never intended to be remembered in the first place, so when we do recall them, we're just getting an unintended glimpse of our brain at work in its off-line mode. "It is a matter of chance, not related to their function, that we are aware of dreams at all," says Winson. Thanks to our capacity for language, humans have developed the ability to distinguish between memories of events we dreamed and events that occur in waking life. We learn to make the distinction as children, when adults explain to us that what felt so real was in fact "only a dream." But for species lacking language, recalling dreamed actions and events could actually be maladaptive. "We and our ancestors might have been protected from mixing illusion and reality by the evolution of mechanisms that made forgetting dreams the normal course of affairs," says psychophysiologist Stephen LaBerge. "Suppose your cat were to dream that the wicked dog was dead and replaced by a family of mice. What would happen if the cat were to remember this dream when it awoke? Not knowing it was a dream, it would probably hungrily jump over the fence, expecting to find a meal. But instead it would find itself a meal—for the dog."

The human ability to distinguish between waking and dream experiences eliminates any peril associated with our occasional ability to recall dreams, and it may give us an advantage, though it's entirely serendipitous. "We can put our recalled dreams to a variety of personal or cultural uses," says Antti Revonsuo, "but no matter how enlightening and meaningful such uses may be, they are invented by us, not by natural selection."

Though humans' developing brain power allowed us to conquer many dangers and create a world in which saber-toothed tigers and venomous snakes were no longer our predominant daily worries, signs of dreaming's ancient origins can be found in our own dream content today. First, consider what is notably absent from our dreams. Studies conducted by Ernest Hartmann, a dream researcher at Tufts University, have shown that in adult dreams, walking, talking to friends, and having sex were represented in dreams about as often as in real life, but reading, writing, and arithmetic rarely if ever appear, even though the dreamers in the study typically spent six hours daily engaged in activities that fall into the three R's category. Revonsuo suggests these parts of waking life aren't reflected in most dreams because they are cultural latecomers. "They were not present in ancestral environments, nor are they neurally hardwired in the human brain in the way that other complex cognitive functions frequently present in dreams are, such as speech comprehension and production," he says.

In contrast, many elements that are not common in waking life but are consistent with simulating primitive threats are universally present in dreams. Content analysis studies show that characters appearing as enemies in our dreams fall into two primary categories: animals filled this role in 82 percent of men's dreams and 77 percent of women's, while male strangers were the fear-inspiring element in 72 percent of men's dreams and 63 percent of women's. Encounters with animals or unfamiliar males aren't linked automatically with danger in modern life, but they were for our ancestors, and Revonsuo argues that this is further evidence that dreams are biased toward simulating threats that were common in prehistoric times. Dreaming of being chased by wild animals or monsters reflects "the threat simulation scripts embedded in the dream production system as default settings, defining the types of threatening events that should be rehearsed most frequently," he says.

In modern life, of course, the threatening experiences from daily routine that the brain tends to process in dreaming are more likely to damage our self-image or lower our bank account balances than to pose true physical danger. But the emotions generated by modern experience nevertheless are incorporated in our dream life along with those DNA-encoded scenarios. What happens in the dreaming brain "may now allow ancient emotional impulses to be integrated with the newer cognitive skills of the more recently evolved brain," according to Jaak Panksepp, head of affective neuroscience research at the Chicago Institute for Neurosurgery and Neuroresearch.

The survival skills rehearsal that accompanied the emergence of REM sleep conferred an advantage that allowed this dreaming phase of sleep to eventually be passed along to humans. Given the complexity of the human brain, though, these nocturnal rehearsals have expanded, reaching a much more sophisticated level that matches the capabilities of our networks of neurons. In fact, intriguing new research demonstrates that dreaming and mental activity in other sleep stages interact in complex ways, playing a vital role in our ability to learn new skills and integrate memories that give us our unique sense of self.

5

Rerunning the Maze

The dream is memory itself changing before your eyes.
—Bert States

MATTHEW WILSON SPENDS HIS DAYS investigating what rats dream about after a rough day in his lab at the Massachusetts Institute of Technology (MIT). "People ask why I'm interested in rats' dreams, and I have to say I'm not, but I *am* interested in how memory is expressed during sleep and how that might relate to what we subjectively experience as dreaming," says Wilson, who started out as an engineering student studying artificial intelligence. He switched to neuroscience when he realized it was impossible to build truly intelligent robots until we had a better understanding of how the brain itself functions. "We want to understand how what you do during the day gets into your sleeping state and if that has any impact other than giving you something to write about in a dream diary. We now believe it does—that the brain's activity at night is a fundamental part of learning and long-term memory formation," he says.

Pointing to the stacks of paper that cover nearly every available surface in his office at MIT, Wilson wryly says, "The challenge of organizing my office is similar to the challenge the brain faces. The process of sorting through all of this information, selecting what I want to store, and organizing it so that it's easily accessible when I need it is something I could squeeze in here and there during the day, but it would be much more effective to do that after hours when I'm otherwise undisturbed." He contends that the hours when the mind slides into sleep and dreaming provide the perfect opportunity for the brain to filter daily experience, evaluate what's relevant, and then integrate it with the vast repository of previous experience in long-term memory. It's a time when we are unencumbered by the need to deal with the outside world.

Wilson's belief is founded in an experiment that provided one of those rare "Aha" moments that mark the high point of any scientist's life. To address his questions about how memory works, Wilson decided that working with rats would be more productive than experimenting with humans because he would have greater control over the experiences the rats were exposed to during waking. He could also more precisely measure how they responded by implanting microelectrodes near individual brain cells, allowing him to eavesdrop on what was happening at that level, in both sleep and waking.

Wilson and his team trained rats to travel a maze in search of chocolate-flavored food rewards. Through the sensors implanted in the rats' brains, they continuously recorded the firing patterns of clusters of neurons responsible for orienting the animals in space. The neurons the researchers were monitoring are located in the hippocampus, a region of the brain initially involved in memory storage in both rats and humans.

But they also recorded what happened in those brain cells as the rats slept—and what they discovered was a remarkable mental replay of experience. The same firing patterns of neurons that they'd seen when the rats were running the maze were reproduced in nearly half of the forty-five periods of REM sleep they recorded, when the rats were presumably dreaming—a vivid demonstration of the nightly survival skill rehearsal described by Jonathan Winson as the biological purpose of the dreaming phase of sleep. The replication was so precise that Wilson could pinpoint where in the maze the rat would be if it were awake and whether it was standing still or running. The amount of time it took for the experience to replay in sleep was the same as it had taken to transpire in the first place.

"Seeing that these animals were literally running through this maze again mentally for over two minutes during sleep was easily the most astonishing thing I have ever experienced and probably ever will experience. What I was seeing was not a report of memory or my guess about memory; it *was* memory in action. The thrill of science is not confirming your hypotheses but rather finding things like this in your data that you had not anticipated," says Wilson.

The results of that study, published in 2001, are a key component of a growing body of scientific evidence indicating that the brain's activity during dream-laden REM sleep is crucial to consolidating memory. Current research, however, indicates that it is not REM sleep alone that helps convert experience into memory but mental activity during other sleep stages as well. Sleep onset, slow-wave sleep, and REM all may play different roles in processing specific types of memories, or they may interact in an intricately choreographed sequence to encode information in a usable, lasting form. Sleeping hours appear to be an optimal time for integrating new memory, not just because the brain is freed from tasks such as ensuring that we're not hit by a truck but also because shifts in brain chemical levels and other physiological changes create ideal conditions for the reorganization and strengthening of memory.

To understand the growing body of evidence about how information processing that occurs in the brain during sleep influences waking behavior, it's helpful to take a closer look at how memory really works. First, toss out any ideas about memories being literal mental videotapes of everything you've ever experienced stored away in some central filing system in the brain. When you experience anything—learning a new computer program, taking a hike in the Maine woods, or simply having a conversation with friends over lunch—the record of that experience is initially held by the hippocampus, a horseshoe-shaped structure in the center of the brain that curves outward and connects with the amygdala, which in turn is crucial both in generating our initial emotional responses and in determining the emotional coloring of memories that we store. The hippocampus takes in all available information about an experience from our senses, as well as from these emotional circuits, thus serving as a kind of superclearinghouse for information needed to construct a memory.

But to become permanently incorporated as memory, information in the hippocampus must be replayed to the higher-level processing systems in the neocortex, where it can be compared with previously encoded experiences and evaluated. Part of this memory consolidation process also involves discarding what the brain judges to be nonessential. In fact, Nobel laureate Francis Crick and his colleague Graeme Mitchison came up with a theory that we actually "dream to forget." In the aftermath of his acclaim as codiscoverer of the structure of DNA, Crick turned his attention to investigating the nature of consciousness. Examining the dreaming process as part of that effort, he proposed in 1983 that memories were indeed consolidated and reorganized during sleep. According to Crick and Mitchison's theory of "reverse learning," the random stimulation of the forebrain by the brainstem would set this memory-reorganizing process in motion. Superfluous information and nonsensical mental associations that were being pruned from neural networks would make an appearance as dream material on the way out, which would explain bizarre elements in dreams. "In order to optimize storage and recall of memories, the brain has to go through a process that in the world of computers is called garbage collection. Getting rid of inessential facts and invalid associations helps to consolidate the facts that *are* important for your future behavior. So this reverse learning theory is one variant of the idea that REM dreams are necessary for memory consolidation," explains Crick's current collaborator, Christof Koch.

Working memory consists of information that you are holding in your consciousness at this very moment—either knowledge you've just acquired or something you've temporarily brought to mind from long-term memory. Our ability to consciously hold information in this short-term buffer is surprisingly limited. If someone were to present you with a random series of numbers and immediately ask you to repeat them, you'd likely be unable to retain and parrot back more than seven digits at a time—the equivalent of a local telephone number.

When we are in the act of holding information in memory, what happens physiologically is that groups of interconnected neurons fire together in a particular pattern that ties together all of the elements of that specific memory. When a memory is replayed, it reactivates the firing pattern of those same neurons and causes an anatomical change in which the connections between the neurons actually grow stronger the more they are replayed. As neuroscientists put it, cells that fire together wire together, and it is this "wiring together" that transforms short-term memories into long-term ones. Patients who've suffered memory loss due to brain injuries reveal that the most fragile memories are the most recent—facts learned or experiences that occurred in a period of days, weeks, or months preceding brain damage—while older memories are less susceptible to disruption because they have had more opportunity to become consolidated. The more often a memory circuit is reactivated, the more deeply it is engrained. Over a period that can range from days to years, memories become encoded in the neocortex and no longer depend on the hippocampus to be set in motion.

We form two basic types of memory. Procedural (also known as implicit) memories, typically involve *knowing how* to do something, such as riding a bike. This kind of memory can be formed and retrieved outside our awareness. For instance, we don't have to stop to remember how to put one foot in front of the other in order to walk or consciously think about where to place our fingers on the keyboard for touch-typing once we've consolidated those skills in memory. And when we first learn to speak, we learn the rules of language without consciously setting out to do so.

Most psychologists also would argue that early childhood memories can be activated as procedural memories by some event in the present and can influence our behavior even though the memory activation has occurred outside conscious awareness. For instance, say that a toddler's parents left him overnight with Aunt Agatha while they were out of town attending a wedding. A transportation glitch delayed their return by a couple of days. It was the little boy's first separation experience, and his overwhelming emotions were unhappiness and anxiety. He has no conscious autobiographical memory of that weekend, but on the rare occasions when Aunt Agatha comes to visit later in his life, his inexplicable knee-jerk emotional reaction is an overwhelming desire to slam the door, based on procedural memories associated with Aunt Agatha.

The brain systems that carry out procedural learning in humans have existed throughout the evolutionary history of mammals and work unconsciously not because of some grand design to conceal aspects of our mental life from us, as Freud might have it, but simply because their operation is not directly accessible by the conscious brain, according to Joseph LeDoux, a neuroscientist at New York University. Well known for his research on the biological basis of emotion and memory, LeDoux points out that procedural learning shapes our most basic characteristic traits: our style of walking and talking, what we notice or ignore, and how we react emotionally when things don't go our way. "Memory does indeed make us who we are," says LeDoux in his book *Synaptic Self*. "Keep in mind, though, that the memories involved are distributed across many brain systems and are not always or even mostly available to you consciously."

The second broad category of memory that most people think of when the word comes to mind *is* available consciously and falls into a category called declarative—*knowing that* rather than *knowing how*. Declarative memories in turn come in two varieties. Factual (semantic) memory is general knowledge about the world, such as the fact that John Kennedy was shot on November 22, 1963, or that a Volkswagen is an automobile of a certain shape and size. Then there is autobiographical (episodic) memory, which is the record of what's happened to you personally, such as what you were doing on that particular November day in 1963 or the details of the road trip you took too many summers ago in a battered red Volkswagen with your best friend from college. Declarative memories usually are recalled explicitly—we know that the information is there and we deliberately bring it to conscious awareness, even though we sometimes go through that frustrating experience of having a name or a song title on the tip of the tongue but still inaccessible. Damage to the hippocampus results in amnesia. While amnesics have access to procedural memory and to some factual memory—they generally remember how to speak and what to do with a cup or a door or a car—they typically lose autobiographical memory.

Human autobiographical memory is a more sophisticated version of the memory system that Matthew Wilson's rats relied upon to replay their travels through the maze. Rats have cells in the hippocampus known as "place cells" that fire when they are in a specific location in space and then fire again whenever they are placed in that same location—or as in Wilson's study, when they mentally replay the experience of being in that location during sleep. Humans also link memory to location in this way. A brain-imaging study of London taxi drivers revealed that merely showing them maps of routes they frequently traveled activated the same areas of their brain that were engaged when they were actually traveling those routes. But as the human brain evolved in complexity, the hippocampus expanded its role to become a key element in the system for keeping track of emotionally tagged autobiographical memory.

All of these various categories of memories are stored in neural networks in different regions scattered throughout the brain. As neurologist Antonio Damasio puts it in his book *The Feeling of What Happens,* "There is no single place in our brain where we will find an entry with the word *hammer* followed by a neat dictionary definition of what a hammer is." Instead, there are a number of records in our brain that correspond to our past interaction with hammers: their shape, the hand motion required to manipulate the hammer, the result of the action, and the word that designates it in whatever languages we know. Yet when we bring the image of a hammer to mind, all of those components are seamlessly stitched together.

Autobiographical memories of events in our lives are stored and recalled in similar fashion. Sounds, sights, and emotions associated with an experience all are encoded in different neural circuits. Calling up the memory of your wedding day or your tenth birthday, therefore, is not a matter of pulling out a single mental snapshot but more like assembling a mosaic with colorful pieces (the smell of the flowers and the sounds of the music in the church; the taste of the chocolate cake, the joy you felt when you saw the puppy with the birthday bow around its neck) pulled from many different storage bins and then instantly welded into a unified memory.

An experience in the present that activates just one piece of that mosaic can set the entire circuit of interconnected brain cells firing to assemble the entire memory. In his literary masterpiece *Remembrance of Things Past,* Marcel Proust beautifully illustrated this process in a scene during which the narrator finds that dipping a petite madeleine into a cup of tea suddenly causes him to feel an overwhelming sense of joy. He then realizes that the mere taste of the tea-soaked pastry has triggered the feeling of intense happiness he felt as a child on Sunday mornings when visiting his beloved aunt, who would dip a madeleine in her tea and give it to him as a treat. He hadn't eaten the pastry since those childhood days, and the taste alone was sufficient to automatically conjure up the emotionally laden memory of those Sunday mornings. "Foreshadowing scientific research by more than a half century, Proust achieved the penetrating insight that feelings of remembering result from a subtle interplay between past and present," says Daniel Schacter, chair of the Psychology Department at Harvard University, in his book *Searching for Memory*.

If our emotions are aroused during an experience, our memory of it will be strengthened by that emotional tagging. There's one exception to that general rule, though. Extreme emotional arousal, particularly stress, increases the concentration of a hormone called cortisol, which actually disrupts the activity of the hippocampus and can weaken our ability to form autobiographical memories of the disturbing experience, even though procedural memories may be recorded—a phenomenon common among people who suffer post-traumatic stress disorder (PTSD). Recall of memories linked to strong emotions also can be greatly influenced by our emotional state at the time we retrieve them. Researchers have found, for instance, that we are more likely to remember unhappy events when we are already down in the dumps. And each time we call up an emotional memory, it may be altered slightly by what we're thinking and feeling at the time we're bringing it to mind. According to Joseph LeDoux, memories are "constructions assembled at the time of retrieval," and information stored at the time of the experience is just one of the building blocks used to build a memory.

What we have seen and heard afterward can also shape what we recall, as commonly occurs when eyewitnesses at crime scenes give accounts that are inaccurate because they are influenced by what others report to have seen. A perfect case in point: when two snipers terrorized the Washington, DC, area in 2002 by randomly shooting victims in public spots such as parking lots and gas stations, an early eyewitness report of a white truck speeding away from the shooting scene led to a string of subsequent reports from witnesses saying they'd spotted the same vehicle at other locations where the snipers had struck. In fact, the snipers' vehicle turned out to be a battered blue Chevrolet, but the power of that first suggestion was strong enough to result in the search being targeted on a mythical white vehicle.

In a very real physiological sense, what we've incorporated in memory from the past also significantly affects how we experience the present and form new memories. "Experiences are encoded by brain networks whose connections have already been shaped by previous encounters with the world," says Daniel Schacter. "This preexisting knowledge powerfully influences how we encode and store new memories, thus contributing to the nature, texture, and quality of what we will recall of the moment." We remember only what we have encoded and what the brain decides to encode depends on our past experiences, knowledge, and needs.

While we certainly consolidate memory and adjust our mental models during waking hours, many studies now indicate that a significant portion of this work takes place during our dreaming time and directly affects our waking behavior. "The brain is constantly evaluating new experience to figure out how it fits into the mental model built through previous memories, testing to see how well that model is working to predict novel occurrences and to guide decisions. Much of this revision appears to occur during sleep," says MIT's Matthew Wilson.

The way in which dreams are woven from memory is reflected in two dream accounts offered by neurophilosopher Owen Flanagan in his book *Dreaming Souls.* The first is a dream he had when he was five years old and the second, a dream he recorded at age forty-eight:

> *Dream in 1955:* A pack of wolves was chasing me. I was terrified and couldn't run away fast enough. I awoke breathless, trying unsuccessfully to scream.

> *Dream in 1997:* I was involved in a military maneuver sponsored by the CIA. My unit was badly positioned relative to the enemy and we were pathetically armed. I was very frightened. I tried to explain to my comrades—between normal trips to get the clutch on

my car fixed—that our nonautomatic rifles, a cross between a musket and an M-1 but with no magazines, were losers. Then I gave an antiwar speech insisting that we not obey government orders to do battle. I had some supporters and was subject to some ridicule. The chair of my department appeared in a feathered cap and wearing a tartan-plaid kilt, his weapon pointed as if he did not know what to do with it. He was clearly our leader. I was amused and scared. I picked up my car and was congratulated by the auto mechanics on our victory.

Deconstructing the memory components of the dreams, Flanagan points out that the plot of the five-year-old's dream is much simpler than the adult version, in part because it is drawing from a much more limited repertoire of experience. It is a typical pursuit dream, and since, at the time, he'd recently learned about wolves from frequently hearing the tales of Three Little Pigs and Little Red Riding Hood, his brain supplied the wolves as the threat pursuing him. The dream he had when he was forty-eight drew upon his far greater memory stores, weaving together elements from several time periods. Coming of age in Vietnam, he had spent time in antiwar protests and then on active duty in the military. He'd had experience dealing with car repairs and at the time of the dream was a university professor, so those elements were also incorporated with earlier memories in constructing the dream. "In both dreams, my mind appears to have put the activated memories and experiences into a story, a narrative structure," he says. "How exactly this is and why is one puzzle that needs attention." Flanagan adds that the emotions that permeate the dreams, especially the fear, most likely were prompted by activation of the amygdala, the brain system that triggers the fight-or-flight response.

Our off-line processing of the day's events involves incorporating autobiographical memories that have a profound influence on who we are. What we record as autobiographical memory and how we integrate it with past experience contributes to the development of what neurologist Antonio Damasio calls the autobiographical self. That sense of self is based on past experience, but it is also what allows us to imagine and plan for the future. "The autobiographical self hinges on the consistent reactivation and display of selected sets of autobiographical memories," says Damasio. "The idea each of us constructs of ourself, the image we gradually build of who we are physically and mentally, of where we fit socially, is based on autobiographical memory over years of experience and is constantly subject to remodeling. I believe that much of the building occurs nonconsciously and that so does the remodeling."

An important component of that consistent reworking of autobiographical memory may indeed occur in dreams, usually outside our conscious awareness, though waking life greatly influences which sets of memories are selected for replay as dream material. "It now seems likely that as we sleep, our brains are working hard to save the experiences that we will carry around with us for much of our lives," says Daniel Schacter. "The important events in our lives that we often review during waking may be frequently 'replayed' during sleep. Experiences that receive little attention during waking probably receive fewer nocturnal playbacks, paving the way for forgetting."

If memory is indeed what dreams are made of, what are the brain's rules for selecting which life events are processed in sleep, and how are those events then integrated with existing memory? A creative experiment to find out how and when daily experience turned up in dreams was devised by Howard Roffwarg and his associates at the Albert Einstein College of Medicine in 1978. Nine college students were fitted with goggles that filtered out blue and green wavelengths in light, so that everything they perceived appeared to be tinted red. The test subjects wore the goggles during waking hours for a period ranging from five to eight days straight, and they gradually became accustomed to this altered world, which they called goggle colored.

The subjects spent each night in the sleep lab, where they were monitored by EEG. The researchers hoped that by tagging all incoming visual images in a distinct color, they could track how the brain processed ongoing experience in dreams via the subjects' reports about when and how the red coloration was incorporated in their dream images. When awakened during REM, the students reported dreaming in goggle color for about half of the scenes in the first dreams of the night, but not in succeeding ones. On the following nights, goggle color appeared in later periods of REM, as well, with nearly half of later dreams incorporating scenes of red coloration and more than 80 percent of the dreams in the first REM period of the night including such scenes.

Researchers had assumed that whatever dream material was not colored in red would be derived from memories of pre–goggle wearing experience, but in some instances, events that occurred before the experiment also appeared in goggle color. There also were combinations in a single dream scene: a setting where the room was normal but the scene the dreamer saw when looking out the window was shaded red. When the goggles were removed and the subjects experienced just one day of normal vision, the red tint disappeared from their dreams. The researchers could conclude only that daily experience is quickly incorporated into dreams in a process that involves a complicated interaction between recent experience and memory. Exactly how that dance was choreographed remained a mystery.

Among those in the forefront of solving that mystery is Robert Stickgold, an assistant professor of psychiatry at Harvard. Stickgold came up with a novel way to try to coerce the brain into revealing its rules by examining a stage of sleep that previously had been overlooked by most researchers. As we're drifting off to sleep, we typically experience what's known as hypnagogic imagery—hallucinatory visual images and other sensations that usually aren't threaded together in narrative as most dreams are. More than a decade ago, Stickgold became fascinated by this sleep onset phenomenon while on vacation in Vermont. "After a day of hiking and rock climbing," Stickgold recalls, "as I drifted off to sleep, I immediately felt I was back on the mountain in one tricky passage where I had to cling to the rocks to pull myself up. I roused myself a couple of times, but each time I dozed off, the feeling of my hands on the rocks returned. Later in the night when I'd awake and try to get those same images back, I couldn't, but when I was first falling asleep they were unavoidable." He began taking note of other instances at sleep onset when he'd get similar strong spontaneous replays of the day's events and found that they tended to occur when his days included out-of-the-ordinary experiences, such as days spent white-water rafting or sailing in rough water.

Stickgold's curiosity was both personal and academic. Though he'd started out as a biochemist, Stickgold became interested in neurophysiology while doing postdoctoral work at Harvard. His career shifted entirely when he took a course on the dreaming brain taught by Allan Hobson and, shortly thereafter, in 1990, joined Hobson's lab. "I wanted to bring the scientific rigors of biochemistry to the study of dreaming, which I view as a route to understanding the waking mind," says Stickgold.

In an effort to learn more about how the brain selects which memories will be activated and when, Stickgold decided to focus on the sleep onset period to see if he could manipulate the content of imagery dreamers experienced as they were drifting off. Since asking subjects to go mountain climbing or white-water rafting as part of a study would have posed legal liability nightmares, Stickgold opted to see if a somewhat tamer novel experience could also induce such images. Even he was startled by the results.

In the first experiment, he recruited volunteers to play a computer game called Tetris, in which players assemble geometric puzzle pieces that are falling down the screen. Twenty-seven people played the game for seven hours over a period of three days. Ten of the players were experts because they'd played a Nintendo version of the game previously, while the rest were novices. Stickgold included among the novices five people who were amnesics, simply to see whether their dream imagery would include anything from the game—something he considered unlikely.

When the volunteers were awakened in the first few minutes of sleep and asked to report what was going through their minds during the first two nights, more than 60 percent reported dreaming about Tetris at least once, and all reported the exact same images: falling Tetris pieces. The majority of dream reports occurred on the second rather than the first night of training. "It's as if the brain needs more time or more play before it decides this is something that needs to be dealt with at sleep onset," he says.

To Stickgold's surprise, the amnesics also reported seeing the same kind of Tetris images, even though in waking they had no memory of the game and had to be reintroduced to the researchers from one day to the next. "I was stunned, because we thought if there's one stage of sleep that depends on episodic (autobiographical) memories, which amnesics lack, it would be sleep onset."

The fact that the amnesics got Tetris images at sleep onset indicates that autobiographical memories—details that link us to reality with specifics such as names, times, and places that we can consciously recall—are not the source of dream images at sleep onset. Instead, the dream imagery is being drawn from the kind of memory that amnesics do have—procedural and factual memories generated in the higher levels of the neocortex, where sensory information from experience is first received and associations with existing older autobiographical memories are formed. Scientists had long suspected that this was the source of imagery and memory for the more hallucinatory dreams we experience during REM and also in non-REM sleep periods later in the night. But since sleep onset seemed to incorporate more transparent replicas of real-life events from the day, Stickgold says his finding suggests that all dream imagery comes from the cortex as it associates fragments of recent experience with older memories. "Now we have experimental evidence about where dreams are coming from, and since the process works the same for normals and amnesics, it meets the kind of hard scientific standards I had as a biochemist," says Stickgold. Indeed, when the Tetris study appeared in *Science*, it marked the first time in thirty years that the respected professional journal had published an article related to dream research.

The amnesics' results also suggest that these unconscious Tetris memories that showed up in their dreams affected their waking behavior. The amnesics had to be taught how to play the game all over again each day, but at the start of one session, a researcher noticed that one of the amnesics instinctively placed her fingers on the three keys that are used in playing Tetris: "She did not quite know what she was doing and yet she did," says Stickgold. "Memories can be activated in our brain that are outside conscious awareness but that nonetheless guide our behavior."

The experiment also demonstrated how the brain edits out information it considers irrelevant: none of the sleep onset dreams included the dreamer or any details of the testing room—only the essential images of the task that had been learned were replayed. And the brain was also busy making connections: rather than seeing falling Tetris images in black and white as they appeared on the screen used in the experiment, one expert player dreamed of the pieces in color and accompanied by music, as she'd experienced them in the Nintendo versions on which she'd first learned to play years earlier. The substitution of those older images for the new reveals that the brain wasn't simply replaying memories of the day's events but transforming them through association.

In a follow-up study, Stickgold and his team had test subjects play Alpine Racer II, a more exhilarating, active arcade-style video game that brought even stronger images at sleep onset. Fourteen out of sixteen players reported images from the game at sleep onset, and so did three subjects who merely watched others play the game, so the study succeeded in inducing the same dream imagery in nearly 90 percent of the subjects.

Trying out the experiment myself in Stickgold's lab, I spent most of an afternoon on Alpine Racer, my hands clenched on controls that feel like ski poles and my feet positioned on platforms that slide and tilt to simulate the feeling of leaning into turns while speeding down steep downhill race courses. All the while, my attention was focused fully on the video screen in front of me as I attempted to whip my way down the mountain, through rocky tunnels and sharp curves. That evening, before I'd even turned out the light, images of a turn where I'd repeatedly wiped out on the Alpine Racer course flashed into my mind when I just closed my eyes briefly. I'd been reading the newspaper in bed and thought the game was the furthest thing from my mind, but that simply proves Stickgold's point.

"We think of our mind as being ours, but the brain has a set of rules of its own for picking out memory traces to reactivate and bring into our conscious mind, and in studies like this, we're tricking the brain into showing us some of those rules," Stickgold says. "Memory is stored in different ways throughout the cortex, and during sleep the brain is literally acting like a computer's Web browser, incorporating new experience by sorting through different memory systems to form associations and connections that help us make sense of the world."

He suspects that in all dreaming, not just sleep onset, access to autobiographical memory is blocked. With no input from the external world or access to the memory system that normally organizes our world during waking, the brain is forced to search for creative ways to associate raw data from new experiences with existing memories. When daily experience is folded into more complex narrative dreams as the night wears on, it does indeed pop up in loosely connected bits and pieces rather than as a true replay of autobiographical memory, as demonstrated in a 2003 study conducted by Magdalene and Roar Fosse, Stickgold's colleagues in the Harvard neurophysiology lab. Over a two-week period, they asked twenty-nine subjects to keep a log of daytime activities, events, and concerns, along with daily records of any dreams they recalled. When the dreams were scored for aspects of waking experience incorporated in the dreams, 65 percent included some aspects of daily events but no more than 2 percent contained autobiographical memory replay, which they defined as dreams that clearly contain at least three features of the real-life experience, including location and any characters, objects, or actions associated with it.

Not all dreams contain elements from that day's experiences—in fact, several studies have shown that only about half contain what Freud would call "day residue." But when the brain does weave elements from daily experience into dreams, it appears to follow a specific pattern in which the day's events make an appearance early on and then in some cases crop up again one week later, according to studies conducted by Tore Nielsen, who directs the Sleep Research Center at Hopital de Sacre-Coeur in Montreal. Nielsen has been exploring how daily experience is reflected in dream life in a series of studies conducted since the late 1980s. His results have consistently revealed a pattern he calls "dream lag effect." This pattern shows that something from the day's experience typically makes an appearance in dreams that same night in the form of characters, setting, or other individual features drawn from networks in the cortex that first received incoming information about the experience. On the following day, however, the chance of any elements from the previous day's events being incorporated in a dream drops by half. If the experience is featured in a dream later on, the replay comes a week later. In later studies, Nielsen has found that this lag effect is more common in women (in men, the experience isn't likely to be processed again after the first or second night) and the dream material that is replayed after the week's delay tends to be emotionally significant. "These are the kind of dreams that people will say affected their mood that day or made them sensitive to things they normally ignore in their lives," he says. "They tend to have sadness or anger in the dream, but not fear—they're dreams of insight, not nightmares."

Nielsen also discovered that for experiences that *are* particularly disturbing or fear inspiring, the dream lag effect is actually slightly delayed. When he showed a group of volunteers a disturbing film of the ceremonial slaughter of water buffalo by Indonesian villagers, the peak times for the film to first be reflected in dreams was three days after it was shown, and then the replay would occur a week later, on day ten. That pattern matches a study of first-time parachute jumpers, whose experience popped up in their dreams three days after their jump and then again on the tenth day following the jump.

The lag time before elements of waking events replay in dreams probably reflects the processing time needed for the hippocampus to gradually relay information to the neocortex, where it then becomes accessible again as fodder for dreams, but Nielsen believes the increased delay before especially stressful events first appear in dreams may indicate that the brain requires more time to process the negative emotions associated with the events. Thus, dreaming's role in memory consolidation, with its roots in mere survival skill rehearsal, has evolved to take on additional layers of complexity in humans, thanks to our gift—and burden—of being tuned in to our emotions.

A SUBSET OF MEMORY CONSOLIDATION is learning, whether it's taking piano lessons for the first time or memorizing dates for a history exam. Dream researchers are rapidly building evidence that the dreaming stage of sleep, in a complicated dance with mental activity in other sleep stages, plays a significant role in acquiring new information and skills. "A lot of scientists I know are also musicians, and they frequently have the experience of practicing a difficult new musical piece and not getting it down, but when they come back to it after a couple of nights' sleep, they suddenly have it, even without practicing in the meantime," says Dan Margoliash, a professor of biology at the University of Chicago. "What does that mean? We're obligated to ask those questions now and examine them as rigorously as we do other aspects of behavior."

Like Matthew Wilson, Margoliash has looked for answers via animal studies, and he has uncovered evidence that just as rats dreamt of rerunning mazes, birds replay and refine their species' courtship songs as they sleep. Margoliash studies zebra finches, tiny birds who first learn their species' song pattern by imitating what they hear from adult birds. "Not only does the bird need to hear itself practicing the song early in life while first learning to sing, but adult birds also have to hear themselves singing regularly to maintain the song correctly. Humans also need to hear their own voices regularly or their quality of speech deteriorates, as it does in people who suffer hearing loss as adults," explains Margoliash.

Scientists previously had assumed the auditory feedback a bird requires to keep its song in top form simply occurred while the bird was singing during waking hours, but when Margoliash recorded signals from the neurons that produce singing signals in the brains of both waking and sleeping birds, he discovered something unexpected—the same firing patterns that occurred when the birds were actually singing began to appear once the birds slipped into sleep. The researchers first discovered that the brain cells' firing pattern was replicated when recordings of the birds' own singing were played back to them during sleep, but they also found that even when the recordings weren't playing, those neurons still fired spontaneously in patterns that suggested mental song rehearsal was occurring, primarily during slow-wave sleep.

And while the auditory signals associated with song replay flowed freely in sleeping birds between different brain areas that control singing, that auditory feedback flow was blocked when the birds woke up, as if a barrier had slammed down. Based on this initial evidence, Margoliash hypothesized that rather than listening to its own song as it is singing and instantaneously doing any mental fine-tuning that might be needed, the finch instead stores the auditory signals from that singing episode in the bird-brain equivalent of the hippocampus to be replayed during sleep—assessing its own performance and adjusting its network of song-producing neurons off-line. In fact, he suggests, it may be difficult for either the human or animal nervous system to modify itself while it is actually in the process of singing or, in the human case, performing a new gymnastic move.

Margoliash—whose aversion to taking himself too seriously is evident in his e-mail tag, "bigbird"—says that at first he was skeptical of his own hypothesis about birdsong being replayed and tuned up during sleep, because it seemed "a bit wild." But now he believes rapidly accumulating evidence from his own lab and from experiments by other researchers indicates that both dream-rich REM sleep and slow-wave sleep play an integral role in learning.

The suggestion that a good night's sleep improves human learning surfaced early on in a scientific report published in 1924, but the results of rounds of experiments conducted after the discovery of REM sleep in the 1950s tossed cold water on that idea. The experimenters required that subjects learn factual information, including memorizing lists of paired words that had no obvious connection, such as cow/stair. They then tested subjects to see whether depriving them of their dreaming time affected their performance. It didn't, so researchers mistakenly assumed there was no connection between sleep and learning.

What researchers have since discovered is that different sleep stages are tailored toward different types of learning, explains Carlyle Smith, who began studying the link between learning and sleep back in the early 1970s, when he joined the stream of American researchers who traveled to France to work in the lab of dream research pioneer Michel Jouvet. "We spent a month sawing little rods to make a maze for mice and then recorded their brain activity twenty-four hours a day for ten days straight. The mice who became smarter at running the maze showed big increases in REM sleep, and the others didn't," recalls Smith, now a psychology professor at Trent University in Peterborough, Ontario, whose studies have continued over more than three decades. "From that point on, I never doubted that sleep and learning were connected, and now there's enough supporting evidence to get other researchers interested in it, too," he says.

A steady accumulation of research by Smith and others has helped explain how dreaming and cognitive processing in various stages of sleep affect learning. Shortly after falling asleep, we enter the light sleep known as stage II, and it is this phase that appears to be responsible for the improvement in performance that musicians, athletes, and dancers often experience a day or two after practicing a new skill.

A 2002 study by Harvard researcher Matthew Walker found that a 20 percent improvement in motor skill tasks was largely dependent on test subjects getting stage II sleep in the final two hours of sleep prior to waking in the morning. "To get the maximum benefit from practice if you're learning a new sport or a new piece of music, you need to get a full night's sleep for at least the first night afterwards so that you don't miss that final period of stage II sleep before waking," says Smith.

Following stage II comes slow-wave sleep, a deeper sleep that precedes REM. Slow-wave sleep is more prevalent in the first half of the night, when it occupies up to 80 percent of sleep time. During the second half of the night, the proportion of REM sleep jumps dramatically and alternates with stage II sleep. Slow-wave sleep is important for learning tasks involving factual memory—the kind of rote memorization you would need for a history test, for instance. Our dream-laden REM sleep, in contrast, is critical for procedural learning—the "how to" category that includes learning a new behavioral strategy. Studies have shown that not only does the amount of REM sleep that subjects experience increase immediately after they have been trained on such tasks, but their performance declines if they are deprived of REM after training, particularly on the first night.

In a well-known 1994 study, a team of Israeli scientists led by Avi Karni and Dov Sagi measured the time it took people to carry out a visual discrimination task—identifying the shape of a striped area flashing against the background of a test pattern on a computer screen. They found that speed in carrying out this procedural learning task improved not during the practice session but in the eight hours following it. If subjects were repeatedly awakened during REM, they failed to learn, but their performance didn't suffer if they were awakened during the deepest stages of slow-wave sleep.

Since then, other researchers have conducted studies using the same learning task featured in the Israeli study, but their conclusions suggest that optimum learning may in fact depend on a combination of both types of sleep, not just REM. One of the studies indicated that improved performance hinged on getting sufficient slow-wave sleep in the first quarter of the night and REM in the last quarter of the night. Matthew Wilson has found the same sort of process occurs in rats, and he surmises that it is during slow-wave sleep that memory traces in the hippocampus are in essence stamped in for further processing later, during dreaming sleep, especially those REM periods in the last part of the night. During late stages of REM, it appears that the hippocampus and related limbic system structures such as the amygdala (which is important in processing emotions) exchange information with the higher-level processing centers in the neocortex in a way that strengthens memory and solidifies learning.

In fact, molecular biological evidence also supports the idea that the brain is learning as well as spinning dream plot during REM. Every cell contains a collection of genes, each of which has a specific function in the body. When a gene is called into action to perform its DNA-ordained purpose, it becomes activated in a way that can now be measured. This measurable activity is called gene expression. A 2002 study revealed that a specific gene that is expressed during waking when a rat is in the process of learning is expressed again most strongly during late stages of REM, indicating that learning-associated changes on a molecular level occur in this phase of sleep. And when the hippocampus is put out of commission through anesthesia, the gene expression associated with learning simply doesn't occur at all in the neocortex.

"It has been hypothesized for some time that memory traces must be passed from the hippocampus to the neocortex for long-term storage, and our study indicates that this may be what's occurring during REM sleep. Especially during the later phases of REM, the hippocampus is talking to the neocortex," says Constantine Pavlides, a neurophysiologist at Rockefeller University who is one of the authors of the study and a protégé of Jonathan Winson, whose theories from the 1970s on the biological function of REM sleep are bolstered by the new molecular biology research.

The research suggesting that learning takes place after we drift off to dreamland obviously gives "Sleep on it" a whole new meaning. "While late periods of REM may be especially beneficial, I suspect it's the full cycle of sleep that's really important for learning," says Smith. And there's wisdom in power napping too. In another recent study by Robert Stickgold and his colleagues at Harvard, subjects trained to carry out a visual task on a computer screen saw their scores steadily decline over the course of four daily practice sessions as mental burnout set in. But thirty-minute naps after the second session prevented further deterioration, and a one-hour nap actually boosted their performance in the third and fourth sessions.

Skeptics who question whether REM sleep really plays a role in learning point to two examples that, they contend, contradict the whole theory. The first is the case of an Israeli man who suffered brainstem damage from a gunshot wound at age twenty. He recovered, but when his sleep patterns were examined at age thirty-three, researchers found that on most nights, he had no REM sleep at all, and on nights when he did, it represented less than 3 percent of his total sleep time. Nevertheless, he appeared to have no memory impairment, having completed both college and law school after his injury. "Clearly you can eliminate REM sleep without disturbing memory, because there's no profession that requires more mindless learning than the law," quips Jerome Siegel, professor of psychology and biobehavioral sciences at the University of California at Los Angeles. Siegel and other skeptics cite another reason to doubt sleep's importance in memory processing: a class of antidepressants called monoamine inhibitors has been shown to dramatically reduce or even entirely eliminate REM sleep, and though the drugs have been widely taken for years, memory impairment is not reported as a side effect.

Carlyle Smith counters that the demands of law school and the tasks used in studies to test the Israeli man's memory all involved declarative memory, which would be impaired by slow-wave sleep deprivation but not REM loss. Similarly, any testing done on patients taking antidepressants also has focused on declarative memory tasks, so people who don't experience REM would have no trouble remembering names, places, and facts. Because learning doesn't take place exclusively during sleep, they would be able to learn procedural tasks as well, but not as efficiently as someone getting a normal amount of REM nightly. The difference in learning results would only become obvious over a period of days or weeks, and no studies of that kind have been conducted, says Smith.

Perhaps the most conclusive evidence demonstrating that we are indeed learning during dreaming time is found in studies using brain-imaging technology. While it's not feasible to record the activity of individual brain cells in humans as Matthew Wilson did with rats running the maze, scientists can use brain imaging to see which regions of the brain are activated while a test subject is in the process of learning a new skill. They can then scan that person's brain again during sleep to see whether those same regions are reactivated, indicating a mental replay of experience.

That's just what Pierre Maquet has done. Maquet, who runs a research lab in Liege, Belgium, conducted experiments in 2002 in which he asked test subjects to sit in front of a computer screen displaying six fixed markers, each of which has its own identifying key on a keyboard. A flashing signal appears beneath one marker, then quickly vanishes and reappears beneath another marker. Whenever the signal flashes beneath a given marker, the test subject must quickly hit the key identifying that marker. For one group of test subjects, the signals appeared randomly, so there really was nothing to learn that could improve their performance. For a second group, there was a trick to the task that they weren't aware of. For this group, the signals did not flash randomly but instead followed a pattern—an artificial grammar of sorts—that the brain begins to recognize and learn implicitly, just as toddlers learn the grammar of their native language. "Subjects don't know *that* they're learning or *what* they're learning, but we can accurately assess *whether* they have learned by measuring their reaction time," explains Maquet.

Members of both groups performed their task at the computer for the same amount of time in the afternoon. That night when they slept, Maquet monitored their brain activity via a PET scanner, which shows which areas of the brain are most highly activated by measuring blood flow, with the most active areas showing up as brightly colored spots on the resulting images. Some members of the group who unwittingly had been learning the artificial grammar of the signaling patterns also were scanned while awake at the computer in order to identify which brain regions were highly charged while they were in the act of learning the task. (To limit subjects' exposure to the radiation involved in PET scanning, subjects were either scanned as awake participants or during sleep, but not both.)

What Maquet found when he scanned the sleeping subjects who had been learning the grammar was that the same brain areas that lit up while subjects were awake and performing the task were reactivated during REM sleep. In the group that had just been responding to random signals, however, there was no such reactivation. The brain apparently judged the experience of merely pushing buttons in response to random signals unworthy of a mental replay.

"The two groups had performed the same task for the same amount of time; both were hitting buttons when they saw flashing signals on the screen, so the only difference was that one group had something to learn and the other didn't," says Maquet. This indicates that the brain reactivates in REM sleep to replay experience only when it has something new to learn. And further underscoring the link with learning, those who had the fastest reaction times in the training sessions while learning the artificial grammar also showed the greatest reactivation of those same brain regions during REM. When viewed as a whole, this growing body of evidence indicates that a tremendous amount of memory consolidation occurs during dreaming time and other sleep stages.

Given the fact that the emotional centers of the brain are its most highly activated areas during the periods when we have our most vivid dreams, it also appears that a specific type of memory is selected for processing when we dream. "My hunch," says Tore Nielsen, "is that emotionally charged memories are what the brain is really targeting when we dream during REM."

That hunch is in fact being borne out by a number of studies that suggest dreaming may serve as a kind of internal therapist, helping us to integrate emotional experiences from the day. Even though these nightly sessions occur largely outside our conscious awareness, they can have a significant impact on our emotional state during waking hours. As Robert Stickgold puts it, "Figuring out what memory means, rather than simply recording events, is the brain's mission at night."

6

Nocturnal Therapy

We do not have emotions about our dreams so much as dreams about our emotions.

—Rosalind Cartwright

AT 10:30 ON A BALMY JULY NIGHT in Chicago, a man in his thirties sits patiently on the edge of his bed in the sleep lab, idly watching TV while electrodes are glued to his scalp to record his sleeping brain's electrical activity. He's here because he responded to a newspaper ad recruiting subjects for a study examining dream patterns among people who are going through divorce. Each time he's in the midst of REM sleep, he will be awakened via intercom by the soft voice of a researcher, in a monitoring room down the hall, who will ask him to describe his dream images and the emotions associated with them. "I only occasionally remember my dreams at home, but in the lab, when they wake me while the dream is still going on, I can always describe the settings and characters, and I realize I must be dreaming like this every night," he says.

This man, whose first marriage ended just six months ago, is one of thirty subjects participating in a study being conducted by veteran dream researcher Rosalind Cartwright to test her theory that dreams are in fact mood regulators, helping us process negative emotions so that we wake up in a better mood than when we went to sleep. When this nighttime mood regulation process goes awry—causing us to experience nothing but bland, emotionless dreams—we wake up even more down in the dumps, a situation common among people who suffer from depression, contends Cartwright, who directs the Sleep Disorder Service and Research Center at Rush-Presbyterian–St. Luke's Medical Center in Chicago. Her long-term study of people going through marital breakups shows that those who are able to recover and get on with their lives do indeed have a dreaming pattern that differs significantly from those who remain mired in depression. And her results fit in with those of researchers using other scientific approaches to examine whether dreaming plays some special role in helping to regulate our emotional lives.

Cartwright has been active in dream research since the early 1960s, when she set up her first sleep lab while going through a divorce herself. "I was feeling depressed and wasn't sleeping all that well, so I thought I might as well do something productive with my nights," she recalls. She'd been fascinated by dreams from childhood on, because her mother, a poet, had vivid dreams that she shared with the family at the breakfast table, while her more practically minded father claimed he never dreamed at all. "I was always intrigued by why some people were big dreamers and others weren't," Cartwright says.

Though she began her career collaborating on research with the well-known psychotherapist Carl Rogers, Cartwright shifted to the study of dreaming after the burgeoning new field came to her attention via her secretary, who happened to be dating William Dement while he was still working in the Chicago lab where REM sleep was discovered. "My secretary would get off the phone with Bill and bubble over with excitement about how they'd found out that eye movements indicated when people were dreaming, and I'd say, 'Well, that's interesting, but we've got work to do.' She married Bill and lived happily ever after, and I eventually caught on to the importance of dream research and have been hooked ever since," says Cartwright.

Her studies of dream content over the years have shown—as have most other researchers'—that the predominant emotions in dreams are negative. A 1991 study comparing reports of emotions in waking-life events versus dreams found positive emotions were less frequent in dreams and the incidence of fear specifically was higher than in waking. Several studies of dreams reported in both lab and home settings concur that more than two-thirds of emotion in dreams are negative. Which specific feelings are most prevalent varies from study to study, but they are all in the same general emotional spectrum regardless of when or where the studies were conducted. For instance, in a 1966 study of 1,000 college students, 80 percent of emotions expressed were negative, and about half of those were classified as feelings of apprehension, while the other half were reported as sadness, anger, or confusion. Similarly, a 1996 sleep lab study by Swiss researchers found negative emotions appeared twice as often as positive ones, with anger, fear, and stress the most frequently reported. And a 2001 analysis of more than 1,400 dream reports by a Tufts University group found dream imagery most commonly reflected fear, followed by helplessness, anxiety, and guilt.

Of course, positive emotions appear in dreams, too. In a 2001 study conducted in Norway, joy/elation was the single most frequently reported emotion, appearing in 36 percent of dream reports, followed by surprise in 24 percent, anger in 17 percent, anxiety/fear in 11 percent, and sadness in 10 percent. The predominance of positive emotion in this study may have something to do with how it was carried out, suggests its lead author, Roar Fosse. Experimenters used portable EEG equipment to monitor subjects in their own homes, awakening them during REM for dream reports and asking the subjects themselves to note the occurrence and intensity of emotions in their dreams. Fosse contends that independent judges scoring dream reports tend to understate the occurrence of positive emotions and that when subjects report dreams after awakening spontaneously, dreams with negative emotions are predominant because they usually interrupt sleep and thus are the most likely to be recalled. Cartwright counters that in her lab studies, dreamers also are awakened in mid-dream and the majority of emotions are still negative, as is the case in most other studies of dream reports. Fosse acknowledges that many other factors, including differing perceptions of emotions and subjects' personality types, could affect results, and such variables should be considered in designing large-scale studies of emotions in dreams. Fosse's study tested only nine subjects, ranging in age from thirty-one to sixty.

The predominance of distressing emotions Cartwright found in dreaming subjects led her to suspect that integrating emotional experiences—particularly ones that are stressful or damaging to our self-esteem—is an important part of what happens during REM sleep, when our most complex, vivid dreams occur. And of course, this negative emotional coloring is also in keeping with the evidence that REM sleep evolved as an off-line way to process survival-related information. "Our brain gives everything we experience an emotional tag, and those experiences that are selected for processing in REM sleep are primarily those that make us angry, fearful, depressed, or anxious. The negative-positive mix may vary from 60:40 for someone who's had a good day and is in pretty good shape emotionally to 95:5 for someone who's working through a lot of problems, but there's no question that the tilt is toward the negative for everyone. They're the emotions we have to work through so we can get up and face the next day," Cartwright explains.

Her conviction was strengthened when imaging studies of the dreaming brain that emerged in the late 1990s revealed that structures in the limbic system—the center of emotional memory—are more highly activated during REM sleep than in waking, while the portions of the prefrontal cortex that direct logical thinking are nearly shut down. Moreover, the areas of the cortex that *are* activated during REM are those with numerous anatomical connections to the amygdala, the portion of the brain that triggers our fight-or-flight response and also plays a critical role in unconscious emotional learning. Pierre Maquet, one of the leading researchers studying REM sleep via brain imaging, concludes that the interplay among these specific brain regions does indeed reflect the processing of emotional memories.

Cartwright argues that when you're dreaming, you're updating your concept of who you are. You may occasionally get a night off just for play in your dreams because life at the moment is relatively uneventful, but on most nights you go to sleep with some emotional issue unresolved. It could be a minor blow to self-esteem after overhearing someone say you're putting on weight, a nagging worry about your job security, or deep distress over an argument with a spouse or child. When you enter REM and the brain's emotional memory system suddenly kicks into high gear, it calls the shots, constructing the dream by piecing together images that are in some way associated with whatever the predominant emotion is at the end of your day. "When we're awake, we're used to thinking in a logical, linear way, one thing leading to the next in a straight-forward line," says Cartwright. "But dreams are constructed more like Scotch plaids, with recent memory placed on top of earlier memories, all linked by feeling, not logic."

Based on her studies, published in 1998, that compared dreaming patterns among sixty normal adults and seventy who were clinically depressed, Cartwright says that for most people, dreams in the first REM period of the night contain the most negative emotion, and in each successive REM period, dreams become both more positive emotionally and also incorporate elements of autobiographical memory that go further back in time. Other researchers also have found that dreams incorporating childhood memories tend to occur later in the night, coinciding with the period when body temperature is at its lowest point.

"If you fall asleep focused on something disappointing in a current romantic relationship, your brain is taking that current information and laying it over experiences that are matches of some sort in the same emotional network of memory," she says. With each succeeding REM period, dream plots become more complex and include older images that are increasingly remote from current reality. That's why your first-grade teacher may make a guest appearance in a dream built around some difficulty with your boss. Your dreams by morning become more pleasant and your mood improves if by the last REM period of the night, your brain finds matches in long-term memories that are associated with the same feeling but that had a positive outcome.

In people who suffer from depression, however, the dreaming pattern differs significantly. They tend to have their first period of REM earlier in the night than nondepressed people do, and the dreams they report at that stage are surprisingly lacking in emotion of any kind. But as the night wears on, their dreams become progressively more negative. "People who suffer from depression tend to ruminate during waking hours," she points out. "If you tell them they're looking great, they can put a negative spin on it by wondering whether you're just saying that because you want to borrow money from them. During REM they also may be running through exclusively negative images from memory, reinforcing the anxiety or fear that triggered the dream in the first place. It makes sense that you wake up feeling even more depressed if the Scotch plaid your dreaming brain weaves consists of nothing but images of one negative outcome after another."

In her latest study, Cartwright recruited subjects who were going through the breakup of a first marriage and whose psychological test scores when they entered the study revealed symptoms of clinical depression though they were unaware of it and weren't being treated. "I wanted to see how they got over it on their own, because a substantial proportion of people going through divorce do have a major episode of depression and most get over it without drugs or therapy," says Cartwright. Over a period of five months, the test subjects' dreaming patterns were periodically studied in the sleep lab. They reported on their moods in the evening, when they arrived, and again when they awakened in the morning. They also met with Cartwright regularly to give progress reports on how their marital problems were being resolved and how they were coping emotionally. At the end, they were again tested for signs of depression, and their results were compared to their scores when they first started. The first twelve to complete the study were monitored over an even longer period—eight months—and of those, nine recovered from symptoms of depression associated with the divorce. Test results for the other three showed that they were still depressed at the end of the study period. There was also a dramatic difference in dreaming patterns between the two groups. Of those who got over their depression, 52 percent reported well-developed dreams that usually incorporated the former spouse or failed marriage in the plot, while in the group that stayed mired in depression, only 24 percent reported such dreams. While Cartwright says dreams can perform this function whether we remember them or not, the dream recall rate in those who recovered was also double that of those who did not, so remembering dream content may heighten dreaming's therapeutic effect.

Similarly, German researcher Michael Schredl has shown in a study of people withdrawing from alcohol in an inpatient treatment program that those who had high recall of dreams about drinking in the period immediately after they had given it up were most likely to stay sober through follow-up a year later. Dreaming of being confronted with the opportunity to drink again and recalling those dreams may contribute to successful therapy because such dreams help develop appropriate coping strategies to prevent falling off the wagon in waking life, concludes Schredl, who conducts studies at the sleep laboratory of the Central Institute of Mental Health in Mannheim.

Cartwright says for those who overcome divorce-related depression, the role of the ex-spouse as a dream character also changes over time: "At the beginning, the ex-spouse in the dream generates feelings of anger or unhappiness, but in dream reports toward the end of the study period, the ex-spouse appears in a way that shows the dreamer is now unhooked from the relationship and is enjoying reclaiming an independent identity and sense of freedom." The following dream report during the final month of the study from a woman who recovered from her depression illustrates Cartwright's point:

> I was hoping that I would be able to make time to go back to school. I was going to call the college to find out what the schedule would be but I couldn't find the number. I think we were on vacation in Disney World. It was just the three of us, my boys and me. It was kind of nice, it was kind of emotional. We haven't had a vacation in a long time. It was weird because usually I have to get permission from their dad to take the children but for some reason, it didn't matter. It was my choice to take them on vacation. I didn't have to ask anybody.

Another subject dreamed his ex-wife was trying various tricks to force him out of a big race in which all contestants were flying in airplanes that looked like World War II bombers. The dreamer was accompanied by another woman in his plane. "In the dream, my wife was speaking French. I was struck by my lack of involvement, my nonattachment. I really wasn't involved enough to care what happened," said the man, who viewed his feelings of detachment in the dream as positive. Cartwright noted that the dreamer didn't speak French himself and agreed that the dream was a dramatization of the man's healthy disengagement from his former spouse. "It was his way of saying, 'My ex-wife can rail all she wants about me seeing another woman but I don't care and I don't even understand what she's saying,'" explains Cartwright.

She concludes that the ability to both form and recall well-developed dreams that make positive associations between your current emotional state and past memories clearly improves your odds of getting over symptoms of depression. In her latest study Cartwright is also testing a new theory about how to make that happen in people whose REM sleep doesn't seem to work properly as a mood regulator. "There's plenty of evidence that interrupting REM sleep in normal people makes them wake up more irritable and fatigued but suppressing REM in those who are clinically depressed actually improves their mood and energy level in the morning," says Cartwright. The REM sleep that depressed people experience actually tends to worsen rather than improve mood, because in their dreams they're reinforcing the negative introspection and rumination that preoccupies them in waking hours.

With that in mind, she wondered whether the very process used to collect dreams in the lab could be therapeutic because it involves repeatedly interrupting REM. For both depressed and normal subjects, Cartwright always follows a strict protocol whereby subjects are awakened five minutes into their first REM period, ten minutes into the second, fifteen minutes into the third, and twenty minutes into all subsequent REMs. The time frames for interrupting REM when a dream is likely to be in progress are set to accommodate the fact that REM periods increase in duration as the night progresses. These constant interruptions prompted one of her study subjects to jokingly express her feelings of frustration on a campaign-style button she gave Cartwright: underneath the large-print words "I Have A Dream" is, in smaller print, ". . . and I wish you'd let me finish it."

Cartwright is exploring whether intentionally disrupting the pattern of repetitive negative dreaming among depressed subjects can jolt their emotional memory systems into breaking through to new associations that provide more positive outcomes in dreams, leading to improved moods in the morning. "By waking them repeatedly during REM, allowing them to recount the dream images to the experimenter, and cutting off the dream's negative ending, when they enter the next REM period, if there is a positive pathway through the memory system, they have a better chance of accessing it," she says. "Also, when you interrupt REM, pressure builds up for the brain to make more and more attempts to get into REM—in our study we see them go from an average of three REM periods to an average of five per night. That gives them more chances for the process to work the way it should."

Shortening REM periods also increases the intensity of emotions when they do occur, which can be measured by eye movements during REM. "It's long been known that sparse eye movement is associated with bland dreams and dense eye movement with more emotionally jazzy ones," she explains. "I really think I've got the problem by the tail now. By interrupting REM periods and breaking that cycle of progressively negative dreaming, we're seeing improvement among depressed subjects in our study without medication and without psychotherapy."

TAKING A DIFFERENT APPROACH to tackle similar questions, Eric A. Nofzinger is examining whether dreaming plays a role in regulating our moods by peering inside the brains of both healthy subjects and people being treated for depression to compare how they function when they're sleeping and when they're awake. What he has found is remarkable evidence that what happens in the brain physiologically during REM sleep among healthy subjects differs dramatically from what occurs in people who are depressed. Nofzinger, a psychiatrist and director of the Sleep Imaging Research Program at Western Psychiatric Institute and Clinic in Pittsburgh, was among the researchers who provided the first images of the dreaming brain back in 1997 via PET scanning. What he saw then led him to suspect that incorporating daily emotional experiences is indeed at the heart of what happens in the brain during REM.

Hanging next to Nofzinger's office door is the first image he ever made of the dreaming brain. The image, created via PET scanning, clearly shows the brain's limbic system operating at full tilt. "When you compare the brain in REM to waking, the activation of the limbic system increases by 15 percent. That is massive, because a 3 or 4 percent increase is what you typically see for regional shifts in brain activation. Clearly, in REM we are tapping into the seat of emotional behavior, and we see that the brain is being flooded with some sort of processing task," says Nofzinger, who increasingly believes that the task in question is integration of immediate and past emotional experience.

His own experience of keeping a dream journal during his college years also gave him insight. "Through keeping track of my dreams for a while during my college years, it became very apparent to me that there's an emotional undercurrent to our lives that shows up in dreams. The same story line would play out over two or three months, and it seemed that what dreams were reflecting was emotional regulation and growth," says Nofzinger.

For his PET scanning studies, Nofzinger scanned subjects two to four hours after they awoke in the morning, because studies on the body's natural daily rhythms indicate that this is the period of the day when we tend to be most alert. He then did scans during both non-REM and REM sleep. In healthy subjects, images showed that during waking hours, the outer regions of the cortex that process sensory information and direct logical thought were more highly activated than were the limbic system and the brainstem. In non-REM sleep, those decision-making, attention-directing areas of the cortex wound down, and the region of the brain that is the sensory gate for information from the outside world also slipped into a quiet state.

During REM the greatest burst in activity appeared in a part of the limbic system called the anterior cingulate gyrus. It is a region on the inner surface of the cortex that Nofzinger says appears to swing into action for any kind of information-processing task and that "may have something to do with sensing changes in our environment and imparting meaning to experience."

Other researchers also have zeroed in on the critical role played by this structure in the front of the brain. In his book *The Astonishing Hypothesis,* which examines the neurological underpinnings of consciousness, Nobel laureate Francis Crick speculates that the anterior cingulate is the seat of free will, where our sense of an independently acting self is generated.

In their initial brain-imaging studies at the National Institutes of Health, Allen Braun and Tom Balkin also found peak activation of the anterior cingulate during REM sleep. A later study comparing the brain first at five minutes after awakening and then again at the 20-minute postawakening mark revealed that the prefrontal cortex was not fully active until twenty minutes after awakening, which Braun and Balkin believe most likely explains the impairment in alertness and cognitive performance that characterizes the period just after waking. By contrast, they found that the anterior cingulate was active immediately upon waking and its activity didn't change over the ensuing twenty minutes, nor did its functional connections with other brain regions. "We interpreted this to mean that the anterior cingulate cortex supports consciousness per se," says Braun. "Crick theorizes that the anterior cingulate is the source of self-awareness, and now, based on our results, I think he may be right," says Braun.

Nofzinger's studies of depressed versus healthy subjects show that not only does this critical brain area linked to our sense of self light up during REM but so do the systems responsible for detecting emotional significance of experiences and for triggering more primitive urges such as fight-or-flight instincts and sexual drive. In nondepressed subjects, these emotional centers are the driving force generating activity in the cortex as we dream. "Dreams seem to be taking emotionally charged information from the daytime and connecting it with a larger body of information in the cortex that's species specific or that comes from each individual's personal base of experience," he says. But then during waking, these areas that are supercharged during REM slow back down to an idling speed.

In depressed subjects, however, a significantly different pattern emerged in the scanning images. During dreaming, the emotional networks in the brains of depressed subjects are even more highly activated than in their normal counterparts—the intensity of the activity is indicative of a stress response. In the depressed, the supercharged state of the limbic system in turn apparently activates the prefrontal cortex and related cortical regions that go into action for problem solving and logical thinking during waking hours. In people who don't suffer from depression, of course, these are the regions that are almost entirely off-line during dreaming and other sleep stages.

"In healthy subjects, the limbic system has free play and emotions are churning during REM sleep, but it is not creating the stress response we see in the depressed, and the executive areas of the cortex are getting a break," Nofzinger says. "But in depressed individuals, it appears that the problem-solving areas of the brain never shut down and the ruminating pattern that characterizes their waking life continues throughout the night." Like Cartwright, he concludes this may explain why REM sleep is not restorative for the depressed but instead can plunge them further into a negative frame of mind.

In fact, some psychologists suggest that a properly functioning dreaming system may actually be more effective than forms of psychotherapy that encourage the depressed to become introspective and ruminate still further. "Freud had a model of the unconscious mind that is very like a cesspool: emotions that weren't fully expressed are held onto in this cesspool of repression, and the job of the therapist is to release the noxious emotions and thereby free the person," according to Joe Griffin, a psychologist in Britain who has spent more than a decade researching REM sleep and the evolution of dreams. "But research has shown quite unambiguously that dreams do this for us every night. In other words, nature actually invented the emotional flush mechanism long before Freud."

If indeed REM sleep is our off-line means of regulating our moods, what happens in the brain when we have nightmares? Nightmares—especially repetitive ones commonly experienced by people who've been through the horrors of war, rape, an auto accident, or other trauma—actually offer an ideal window for understanding how all dreams function by making broad connections in our memory system and creating visual images that reflect our predominant emotions at the moment, says Ernest Hartmann, a psychiatry professor at Tufts University and director of the Sleep Disorders Center at Newton-Wellesley Hospital in Boston. Though Hartmann's father was a colleague of Sigmund Freud, his own theory of how and why we dream—based on extensive studies of trauma victims' dreams—contradicts Freud's central thesis that every dream is a fulfillment of a hidden wish. Freud's notion that dreams serve as a royal road to the unconscious activities of the mind, though, is compatible with Hartmann's findings.

"For many of us leading fairly ordinary lives, there are many emotional concerns active at any one time and it is not easy to determine one dominant emotion, so our dreams may seem confused and almost random," says Hartmann. In someone who has recently experienced a trauma, however, the emotion to be processed is both strong and obvious, making it easier to follow how the brain translates that emotion into moving visual images that serve as metaphors for what we're feeling. For example, a woman who was brutally raped provided Hartmann with the following dreams she recorded over the course of several weeks following the attack:

> I was walking down the street with a female friend and the woman's four-year-old daughter. A gang of male adolescents in black leather started attacking the child. My friend ran away. I tried to free the child, but I realized my clothing was being torn off. I awoke very frightened.
>
> I was trying to walk to the bathroom when some curtains began to choke me. I was choking and gasping for air. I had the feeling I was screaming, but actually I didn't make a sound.
>
> I was making a movie with Rex Harrison. Then I heard a train coming right at us, louder and louder; it was just about upon us when I woke up.
>
> The dream is all in color. I'm on a beach. A whirlwind comes and envelops me. I'm wearing a skirt with streamers. The whirlwind spins me around. The streamers become snakes which choke me and I wake up frightened.

While the woman's dreams include some actual details of her rape—the eighteen-year-old rapist entered her window through curtains and threatened to strangle her with them—she is primarily dreaming about the terror and vulnerability she felt: a child is attacked, she is choked, a train rushes at her, a whirlwind envelops her.

In fact, Hartmann says, dreams serve to "contextualize" emotions in visual form, and whirlwinds or tidal waves frequently appear as metaphors for overwhelming feelings of fear. He reports that several people who escaped from fires first dreamed about fire but then of tidal waves or being chased by gangs of criminals.

Over a period of weeks as the trauma gradually is resolved—in significant measure due to the emotional processing carried out during dreaming—survivors' dreams follow a discernable pattern, Hartmann has found. First, the incident is replayed vividly and dramatically but often with at least one major change—something that did not actually occur. Then fairly rapidly the dreams begin to connect this traumatic material with other information or autobiographical memory that appears emotionally related. Often a person who has been through one kind of trauma dreams of all kinds of other traumas that may be related to the same feelings of helplessness or guilt. If the dreamer has survived a trauma in which others have been killed or injured, the theme of survivor guilt almost always emerges. For instance, a dreamer who escaped a fire in which his brother died reported: "In my dreams, most of the time I am getting hurt in some way by my brother or I get hurt in an accident while my brother is safe."

For most people, the nightmares gradually change into modified versions of the event as the original experience is linked by the neural networks in the cortex to other emotionally related material from the dreamer's life or imagination. Over a period of a few weeks or months, the trauma figures less and less in dream life, and eventually content returns to normal as the disturbing experience is integrated into memories of other, positive experiences and the negative emotions associated with it are toned down.

Hartmann likens this dreaming pattern to a form of automatic internal therapy. Initially, the emotional message reverberating through the dreamer's mind is "This is the most horrible thing that has ever happened to anyone! How can anyone survive this?" Hartmann says the dreaming brain's ensuing attempts to replay and connect various images, in essence provide the following response:

> Well, let's take a look at what happened. Let yourself picture it, and any other pictures that come to mind. Picture whatever you want, picture other catastrophes. You're beginning to see other people in similar situations, too. All these scenes are horrible but

> not unique; people seem to survive. In fact, does this remind you of anything else? Let's look at other times when you felt terrified. Not quite the same? No, but let's keep looking; wasn't there some similar feeling? Let's see what else is related. And you survived. In fact you seem to be surviving this time.

Both good psychotherapy and dreaming offer the same therapeutic benefit: allowing connections to be made in a safe place. "The therapist allows the patient, especially the traumatized patient, to go back and tell her or his story in many different ways, making connections between the trauma and other parts of the patient's life—overall making connections and trying to integrate the trauma," Hartmann says. "Dreaming performs at least some of these same functions." As connections are made between the recent disturbing event and previous experiences, the emotion becomes less overwhelming and the trauma is gradually integrated.

This kind of posttrauma dreaming pattern is clearly apparent in post–September 11, 2001, dream reports compiled by Deirdre Barrett, a Harvard psychology professor and editor of the book *Trauma and Dreams*. One of the most dramatic examples she cites is the case of air traffic controller Danielle O'Brien, who guided the takeoff of American Airlines flight 77 from Dulles International Airport on that tragic morning. An hour later she watched the plane—a blip on her radar screen—head straight for the White House, then veer off and crash into the Pentagon. For several nights afterward, O'Brien had nightmares. "I've sat up straight in bed many times, reliving it, reseeing it, rehearing it," said O'Brien. But within a couple of months, the therapeutic process Hartmann describes appears to have occurred, for O'Brien reported her dreams had changed. She dreamed of the radar scope as a green pool in front of her: "It was a pool of gel and I reached into the radar scope to stop that flight," she said. "But in the dream, I didn't harm the plane. I just held it in my hand, and somehow that stopped everything."

Similarly, a woman in New York City who emerged from the subway onto the street by the World Trade Center only to see people jumping to their deaths from the burning towers replayed the horrific images in her first dreams just as she'd seen them. After several weeks passed and her own traumatic reaction was subsiding, however, the dreams were also transformed, and instead of watching helplessly, she supplied all of the people leaping from the buildings with colorful parasols that allowed them to drift down gently to safety.

The natural therapy that dreaming provides can of course be accelerated and strengthened in waking life by support from a network of family and friends or therapy focused on resolving the trauma. "When there's no therapy involved and researchers are just tracing what happens after trauma, people who get better are most likely to be the ones that are having dreams which work through the issue and also tend to be the ones who have good social support," says Barrett.

Of course, there are some trauma survivors for whom these emotional regulating processes during REM don't seem to work. About 25 percent of people who go through emotional or physical trauma experience post-traumatic stress disorder (PTSD), which is frequently accompanied by repetitive nightmares that replay the trauma approximately as it occurred, though sometimes there is an added emotional element that transforms the scene in some way. One of Hartmann's subjects, a Vietnam War veteran whose battlefield duty was to open body bags to identify dead American soldiers, had a difficult job as it was, but he became severely traumatized by unexpectedly finding his best buddy in one of the bags. The dream that kept rerunning in his brain afterward didn't simply replay the experience but instead incorporated a plot twist that Hartmann says contextualizes survivor guilt:

> I'm doing my job opening the body bags one by one . . . all kinds of screaming and helicopter noises. I open the bags and the last bag I open contains myself and I wake up screaming.

Several researchers are examining PTSD dreams to understand how the brain gets stuck in these disturbing replays and how to help it break free. Eric Nofzinger at the University of Pittsburgh plans to extend his brain-imaging studies to focus on people who suffer from PTSD. "We want to see what the brain looks like when it has these thematic repetitive dreams that seem to be hardwired to replay night after night," says Nofzinger.

The dreaming brain's broad search for contextualizing metaphors and connections with positive memories that help calm the emotional storms generated by trauma is just the most dramatic example of a process that is continually at work in ordinary dreams as the brain builds dream imagery around more mundane concerns, according to Ernest Hartmann. For instance, pregnant women typically have dreams early in pregnancy that incorporate imagery reflecting their anxiety about the changes occurring in their bodies and fears about whether they are still attractive. Later in pregnancy, dreams often portray fears about what the baby will be like or anxiety about not being equipped to handle the demands of motherhood.

Long-standing anxieties may also be expressed metaphorically. Hartmann offers an example of a mother with two young children who seemed satisfied with her career and husband but was herself the child of parents who were hypercritical, making her feel that no matter what she did, she could have done it better. When she became a parent herself, her childhood anxiety about being inadequate suddenly was triggered, and she developed repetitive dreams featuring the same theme. Her fears about not being a good enough mother were expressed in dream reports such as these:

> I leave my son alone and a big cat is clawing him, killing him.
>
> I'm at a hotel by the seashore in Maine. My two children are off in separate rooms and the tide is coming up fast. I wake up panicked that they'll drown.

Skeptics question how these internal dramas enacted by the brain at night can be of any use if they're nearly all forgotten within minutes after the curtain falls. But researchers such as Hartmann and Cartwright argue that what's crucial in dreaming is the forming and reforming of connections in various neural networks—a physiological process that in some cases reinforces older memories and in others makes new associations, thereby weaving in fresh experience that updates our mental model of ourselves and our world. This nightly rewiring fits in with theories that have been proposed about the evolutionary purpose of dreaming—to integrate information crucial to survival—and it can occur regardless of whether we remember dream content.

That's not to say that trying to recall dream content is fruitless, however. While some dreams are indeed nonsensical, a remembered dream may also give us insight about the emotional issues we're wrestling with that we overlook during the day. Being able to recall and reflect on dream content in some cases has been shown to have an impact on both future dreaming patterns and waking behavior. Several studies by researchers over the past decade have shown that recording nightmares and then thinking about them in a relaxed state or visualizing them with a changed ending helps break the pattern. In a technique called imagery rehearsal treatment, subjects plagued by repetitive bad dreams are asked to rehearse a positive dream ending once a day over a two-week period. The amended plot forms a new coping strategy that effectively short-circuits the nightmares. Not only does converting nightmares to "mastery" dreams reduce or eliminate disturbing dreams, but daytime symptoms of reaction to trauma such as flashbacks, heightened startle response, and generalized anxiety also tend to subside automatically, according to Deirdre Barrett.

Rosalind Cartwright has found that even for her study subjects who aren't suffering trauma symptoms, training them to reflect on negative dream scenarios and imagine more affirmative outcomes can lead to more positive dreams the next time around, as well as an improvement in attitude during the day. As an example, she cites a woman who was ending a marriage to a domineering husband at the same time that she was having troubles on the job with a male coworker who she said was "walking all over her." After the woman had a dream of her ex-husband coming into her new apartment wearing muddy shoes and ruining her white carpet, Cartwright urged her to think about changing her dream imagery so that she wasn't cast in the role of victim. In a subsequent dream, the woman found herself lying on an elevator platform with no walls, terrified as she rose through the air above Lake Michigan with no protection.

But the memories of the mental instructions she'd rehearsed during waking about not playing the victim also were triggered, and in the dream she decided to stand up, despite her fear. "As soon as she stood up, the elevator walls came up securely around her, and she realized that all she'd had to do was stand up for herself and she'd be OK," says Cartwright. Working through her passivity in the dream imagery appeared to create an emotional shift that carried through to waking life as well: the woman decided to speak to her boss about the colleague who was trying to undermine her, and the situation was resolved.

"Therapists would have a good wedge into what isn't getting worked out on its own, what needs attention, if they could get subjects to remember the last dream of the night, which in the depressed tends to be the most negative," says Cartwright. "Contrary to Freudian theory, the key issue isn't hidden. It's right there, very obvious."

To examine your dreams, of course, you actually have to remember them, and most of us recall no more than 1 percent of our dreams. While memory of one to two dreams per week is the average for adults, there is a great range of variability among individuals, with some saying they never dream at all and others who regularly recount their nightly adventures in elaborate detail. Studies examining why some people tend to remember dreams more often than others have shown that recall has nothing to do with intelligence but may be influenced somewhat by other personal traits. People who are frequent dream recallers have better-than-average recollections of childhood memories, are frequent daydreamers, and tend to have creative interests, especially in visual arts.

Dream researchers suggest some simple but effective steps for their subjects to improve dream recall. Autosuggestion works wonders, just as it does when you plant the idea in your mind that you have to awaken at a certain hour the next morning. Harvard psychologist Deirdre Barrett advises getting into your most comfortable sleeping position and then reminding yourself a few times that you will be dreaming and you intend to remember your dreams.

Anytime you wake up during the night or in the morning, immediately ask yourself what you were just dreaming, without shifting your position or allowing general waking thoughts to creep in yet. If a single dream scene sticks in your mind, try to remember what came before or after it, what else you saw, who the characters were, what your mood was. Keep a journal on your nightstand to jot down whatever you remember—or better yet, a voice-activated tape recorder so you don't have to move at all.

Scientists running dream studies also find that subjects' recall increases most dramatically merely as a result of writing dream reports or keeping a dream journal. Timing is the key. While something you see or hear during the course of the day may occasionally trigger a memory of a previously forgotten dream you had that night, most dreams are lost to us if we don't make a conscious effort to recall them within minutes after they end. Several studies have shown that people who awaken frequently during the night due to disorders such as sleep apnea also tend to have above-average dream recall. That's why Harvard neuroscientist Robert Stickgold isn't joking when he suggests that one of the best ways to recall more of your dreams is to drink lots of water before bed. Odds are you'll have to get up more often during the night, hopefully at least once or twice in middream.

But simply having an interest in dreams and therefore a motivation for remembering them is the variable that more than anything else correlates with high dream recall in most studies. Since dream periods get longer as the night goes on and late morning dreams are the most vivid of all, working on improving your memory of dreams during weekends or anytime you can sleep late also will increase your odds of success.

As your recall improves, you may be surprised at what you find, especially if you think of yourself as someone who rarely dreams. "We send our study subjects transcripts of the dreams they've reported in the lab along with questionnaires asking if they recognize anyone, if there are any relationships between one dream and another, any connections to what's going on now in their lives," says Rosalind Cartwright. "And even the subjects who deny that dreams have any importance or meaning—boy, do they go to town and write and write. It's do-it-yourself psychoanalysis."

7

The Ultimate Spin Doctor

Freud was 50 percent right and 100 percent wrong.
—Robert Stickgold

"WHAT ALWAYS FASCINATED ME about dreams was how your brain created something that was surprising to itself," says John Antrobus, a cognitive psychologist at City University of New York. Antrobus entered dream research in the 1960s after conducting experiments exploring how the mind wanders during waking hours. He found that if you check in with a test subject every ten or twelve minutes during the daytime to get a report on what's running through his or her mind, there are more discontinuities and scene changes in waking consciousness than there are in REM dreams.

Antrobus and his colleague Jerry Singer also conducted experiments in which they gave people a task to focus on and then asked them to signal when their minds began to wander. "We thought people's thoughts would start to wander after a few minutes, but when we studied them in the lab, the interval was much shorter—a matter of seconds," Antrobus says. As James Joyce illustrated in his groundbreaking novel *Ulysses*, consciousness is largely comprised of a stream of continually shifting internally generated associations and thoughts. "You shift your attention away from that inner world only when something else in the external world is judged by the brain to be more important. We now think that judgment call is made by neural networks in the limbic system," Antrobus says.

Thanks to brain-imaging studies showing the dreaming brain in action, it also is becoming clear that in dreaming consciousness, the limbic system—the command center for directing emotion and storing strong emotional memory—is directing the dream show. Clearly, a dream is a product of multiple layers of mental activity. The brain is running tests of genetically programmed, survival-related behavior, as well as reviewing recent experience and integrating significant bits of new information with what's already in the memory database in order to update our individual concepts of how the world works and how we fit into it. And having the brain's emotional center in the driver's seat means that the memories that are being singled out most prominently for processing are those that are emotionally charged: anxieties, feelings of loss, blows to self-esteem, and physical or psychological trauma. Meanwhile, all of this is taking place under unusual physiological conditions, in which the neuromodulators that help focus attention are in short supply and the brain responds only to its own internally generated signals.

All of this activity happens and serves its purpose whether we remember any of it or not. But understanding how the brain spins its dream narratives and examining them can be both entertaining and enlightening. Making an effort to recall and examine what happens in the mind at night not only can provide personal psychological insight (as research discussed in the previous chapter has shown) but can also offer a greater understanding of the nature of consciousness itself—especially if you learn how to become aware of a dream while it's in progress—and sometimes even lead to creative breakthroughs. Equipped with an accurate scientific understanding of what's happening in the brain during dreaming, you can progress beyond simplistic dictionaries of dream symbols to achieve a more sophisticated level of dream interpretation that intelligently answers the basic question we all ask when we awaken from a vivid dream: what did that mean?

Unraveling the mystery of how the brain constructs dream narratives provides fascinating insight not only into how meaning can be extracted from them but about how the mind works in waking hours as well. While researchers such as Mark Solms and Allan Hobson focused on the physiological processes that triggered the dreaming process, John Antrobus and other cognitive psychologists zeroed in on exactly how the bits and pieces of the end product are assembled and connected into a story that the dreamer views as if it were created by someone else. When Antrobus first began studying dreaming in the 1960s, neuroscientists viewed the brain as being divided into different "boxes" or regions, each of which had a specific function. But in the 1980s the revolutionary notion of neural networks was introduced, which compared the operations of the brain to the workings of a computer. The big difference is that computers have a relatively limited number of processors for data storage, while the computational power of neurons operating in networks within the brain is astoundingly more powerful. "It's beyond imagination the amount of stuff the brain is processing. Everything we see, everything we think, is based on the computations of millions of neurons for any given perception. They work together to say this is a person or this is a house, and despite variations between people's faces and between one house and another, neurons can abstract the essential features needed to identify a house or a person," says Antrobus.

When he grasped the complexity of how neural networks function, Antrobus says the realization struck him like a bolt of lightning that the operating rules for those networks explained some aspects of dreams that puzzled him: How could the brain take material from memory that was thoroughly familiar and end up concocting images that were entirely novel and plots that surprised the dreamer? And why did characters and objects often go through Houdini-like disappearances, reappearances, and transformations? He realized that while the same neural networks that make associations and plan our actions in waking are directing brain activity during sleep, the surprise element in dreams stems from the fact that the networks during dreaming have no sensory input from the outside world to constrain the possible combination of neural patterns that can be activated.

Pieces of many houses or features from a variety of faces are combined and assembled into one image that is not anything we have ever seen before.

He even developed a series of neural network models to simulate how the brain produces dreams. "The brain makes the best sense it can of the barrage of internally generated neural signals it receives, including random neural noise, and passes it on to the next part of the system. If a visual image of two dots is created in the visual cortex, the parietal cortex is likely to turn them into a couple of eyes, and then put those two eyes into a face. If that face isn't recognized, the limbic system says, 'Ah, that's worrisome; let's run.' That signal goes to the motor system and the dream plot takes off," explains Antrobus. He insists that Allan Hobson and Robert McCarley's theory about how dream plots were created was faulty because it suggested that there had to be input from the brainstem that the cortex somehow synthesized into a dream. "They have never understood that the brain can create pattern out of *any* noise," says Antrobus.

The brain's relentless drive to create some sort of meaning out of whatever it encounters—even the nonsensical—also predominates during waking hours, though we're usually unaware of just how much we are being conned by the story spinner in our brain, according to Michael Gazzaniga, director of Dartmouth College's Center for Cognitive Neuroscience. He bases his views on hundreds of remarkably revealing experiments he and other researchers have conducted on split-brain patients—people whose severe epilepsy was brought under control by surgically severing the bundle of fibers that connect the right and left hemispheres of the brain.

As Gazzaniga's mentor Roger Sperry demonstrated through research that earned him a Nobel Prize in 1981, the left hemisphere specializes in verbal skills, writing, complex mathematical calculations, and abstract thought. The right hemisphere is essentially nonverbal, but its specialties include processing anything to do with geometric forms and spatial relationships, perceiving and enjoying music in all its complexity, recognizing human faces, and detecting emotions. The right side of the brain basically is engaged in perceiving the world, while the left brain is geared toward analyzing those perceptions, solving problems, and communicating with the outside world, especially via language. In over 95 percent of right-handed people, the left hemisphere governs speech, as it also does in 70 percent of left-handers.

Based on experiments with split-brain patients, Gazzaniga contends that the left hemisphere contains a neural system that he labels the "interpreter," which continually seeks and provides explanations for both internal and external perceptions and experiences. His studies clearly show this spin doctor at work. Because there is no communication between the right and left sides of the brain in split-brain patients, it's possible to see how the two hemispheres process their specialized brands of information independently, each completely unaware of the other. When the analytical left brain doesn't have the correct answer, it will simply make up something based on the information it does have, just as the dreaming brain pieces together strange combinations of images into a narrative with its own form of logic.

In one classic experiment, a split-brain patient was shown two different pictures, with his visual field restricted so that the left hemisphere received only the image of a chicken claw, while the picture viewed exclusively by his brain's right hemisphere was a snow scene. With the hand controlled by the left hemisphere the patient selected a picture of a chicken to match the claw, and with the other hand, he chose a shovel to go with the snow scene. When he was asked to explain the two choices, his left hemisphere response was that he had seen the claw and naturally picked the chicken to go with it and that the shovel had been chosen because it was needed to clean out the chicken shed. He couldn't explain the real reason for choosing the shovel because his left hemisphere hadn't seen the snow scene, but the interpreter in that side of the brain nevertheless offered an explanation for his selection—and that explanation was expressed not as a tentative guess but as a confident statement of fact.

In another split-brain experiment, Gazzaniga asked the subject to get up and take a walk, but that request was communicated only to the right side of the brain. When the subject was asked why he was pushing back the chair and getting up to leave the room, he replied without hesitation, "Oh, I need to get a drink." Again, even though the left hemisphere has no clue why the subject is leaving the room, it cooks up a reason. "The left brain, which asks how A relates to B and constantly does that when solving problems, is also the hemisphere that provides our personal narrative for why we feel and do the things we feel and do," explains Gazzaniga in his book *The Mind's Past*. "The interpreter constantly establishes a running narrative of our actions, emotions, thoughts and dreams. It is the glue that unifies our story and creates our sense of being a whole, rational agent."

Of course, that doesn't mean the stories it spins are necessarily reliable. Gazzaniga points out that the interpreter influences other mental capacities, such as our ability to accurately remember past events. When a split-brain subject is shown a series of pictures representing a simple activity such as making cookies and is later asked whether pictures in another series of illustrations had appeared in the first group, both hemispheres were equally accurate in recognizing the previously viewed pictures and rejecting unseen ones. But when the subject was shown related pictures that had not been included in the first group, only the right brain correctly rejected images it had not seen before. The left hemisphere incorrectly recalled more of these pictures, presumably because they fit into the pattern it had constructed regarding cookie making. "Once you realize the brain is so gullible, you don't want to believe a damn thing it does. It's always trying to make sense, and in doing so, it fabricates more than just dreams," says John Antrobus. Nowhere does this spin doctor in our brain give us more done deals than in emotional matters, according to Gazzaniga. "Our automatic brain files away gain and loss experiences, and when we encounter a new decision, the emotional brain helps us sort out which cognitive strategy to use, even though for a startlingly long time we remain unaware of why we are doing one thing rather than another," he says.

Only humans have this interpretative system, and it developed because it gives us a competitive edge for survival, Gazzaniga contends. While all animals can learn to avoid food that makes them ill, for instance, only humans have the capacity to ask why the plant made them sick and to devise strategies to avoid having it happen in the future. This ability to reason, based in the left hemisphere, is the foundation from which the interpreter evolved to spin narratives about what happens in our waking experience, as well as to construct the tales that comprise our dream life. As Gazzaniga puts it, "the very device which emerged to help us conquer the vicissitudes of the environment enabled us to become psychologically interesting to ourselves as a species."

Though Gazzaniga's experiments focused on subjects during waking, researchers who find his work illuminating in understanding the dreaming process include David Foulkes, the premier investigator of children's dreams. "Everything that Gazzaniga is talking about in terms of the interpretive system is exemplified in dreaming," Foulkes says. "The interpreter is doing an even more spectacular job of story making than it does in waking, because the brain in sleep is activated but the raw material it has to work with is much different. You lose yourself, you lose the world, and thought is no longer directed. The brain has quite a challenge making sense under those operating conditions, but it does what it always does—it spins a narrative." In essence, the dreaming brain jumps to conclusions based on incomplete evidence, just as it does during waking; but during sleep, the material it has to work with can be even more incomplete and disorganized. While some dream content may reflect information that correlates with the dreamer's current waking concerns, represented in mental activity that is thoughtlike, other portions may be metaphoric expressions of those concerns, and others may be simply a confabulated, wing-it kind of filler supplied by the left-brain spin doctor that provides our ongoing narrative in waking life.

While the dreaming brain obviously is using the same cognitive abilities it relies upon during waking, there also are clearly some differences in its operational rules that can lend a bizarre quality to dream life. Setting is the dream element that most often is incongruous with the real world. Scenes change without warning, or one setting itself may be a strange conglomeration of many: you're in a house that seems to be your home, but it's on the beach instead of in the city, and some of the rooms seem to be part of a museum or hotel. Tufts University dream researcher Ernest Hartmann found that in a sample of one hundred of his own dreams, 60 percent of the settings involved a generic house that was a combination of his own home and an unrelated structure such as a lecture hall or lobby. Hartmann and a growing number of neuroscientists suggest that the explanation for this phenomenon of confusion and conglomeration in dreams primarily lies in how the brain's normal operating rules are altered due to physiological changes during sleep.

In waking as well as in sleeping consciousness, a thought or fantasy stems from the firing of a widely distributed network of neurons. But when thinking of a house in waking hours, we generally are directing the brain to activate a network of neurons that call up the image of a specific house—where we lived during high school, or where our children grew up, or where we live now. In the dreaming process, however, with the logic-oriented prefrontal cortex deactivated and sensory input from the outside world shut off, the brain makes much broader connections. When the neuronal pattern representing "house" lights up, the brain doesn't seek out a specific memory of house but activates several neural nets representing a variety of houses and similar structures.

These dreams that have a more hallucinatory quality occur most frequently in REM sleep, when the supply of the neurochemical norepinephrine is dramatically reduced. Norepinephrine has been shown in several studies to enhance the cortex's ability to tune out the noise of the many competing signals of neurons firing at any given point and home in on one specific signal. Its low levels in REM may also contribute to the hyperassociative quality of dreaming. Not only do settings shift, but characters also sometimes transform without warning: the person traveling with you on the train may have started out as your sister, but when you turn to look at her again, you realize she's become your mother or perhaps has simply disappeared altogether. One study by researchers in Allan Hobson's lab at Harvard examined four hundred dream reports and found eleven instances of one character changing into another and seven inanimate objects becoming another object, but no examples of characters changing into objects or vice versa. Yet in a content analysis of more than 3,000 dreams supplied by a woman given the pseudonym "Barb Sanders," Bill Domhoff found seven instances of animals or objects transforming into people, including a yellow wooden horse transforming into an artistic man and a spider becoming a miniature man who then morphs into a light bulb, so there may be no hard and fast rules governing dream imagery.

Such metamorphoses have long intrigued scientists, and they were in fact analyzed at the end of the nineteenth century by Belgian psychologist Joseph Delboeuf. Delboeuf noticed that when we recount a dream to others, we do not say that a cat turned into a young woman but rather "I was playing with a cat, but after a while it wasn't a cat any more, it was a young lady." He theorized that we first dream of the cat and then quite separately of a woman, and our minds afterward create the transition to provide continuity to the dream. "Delboeuf clearly stated that dream inconsistency is nothing special, since our waking thoughts are in fact as chaotic as dreams are. But because waking thoughts are accompanied by perceptions that are logically linked together they seem to be more coherent," explains Sophie Schwartz, a dream researcher in the Departments of Physiology and Clinical Neurosciences at the University of Geneva in Switzerland.

Given all of the spin-doctoring and mental sleight of hand involved in creating a dream, how much meaning can we actually glean from the end product? First of all, the answer depends on the dream. To believe that every dream is worthy of interpretation would be the equivalent of assuming that every sentence you utter is equally interesting or meaningful. As laboratory studies have shown, many dreams are so mundane that we sleep through them and never recall them. In fact, a study by National Institutes of Health researcher Frederick Snyder in the early days of dream research showed that 90 percent of dreams reported when subjects were awakened in the lab involved "coherent accounts of realistic situations in which the self is involved in mundane activities and preoccupations." Vivid, emotionally charged, or complex narrative dreams are more likely to occur toward morning, when the chances of awakening while they're still going on or after they've just concluded are higher. Those more cinematic productions, therefore, are the ones we tend to recall, and are probably the ones most worth recalling.

As studies by researchers with a psychological bent have indicated, the nightly dramas our brain concocts sometimes can shine a spotlight on the emotional issues that are most active in our minds at a given point in time. Even scientists who don't buy the argument that dreams serve any biological function nevertheless acknowledge that we can glean meaning from them. "Dreams have meaning because they express our emotional preoccupations as well as our conceptions of ourselves and the people close to us," says dream content analysis specialist Bill Domhoff. "While some meaningful psychological information can be extracted from dream reports, we also should recognize that some aspects of dream content may turn out to be nothing more than frivolous products of the freewheeling improvisation the brain undergoes when input from the external world is shut off while the forebrain is activated."

But making sense of a dream can't be accomplished by consulting a one-size-fits-all dream dictionary, whether it's based on Freudian theory, ancient Chinese beliefs, or any of the other decoding systems used in the dream guidebooks you'll find on bookstore shelves today. The effort to find meaning in this simplistic way dates back to the Greeks. The first comprehensive guide to dream interpretation was a five-volume encyclopedia compiled in the first century A.D. by Artemidorus, who collected dream reports from people he met on his travels throughout Greece, Italy, and parts of Asia. Dream interpretation books from Artemidorus through the present are based on the assumption that all material in dreams is symbolic and that symbols have universal significance. According to Freud, dreaming of teeth falling out symbolizes castration, while an early Chinese dream guide says the same dream symbol means one's parents are in danger.

All such rigid approaches to dream interpretation have a common failing, which dream content expert Calvin Hall described succinctly: "We read in Artemidorus that to dream of eating cheese signifies profit and gain to the dreamer. It is not stated that *sometimes* this is its meaning, or that it depends upon the state of the dreamer or upon the context in which this activity appears. The meaning of eating cheese in dreams is univocal, universal, and timeless. It is this feature of universal symbol-referent connections that accounts for the popularity of dream books. Since they do not make qualifications and exceptions, which would require the use of judgment and discrimination, anyone can decode dreams and foretell the future if he has a dream book handy."

Relying on universal dream symbols to derive meaning from our dreams amounts to underestimating the brain's creativity in conjuring dream scenes to reflect our unique daily concerns. A perfect example is a dream incorporating a clever visual pun that was reported by Ann Faraday, a British dream researcher. The night before she was to appear on a radio show hosted by a man named Long John Nebel, Faraday dreamed that a man in long white underwear was shooting her down with a machine gun. She had never met Nebel, but she knew he had a reputation for sharp-tongued critical attacks on his guests, and her anxiety about her appearance on his show was captured in the visual dream pun of being shot down by a man in long johns—obviously a play on the radio host's name. Whatever meaning you might find for guns or long underwear in a psychoanalytic book or dream symbol dictionary obviously would have little relevance to this particular dream. "It is as though the mind while dreaming is deliberately searching for opportunities to pun, so that it can present abstract ideas though imagery," says Patricia A. Kilroe, a professor of English at the University of Louisiana who has examined the linguistics of dream puns. "The relatively easy identification of puns in dreams suggests that dreams are not meaningless, that the mind is motivated to put abstract concepts into concrete form during sleep."

Freud obviously borrowed the age-old reliance on using universal symbols for dream interpretation but put his own spin on it by proposing that the symbols all were designed to disguise fears and desires that would be unacceptable to us in waking life. Since he believed the buried wishes fueling dreams were nearly always sexual in nature, it's not surprising that a review of psychoanalytic literature conducted by Calvin Hall found that out of 709 symbols commonly identified by psychoanalysts in dreams, 102 objects were categorized as representing the penis, while 95 different symbols were interpreted as standing for the vagina and another 55 were supposed to be symbols for sexual intercourse.

Clearly, scientific evidence now indicates repressed sexual wishes or fears are not the driving force behind dream creation. Sometimes a cigar really is just a cigar, as anti-Freudians like to point out. Freudian scholar and psychoanalyst Mark Solms concedes that Freud "may have been wrong" in claiming that the bizarre elements in dreams result from the mind's attempt to censor and disguise taboo wishes and desires. Instead, they may simply result from the brain's strange physiological state during dreaming, when the rational systems in the brain's frontal lobes are not fully operational.

But Freud was also right on some other important scores. As evidence from brain-imaging studies and investigations of patients whose dreaming is altered by brain damage has demonstrated, dreams are driven by strong emotion and primitive instincts and they draw on memory, both recent experiences and those dating back to childhood. Even anti-Freudian Allan Hobson gives his nemesis credit for being on target about another crucial issue: "Freud was also correct in insisting that much more of waking consciousness than we were prepared to accept comes from our instinctive/emotional brains (or as we would now say, our limbic systems). Moreover, we can expect to learn more about this part of ourselves by paying attention to our dreams and, perhaps, by using dreams as starting points in tracking associative trains of thought back to their imagined source in our instincts."

Hobson offers one of his own dreams as a good case study in this kind of interpretation. In his dream journal Hobson recorded the following dream for December 3, 1980:

> I arrive at a meeting and am greeting colleagues. Suddenly I notice that Jouvet is there. He recognizes me and smiles broadly (not his usual greeting). I am about to call out to him when I suddenly lose muscle tone in my legs and sink to the floor. I cannot communicate and feel lost.

Jouvet refers to the French dream researcher Michel Jouvet, with whom Hobson had a somewhat contentious relationship early in his career when he worked in the French scientist's lab. Hobson also recorded comments in his journal about his interpretation of the dream's meaning. They included the following:

> —Limp legs: I first heard the French expression for this on the day that I went to a romantic rendezvous that needed to be discreet, to the Hotel de Beaux-Arts in Villefranche. When I returned to the lab, Jouvet said I looked like I had *les jambes coupees*—an expression used to describe one who is sexually exhausted. . . .

—Jouvet's smile: a beginning reconciliation after almost ten years of tension over personal and professional rivalry. . . . Today I received a cordial letter from Jouvet—formal, but cordial.

—Atonia: Jouvet's great discovery, the abolition of muscle tone associated with REM sleep, is represented in my dream cataplexy. Like narcoleptics in real life, strong emotion—especially surprise—produces atonia. Perhaps I now recognize Jouvet's achievement in my behavior.

Reflecting on the journal entries years after the dream, Hobson says that while his interpretation seems to ring true, there's no way of knowing whether it accurately explains why he concocted this particular dream. Even so, the kind of personally meaningful associations Hobson made in an attempt to make sense of the dream constitutes a more reasonable strategy than mechanically decoding dreams based on someone else's definitions of symbols. This search for individual meaning is what Jung advocated, and research on the role of emotional processing in dreams supports this approach more than it does Freudian-style interpretation.

As evidence on the evolutionary history and biological functions of REM sleep suggests, Jung may also have been on target in his notion that elements in dreams can reflect the experiential history of our ancient ancestors. Certainly not all dreams fit that bill, but survival-oriented dreams of being the hunter or hunted do appear to emanate from genetically encoded, collective ancestral experience. Content analysis expert Bill Domhoff concludes that overall, Jung's observation of some commonality in dream content across individuals and cultures is "plausibly encompassed by the idea that metaphorical concepts are acquired through both developmental experiences shared by all human beings and gradual linguistic socialization into the huge treasure trove of conceptual metaphors that are part of our cultural heritage."

From a scientific standpoint, it's unlikely that it will ever be possible to say definitively that a given dream means A, B, or C. Perhaps the best we can do is to use dreams as helpful tools to gain insight into our emotional preoccupations, realizing that the left brain's interpretative system is spinning a story about the dream's meaning, just as that same story spinner cooked up the dream narrative in the first place. Meaning to a great extent is in the eye of the beholder. Says psychophysiologist Stephen LaBerge, "If what people see in inkblots can tell something about their personal concerns and personality, how much more revealing should dreams be, because they are the worlds we have created from the contents of our minds. Dreams may not be messages, but they are our own most intimately personal creations. As such, they are unmistakably colored by who and what we are, and could become."

Creative Chaos

Dreaming is, above all, a time when the unheard parts of ourselves are allowed to speak.

—Deirdre Barrett

PAUL MCCARTNEY WOKE UP ONE MORNING in May of 1965 with a haunting tune running through his mind. In the dream he'd just awakened from, he'd been listening to the same melody being played by a classical string ensemble. He was so taken with the sound that he immediately got up and began playing the notes he'd heard on the keys of the upright piano next to his bed in his mother's home in London, where the Beatles were filming *Help!* Because he'd dreamed the tune, he was convinced it must be someone else's song that he'd heard somewhere along the way.

He began checking around to try to identify the music, but there was no evidence that it existed outside his own head. When he tried playing the song for other people, they not only said they'd never heard it before but insisted it sounded like the sort of melody that would come from McCartney himself. He'd been so hesitant to believe he could have come up with original music via dreaming that he'd only bothered to come up with a few nonsense lyrics for the song: "Scrambled eggs, oh my baby, how I love your legs. . . ."

When he decided he could rightfully claim ownership of the melody from his dream, he finally plunged in and composed the lyrics to "Yesterday," which was then recorded with a string arrangement just as he'd originally heard it in his dream. Nearly forty years later, "Yesterday" still ranked as the most frequently played single of all time on American radio. Reflecting on the song later in life, McCartney said it was "the most complete thing" he'd ever written. "For something that just happened in a dream, even I have to acknowledge that it was a phenomenal stroke of luck," he concluded.

While art may seem to have a natural affinity with dreaming, creative innovations in the scientific field also have come via dreams. Case in point: a breakthrough drug that can greatly reduce risks for people who suffer from life-threatening allergies to peanuts made headlines when its effectiveness was demonstrated in the spring of 2003, but the idea that led to its successful lab development actually was hatched in a dream. Tse Wen Chang and his wife, Nancy, moved from Taiwan to study at Harvard and in 1986 started a biotech company called Tanox. They funded the start-up themselves, with their garage serving as home for mice used in their research. An immunologist, Tse Wen was searching for a new way to treat allergies and asthma. Previous allergy drugs such as antihistamines worked by absorbing chemicals that are released in the wake of an allergy attack, but his groundbreaking notion was to use an engineered protein that would bind to substances in the body that set off allergic reactions and thereby prevent the attack from occurring in the first place. As Tanox chief executive officer Nancy Chang tells it, that out-of-the-box approach came in the dead of night. "He actually concocted that in the middle of the night in a dream, and he woke me up and told me," she recalls. "We didn't go back to sleep for the rest of the night."

Accounts of such moments of inspiration or breakthroughs during dreaming time have been reported by other scientists, musicians, athletes, mathematicians, writers, and visual artists. Many of them have been chronicled by Harvard psychologist Deirdre Barrett in her book *The Committee of Sleep*. For Barrett, who has been a prolific and vivid dreamer since childhood, the idea that creativity can spring from a state some people don't even regard as consciousness makes perfect sense. "During dreaming, we're tuned inward, we experience vivid visual imagery, our conventional logic system is turned down, and social norms are loosened, all of which can lead to making more creative associations than we make when we're awake and our brain is censoring the illogical," she says.

While it's hard to make the case that the brain was designed to be creative at night when dreaming (there certainly are more straightforward ways to make intellectual or artistic breakthroughs), the unique physiology of sleep may make us especially prone to nocturnal creativity, which amounts to a serendipitous bonus that comes along with dreaming. Among those who report regularly reaping this bonus is Roger Shepard, who won a National Medal of Science for a research career that has provided breakthrough insights on the nature of visual and other mental processes and has influenced fields ranging from computer science to linguistics, philosophy, and neuroscience. Shepard says that several of his research breakthroughs had their origins in visual imagery that came to him shortly before awakening in the morning, including a kinetic image of three-dimensional structures "majestically turning in space" that formed the basis for a landmark experiment in the early 1970s on how the brain performs mental rotations to identify three-dimensional objects. He also says short musical scores have come to him in dreams, as well as whimsical images that he has replicated in drawings that play with visual illusion, such as the one shown in Figure 8.1.

Shepard has kept a dream journal for many years, and the high level of creativity springing from what feels like an independent self in the dreaming brain is evident in this early-morning dream he recorded in January 1979:

> I am with my wife, who is consulting with the physician. My wife has expressed concern about how much her teaching job is cutting into her time with our children. Then, at the end of the consultation, she asks, "Do you think I should have a mammogram?" The doctor replies, "No, I don't think that's necessary," and then, with an impish smile slowly spreading across his face, he adds, "but given the professional demands on your time, your kids could use a gramma, ma'am."

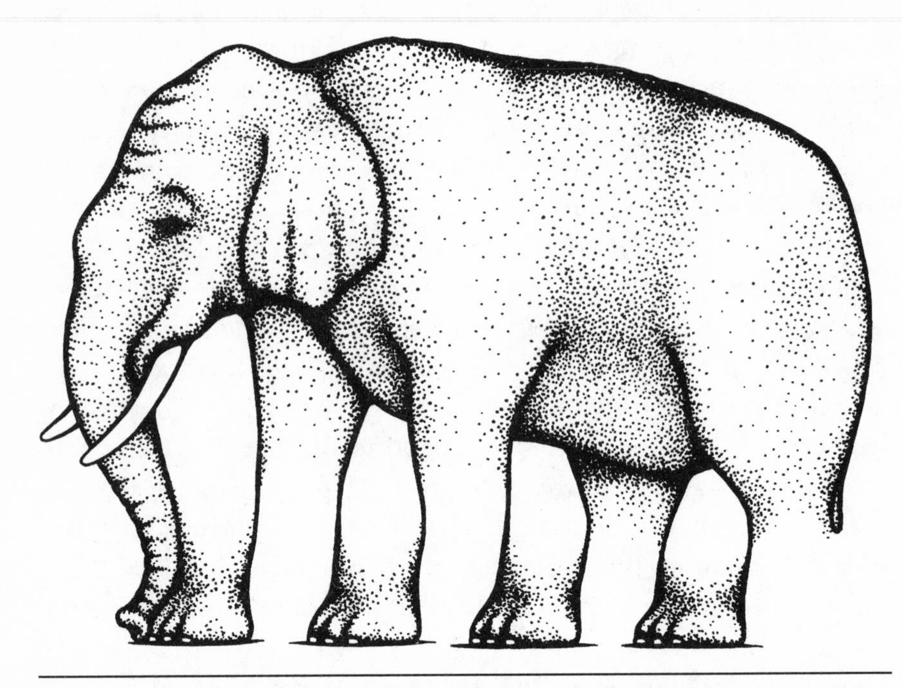

FIGURE 8.1 This drawing, entitled "L'egs-istential Quandary," sprang from a visual image that came to scientist Roger M. Shepard just before he awakened one morning in 1974. The quick pencil sketch he made when he awoke became the basis for this ink drawing, for which Shepard holds the copyright. The drawing first appeared in Shepard's book *Mind Sights* (W. H. Freeman, 1990).

> Doing a double take, I am greatly amused to realize that relative to *mammogram, gramma, ma'am* is a phonetically perfect anagram.

Shepard was intrigued by the fact that he himself was surprised by the dream's punch line, which seemed to require premeditation for its clever humor. Such a dream "suggests that another mind, of which 'I' am not conscious, is operating, so to speak, within 'my' own brain," said Shepard. He observed that his dream experience was akin to the mental workings in experiments of patients with split brains.

Cognitive psychologist John Antrobus suggests one reason that new ideas popping up in dreams may seem foreign to our waking state of consciousness: "In problem solving, you often set constraints around the problem that limit the options you consider as possible solutions. But in dreaming, all constraints are relaxed, so you may see a solution that wasn't apparent before," explains Antrobus. Still, when an innovative breakthrough comes during that altered state of consciousness rather than in ordinary waking thought, the dreamer understandably often feels so disconnected from the creative process that in the dream, he or she plays the role of an observer, according to Barrett.

A prime example: Harvard physicist Paul Horowitz designs control mechanisms for telescopes used in astrophysics, and at several points when he had reached a stumbling block in building a new type of laser telescope, Horowitz says he had dreams in which a new way of approaching the problem presented itself. As he puts it, "These dreams have a narrator who's sketching the problem verbally. Then the voice is giving the solution. I'm also seeing the solution. I watch a man working on the mechanical device—arranging lenses for the optics or building the circuit—whatever it is that I'm stuck on at that point." Horowitz says he keeps a pen and pencil next to the bed to write down what he's seen, because like his more run-of-the-mill dreams, they're gone forever if he doesn't record them immediately when he awakens. He then takes the notes to his colleagues at work, announcing that he's literally dreamed up a solution—a routine to which they've now become accustomed.

Similarly, when mathematician Donald J. Newman was working on a tough new theoretical math problem when he was at the Massachusetts Institute of Technology in the 1960s, he found he was completely stuck. At the time, Newman was part of a group of highly competitive mathematicians on campus, including John Nash, whose life later became the subject of the popular book and film *A Beautiful Mind.*

As Newman, now retired in Philadelphia, recalls, "I'd been mulling over this problem for a week or so and just couldn't get anywhere with it when I had a dream that I was at a restaurant in Cambridge with Nash. I asked him about this problem in the dream and I listened to his explanation of how to do it. When I woke up, I had the solution."

Newman says he's never had such an experience before or since and felt so strongly about it that when he published a paper elucidating the problem, he actually gave John Nash credit for contributing to the work, even though the help came via a dream. "I dreamed of him because this particular problem was the sort of thing Nash was into. I feel that if I hadn't been friends with him, I wouldn't have solved it," says Newman.

New approaches to problems that materialize in dreams aren't limited to intellectual conundrums. Like the birds who improved their songs by rehearsing in their sleep, athletes sometimes find a new way to improve their performance when their logical brains are off-line. Pro golfer Jack Nicklaus was going through a period in the mid-1960s when his game was off, causing him to shoot in the high seventies. As he recounted to a reporter at the *San Francisco Chronicle,* he eventually had a dream about his golf swing that helped him get back in top form. "I was hitting them pretty good in the dream, and all at once I realized I wasn't holding the club the way I've actually been holding it lately," said Nicklaus. "I've been having trouble collapsing my right arm taking the club head away from the ball, but I was doing it perfectly in my sleep. So when I came to the course yesterday morning, I tried it the way I did in my dream and it worked. I shot a sixty-eight yesterday and a sixty-five today."

And out-of-the-box thinking that emerges during dreams sometimes involves more mundane matters too. When Kathy Hurxthal was a Peace Corps volunteer in a Moroccan village during the 1960s, she was teaching local women how to knit. While she knew how to knit sweaters or mittens, one of the women was bent on knitting a pair of socks—something Hurxthal had never done before. "The part I couldn't figure out was how to turn the heel. I was completely preoccupied with that challenge, and finally it came to me while I was dreaming one night. I was knitting in the dream, and in the dream it was very clear what to do to turn the heel. I woke up, went to the center, and showed them all how to knit socks, exactly as I had done it in my dream." Hurxthal, who is now a nurse practitioner in Cambridge, Massachusetts, says she doesn't have particularly good dream recall now and has never had a repeat of that kind of creativity during dreaming, so the incident stands out in her mind all the more. "Learning to do something I'd never done before in a dream was such an unusual experience that all these years later I still find myself telling people about it," she says.

Often, a creative breakthrough provided in a dream comes via a visual metaphor. For example, when Elias Howe was working on inventing the sewing machine, he was stymied by how to secure the needle to the machine in a way that allowed the needle to easily pass through the fabric, because he was still following the model of hand-held sewing needles, where the hole for the thread is located at the end opposite the needle's sharp point. The answer came to him via a dream in which he was surrounded by savages painted with war paint who were leading him to be executed. As he was being led to his death, he noticed that the warriors were carrying spears with eye-shaped holes near their pointed tips. Awakening from the dream, he realized that the needle for the sewing machine should be modeled after the spears in his dreams, with the hole for the thread located near the pointed end, and that was indeed the solution that worked.

In a more recent example of dreaming an invention, Allen Huang, head of optical computing research at AT&T Bell Laboratories, hit a dead end while trying to design circuitry for a new computer. He was dreaming repeatedly of two armies of sorcerers' apprentices marching toward each other carrying pails filled with data. They always stopped short of colliding until one night, instead of stopping, the two armies kept marching forward and then magically passed through each other. The phrase that ran through Huang's mind in the dream was that they were like light passing through light. When he woke up, he was confident that the dream's visual metaphor had shown him the way to design unconventional computer circuitry using lasers. Like the sorcerers' apprentices, laser beams could pass though each other so they didn't need their own separate pathways, as electric currents did, and that became the key to his invention. Deirdre Barrett notes that lasers are heavily represented in invention dreams, "perhaps because they are both cutting-edge technology and lend themselves to visual imagery."

The types of associations and connections the dreaming brain makes don't appear to be conducive to conventional problem solving, however. In a series of experiments in the early 1970s, veteran dream researcher William Dement gave five hundred undergraduate students a copy of a problem that they were supposed to spend exactly fifteen minutes trying to solve before going to bed. In the morning, they recorded any dreams they recalled from the previous night, and if the problem had not been solved, they spent another fifteen minutes trying to solve it. In 1,148 attempts the problem was solved in a dream only 7 times, a success rate of less than 1 percent. Interestingly, however, in one experiment a male subject appeared to solve the problem via visual dream imagery but wasn't aware that he'd done so. Dement presented the following brainteaser: "HIJKLMNO: What one word does this sequence represent?" The correct answer is water, because it equals H_2O, or the letters H to O. The subject thought he'd solved the problem before he went to sleep when he came up with the answer "alphabet." Then he proceeded to have four dreams that all involved water imagery, including scenes of heavy rain, sailing, and scuba diving in the ocean. His brain apparently was providing the answer by creating associations in that dreamy way that makes a curious kind of sense, though not by conventional rules.

This unconventional mode of operation seems to be the key to the breakthroughs that do occur via dreaming. "When you are in REM sleep, you are operating without the anchors of logic or episodic memory, and you're lacking neurochemicals needed for focusing attention, so all things considered, it smells like the brain wants you to think outside the box, to brainstorm," says Robert Stickgold, the Harvard dream researcher who conducted the groundbreaking Tetris game study. The conditions in REM sleep are ideally designed for identifying and forming new associations, ones we wouldn't normally come up with in waking hours. "During the day, if you're driving in traffic and some guy suddenly cuts in front of you, you want to react immediately," he says. "You don't want your mind wandering to associate that with the time you were square-dancing and someone cut in front of you, and didn't that guy remind you of someone else, some actor, or was it a singer? But REM sleep seems to be a safe time set aside for the mind to wander and make meaning in a rich and exploratory way."

This nonlinear meaning making that occurs during dreaming may actually be an example of chaos theory at work in the brain, according to a paper published by Allan Hobson and his colleague at Harvard, David Kahn. Chaos theory emerged in the 1970s as a new way for physicists, mathematicians, biologists, and other scientists to comprehend the patterns of order that exist within what appears to be disorder, allowing them to use mathematical formulas and computer modeling to examine questions ranging from how clouds form, to how infectious diseases spread within a population, to how galaxies are created.

This way of understanding how the world works tells us that all complex systems stabilize, or self-organize, when their equilibrium is disturbed, creating a new order. Just a small change in the initial condition of a complex system can rapidly and dramatically change its eventual outcome. The concept is illustrated concretely in an example known as the butterfly effect—the proposition that the flapping of a butterfly's wing stirring the air today in California can have an effect on storm systems months later on the other side of the world. It is also expressed in the following well-known passage from British poet George Herbert:

For want of a nail, the shoe was lost;
For want of a shoe, the horse was lost;
For want of a horse, the rider was lost;
For want of a rider, the battle was lost;
For want of a battle, the kingdom was lost.

Chaos theory also says that even within seemingly random systems lurks a detectable order created by self-organization. The brain is a complex, chaotic system, and small shifts in its input during any state can indeed dramatically alter how it operates. Recent studies of epileptic seizures using methods derived from chaos principles found that seizures do not, as the medical community has always believed, come on without warning. Instead, they begin with a tiny surge of electrical activity and follow a pattern that is predictable. Studying EEG results collected from epilepsy patients whose brain-wave patterns were routinely measured prior to undergoing surgery, researchers using standard methods of analysis could find no warning signs prior to seizures. But using a computer program derived from chaos theory to analyze the brain waves, scientists at Arizona State University found that they could predict more than 80 percent of seizures based on a change in electrical signals in the brain that occurred on average an hour before physical symptoms appeared. Finding this pattern within what had seemed to be random activity in the brain may allow development of a type of brain pacemaker to detect and prevent an impending seizure.

Dreaming can also be understood via principles of chaos. Most of the time when we're awake, neuromodulators such as serotonin act to restrain cerebral chaos, but in REM, the physiological shifts that occur bump the brain into a chaotic state, and vivid, complex dreaming is the outward sign of its self-organizing response, argue Hobson and Kahn. The only constraining forces come from internal memories and traces of recent experience, leaving the door open for a broad repertoire of possible combinations in forming dream imagery and story lines.

"Dreaming may be our most creative conscious state, one in which the chaotic, spontaneous recombination of cognitive elements produces novel configurations of information: new ideas. While many or even most of these ideas may be nonsensical, if even a few of its fanciful products are truly useful, our dream time will not have been wasted," says Hobson.

In fact, suggests long-time dream researcher Stephen LaBerge, the creative and novel neural connections that are possible in REM may serve an even more fundamental purpose that gives us an edge in the Darwinian scheme of survival of the fittest. "Perhaps dreaming generates a wide range of behavioral schemas or scripts guiding perception and action from which to select adaptive fits to changing environments," says LaBerge.

The altered state of self-organization that produces dreams also may be quite similar to what happens in the brain when a writer, painter, scientist, or theoretical mathematician is in the throes of the creative process during waking consciousness, suggests Bert States, a former professor of English and theater at both Cornell University and the University of California at Santa Barbara. States has had a lifelong interest in dreaming and has written about the relationship between dreaming and art in his book *Seeing in the Dark: Reflections on Dreams and Dreaming*. Now retired, States indulges another passion, creating striking oil paintings in a studio in the garden behind his house. The paintings have a dreamlike quality—landscapes dramatically dominated by images of the sky in its infinite patterns of light, clouds, and subtle color variations. Seated in his garden, with hummingbirds darting among the flowers that surround him, States suggests that PET scans or other imaging studies of a painter or writer at work may well reveal the same activation patterns seen among people spinning a dream during REM sleep.

"The mind state that arises in waking imaginative production for an artist, scientist, writer, or even someone engrossed in reading a novel is akin to that of a dreamer: they are immersed in another world and only minimally attending to practical matters in this one," says States. "Being in the world of the imagination is accompanied by a dreamlike state of disorientation, which is largely why one shouldn't perform surgery or defuse a bomb while reading a book or daydreaming." In dreaming, just as when you are lost in a book, seeing and the seen are the same: you actually see words on a page, but they disappear into a mental image of the things the words refer to—at least until you are called back into that other reality by the ring of the telephone or your spouse's voice. In the dream state, however, images can continue to materialize undisturbed by external-world input.

The end products of the dreaming brain and the virtual worlds created by writers or visual artists also share similar features, he points out. States says that both dreaming and art, in all its varieties, are manifestations of the same biological need to convert experience into some form of structure. "Dreaming uses the cinematic resources of vision to present a theater of the self to itself," he explains. "In the virtual world of dreams and fictions, we get to drive off a cliff into the sea many times in a lifetime, whereas in the actual world we can do it only once."

States points out that universal dreams such as being naked in public or falling off a cliff are the dream equivalent of literary archetypes, akin to stories of jealousy, desire, and revenge that have unfolded from Greek mythology through modern literature. "No one wants to fall from a bridge into a raging river; no one wants to be alone, ignored by the world, humiliated, caught naked, unprepared, lost, or paralyzed before an oncoming menace. And because we are inescapably susceptible to these things, we dream about them, and such dreams the world over vary only in the specifics of the individual's experiences in a particular culture or environment."

The no-holds-barred freedom of the dreaming brain that allows you to leap off a building and soar above the cityscape below is also what the creative process requires, so it should not be surprising if prolific dreamers also tend toward creative pursuits in waking life. States speculates that people who are drawn to the arts, theoretical science, and mathematics may have neural circuitry that has "an unusual capacity to make connections that do not involve serial and analytic reasoning—the very liberty acetylcholine [the neuromodulator that is predominant during REM] apparently enables in our dreams."

In fact, States's theory is in keeping with results of a study conducted by James Pagel, director of the Rocky Mountain Sleep Disorders Center in Pueblo, Colorado. Pagel conducted a study examining the association between dreaming and creativity among participants at the Sundance Film Institute in Utah from 1995 to 1997. Among the study participants were sixty-two screenwriters, directors, and actors. Pagel found that in this creative group, dream recall was nearly twice what he'd found among the general population in earlier studies. Moreover, the frequency with which they said dreams had an effect on their creative activity in waking life was more than double the norm. "There's no question this group of successful filmmakers is different from any other group I've studied, because they showed significantly increased dream use and dream recall," says Pagel. "What I found supports the idea that people who are successful in creative fields may have a functional use for dreaming and are more likely to be psychologically close to their dreams."

He says another study he conducted at his clinic on a group of otherwise normal people who claimed not to dream at all may lend support to this idea. "We only pick up five or six people a year who claim they never recall having had a dream, so over a five-year period, I was able to come up with sixteen who said they were nondreamers to participate in a lab study testing whether they truly dreamt or not," Pagel says. Though subjects were awakened in the middle of the night as well as in the morning, not a single dream was reported among those who claimed not to dream. In another group of people who said they seldom recalled dreams, there were two who did in fact report dreams when awakened in the lab. In examining the nondreamers to look for some common connection that might explain why they didn't report dreams, he said the one difference that surfaced is that none of them had any real creative outlets or even hobbies in waking life. "Perhaps people who don't have a creative drive or creative roles in waking life are able to function without dreams," says Pagel. He says he also would like to do studies investigating whether nondreamers lack the visuospatial abilities essential for dreaming, much like two boys in David Foulkes's studies of children's dreaming whose dreams were infrequent and bland compared to others in their age range of eleven to thirteen years old. Though the boys were average students with normal verbal skills and memory ability, they had abnormally low scores on block design tests that measure visuospatial ability, and unlike others their age, they seldom reported dreaming when awakened during REM sleep.

The capacity for exercising visual imagination may also contribute to the unusual dreaming characteristics Pagel found among filmmakers. Film is a dreamlike medium, and the dark rooms where films were first shown originally were called "dream palaces." Many well-known directors say they frequently incorporate dreams in their films. Among them is Luis Bunuel, who transformed his own dream of having to go on stage to play a role for which he hasn't rehearsed or memorized lines into a scene in which an impatient audience is hissing in *The Discreet Charm of the Bourgeoisie*. Federico Fellini, who went so far as to say "dreams are the only reality," used a childhood dream about a magician as the final scene in his film 8 ½. Ingmar Bergman reports that he transferred a dream exactly as he had dreamed it to a scene in *Wild Strawberries*. The dream-inspired scene builds to a climactic moment when the protagonist is seized by a hand reaching out of a coffin and then sees that the face of the corpse is his own. "I discovered that all my pictures were dreams," Bergman stated. More recently, director Richard Linklater's innovative film *Waking Life* was in its entirety a dream that the film's protagonist and the audience experience simultaneously. His film was a new twist on an observation by Jean Cocteau: "A film is not a dream that is told, but one that we all dream together."

Pagel explains that the participants in his study of filmmakers often deliberately set out to use their dreams to help break through creative blocks in waking life. "Screenwriters said they use dreams in trying to decide what the next step in a story will be, while actors dream all across the board, recreating themselves each time they take a new role," Pagel says.

The participants relied on a technique called incubation, which can be used to focus on any sort of problem prior to sleep in hopes of encouraging the brain to find an out-of-the-box solution in its chaotically creative state during the night. Deirdre Barrett suggests a set of instructions for incubation, beginning with briefly describing in writing the problem you're stuck on and taking a look at what you've written before going to bed. When you're in bed, visualize yourself dreaming about the problem and tell yourself that you will do so just as you're drifting off. Keep a pen and paper at your bedside, and upon awakening write down traces of any dream you recall.

Any success you have is not likely to come through the logical, linear thinking process that you rely on in waking, because the dreaming brain generally isn't physiologically geared for that. Instead, if incubation works, the solution is likely to come in nonlogical, unexpected ways, much as the dreamer who solved the brainteaser in William Dement's experiment came up with the correct answer—water—without realizing it via the collection of water imagery in his dreams.

A similar nonconventional answer that came via dream incubation is illustrated in a story Deirdre Barrett recounts about a chemist in India who was trying to develop enzymes to refine crude oil. When he set out with the intent to focus on solving the problem as he went to sleep, he proceeded to have a dream about a big truck heaped with a load of rotten cabbages. The dream seemed useless at first. But upon returning to work on his project, he suddenly realized that the dream was significant after all: decomposing cabbages would break down into exactly the type of enzyme that would work for the crude-oil refinement project he was developing. Concludes Barrett: "Dreaming is, above all, a time when the unheard parts of ourselves are allowed to speak—we would do well to listen."

9

Altered States

Once I, Chuang Tzu, dreamt that I was a butterfly, a butterfly flying about, feeling that it was enjoying itself. It did not know that it was Chuang. Suddenly I awoke and was myself again, the veritable Chuang. I do not know whether it was Chuang dreaming that he was a butterfly or whether I am now a butterfly dreaming that it is Chuang.

—*Chuang Tzu, Taoist philosopher (fourth century* B.C.*)*

IN HIS OFFICE IN PALO ALTO, California, Stephen LaBerge is surrounded by what feels like a dreamscape: billowing white clouds on sky-blue walls, the kind of serene scene you delight in when you're stretched out on the grass on a perfect summer day, arms behind your head, watching a white armada drift by overhead. This surreal workspace is especially fitting for LaBerge, whose research over the past two decades suggests that the line between our experiences in the dreamworld and in waking reality may not be as starkly defined as many people believe it to be. Just as the discovery of REM had required a rethinking of previous notions of sleep as a state in which the brain essentially shut down, LaBerge's research into an unusual phenomenon known as lucid dreaming eventually shifted scientific thought about the nature of the dreaming mind.

When he was a child, LaBerge loved matinee adventure serials, eagerly awaiting each week's new episode at his local movie theater. One morning when he awoke from a particularly exciting dream in which he played the role of an underwater pirate, he decided it would be fun to return to the same dream the next night, advancing the plot further, like the next installment in one of his beloved adventure serials. Not only was he able to continue the pirate dream he'd begun the night before, but once it resumed, he was fully aware of being both a character in and the director of all of the action. "When I looked up and saw the ocean's surface far above me, I panicked at first, but then I realized I didn't have to worry about holding my breath because I was in a dream and I could just breathe in the dream water," he recalls. "No one had ever told me controlling my dreaming was impossible, so I continued my adventure for weeks, completely aware that I was in a dream and that I could make my own fun in it." Without having a name for what he was doing at the time, LaBerge was experiencing lucid dreaming—a state in which a dreamer becomes aware that he's dreaming while the dream is still in progress. Some lucid dreamers also can consciously manipulate the setting, characters, and action taking place in their internal dramas, just as LaBerge did.

This phenomenon, while fascinating in its own right, also suggests that dreams are a promising window into the secrets of consciousness. Studies in this relatively new area of research suggest that lucid dreaming is the result of physiological shifts in the brain combined with volition and intent developed by the dreamer that introduce an element of self-awareness during REM sleep. While the majority of dreamers are unaware that they're dreaming while the dream is in progress, something unusual happens during lucid dreaming to trigger awareness, though what that trigger for lucidity is remains a mystery that researchers are still working to understand. The answer could also be the key to the larger question of what gives us our unique sense of reflective self-awareness in waking life.

The pursuit for answers about lucid dreaming continues to be led by LaBerge. After earning his undergraduate degree in mathematics at the age of nineteen after only two years of study at the University of Arizona, LaBerge enrolled in Stanford University in 1967 as a graduate student in chemical physics. Though he'd left lucid dreaming in the past along with childhood toys and games of pretend, he still had a keen interest in exploring how the mind works, and Eastern thought intrigued him as much as science did. In fact, the first lucid dream he recalls in adult life occurred shortly after he returned from a workshop at the Esalen Institute, an alternative education center blending Eastern and Western philosophy located on the California coast near Big Sur. The workshop was taught by a Tibetan Buddhist, who urged participants to try to maintain consciousness throughout a twenty-four-hour period, holding on to self-reflective awareness even while dreaming.

A few nights after the workshop ended, LaBerge dreamed he was climbing in the Himalayas, dressed in a short-sleeved shirt as he made his way through snowdrifts. He wondered why he wasn't feeling cold, given how he was dressed, and that incongruity triggered his sudden knowledge that he was in the dreamworld, just as his realization that he didn't need to worry about breathing underwater was the key to lucidity in his childhood pirate dreams. Indeed, for many dreamers, it is some startlingly bizarre twist in plot or setting that manages to break the spell the dreaming brain has cast, so that for the first time they become aware that the world in which they find themselves is entirely of their own making. Among the common catalysts for lucidity are the appearance of a long-dead friend as a dream character, scenery that is so out of the ordinary that we are forced to question its reality, or a chase scene that terrifies us into realizing with relief that we're just dreaming. Often, this sudden insight causes us to wake up, but with luck or practice, it's also possible to keep the dream going. When LaBerge became aware that his mountain-climbing adventure was a dream in progress, he chose to fly off the side of the mountain rather than climb upward, completely exhilarated to be experiencing this natural form of altered consciousness again for the first time since childhood.

LaBerge continued to experiment informally with lucid dreaming over the next few years, during which time he also took a detour from academia—a period in his life that he later described as a hiatus "in search of the Holy Grail in hippiedom." In the late 1970s, however, he decided to return to the scientific world by pursuing his doctorate in psychophysiology at Stanford, and lucid dreaming was the topic he chose for his dissertation. He began keeping a journal of his lucid dreams in February 1977 and, by the mid-1980s, had chronicled nearly nine hundred lucid dreams.

Most Western scientists at the time doubted the phenomenon was real, despite its considerable history. In the fourth century B.C., Aristotle made an apparent reference to lucid dreaming when he wrote of "something in consciousness which declares what then presents itself is but a dream," and as LaBerge discovered at the Esalen workshop, Tibetan Buddhists for more than 1,000 years have incorporated a form of lucid dreaming called dream yoga as part of their spiritual practices. Europe also has long been fertile ground for the exploration of this brand of dreaming. In 1867 the Marquis d'Hervey de Saint-Denys, a Frenchman who was an accomplished lucid dreamer, wrote about his experiences in a book entitled *Dreams and How to Guide Them*. The term *lucid dreaming* itself was coined in a 1913 paper written by Frederik van Eeden, a Dutch psychiatrist who kept a diary of 352 lucid dreams he experienced from 1898 through 1912. Interest in lucid dreaming was kindled in the United States in 1969, when van Eeden's paper was reprinted in *Altered States of Consciousness*, an anthology of scientific papers compiled by Charles Tart, a professor at the University of California at Berkeley, who mentioned in the book's introduction that he had experienced lucid dreaming himself.

Nevertheless, when LaBerge was about to launch into his doctoral dissertation research in 1977, the majority of contemporary researchers discounted lucid dreaming, theorizing that those who claimed to have such dreams weren't truly asleep but were simply reporting mental experiences that occurred during "microawakenings" from REM or other sleep stages. Among the skeptics was William Dement, the dream research pioneer who began his career in Chicago assisting Eugene Aserinsky and Nathaniel Kleitman in the experiments that proved the existence of REM sleep. Now the director of the sleep lab at Stanford, Dement was approached by LaBerge, who wanted to use the lab to conduct lucid dreaming experiments for his dissertation. He had the support of Lynn Nagel, another researcher in Dement's lab, who also was interested in studying the subject. "Everything I'd read in contemporary dream research said achieving lucidity during dreaming was impossible, but since I'd done it myself so often, I told Bill I wanted to prove scientifically that it was real," says LaBerge.

To his credit, Dement was sufficiently open-minded to agree to LaBerge's plan, and Nagel became his adviser and collaborator. The key to establishing whether lucidity occurred when dreamers were really asleep was coming up with a way for the dreamer to signal to experimenters the beginning of lucidity. The dreaming subject would be wired to equipment to monitor his or her brain waves, eye movements, and other physiological indicators of sleep state. LaBerge decided to serve as the first subject, since he knew he could control his own eye movements in a lucid dream, moving them left to right in a specific series of movements that could easily be distinguished from the involuntary eye movements that characterize REM. On Friday the 13th, January 1978, LaBerge for the first time succeeded in communicating to Nagel via prearranged eye signals that he was in the midst of a lucid dream. He had been asleep for seven and a half hours when he suddenly realized middream that he must be asleep because he couldn't see, feel, or hear anything. He then recalled that he was in the sleep lab and was able later to describe in detail his lucid dream:

> The image of what seemed to be the instruction booklet for a vacuum cleaner or some such appliance floated by. It struck me as mere flotsam on the stream of consciousness, but as I focused on it and tried to read the writing the image gradually stabilized and I had the sensation of opening my (dream) eyes. Then my hands appeared, with the rest of my dream body, and I was looking at the booklet in bed. My dream room was a reasonably good copy of the room in which I was actually asleep. Since I now had a dream body, I decided to do the eye movements that we had agreed upon as a signal. I moved my finger in a vertical line in front of me, following it with my eyes. But I had become very excited over being able to do this at last and the thought disrupted my dream so that it faded a few seconds later.

Afterward, there were two large eye movements on the polygraph record just before LaBerge awakened from a thirteen-minute REM period. This was objective evidence that at least one lucid dream had taken place during what was unquestionably REM sleep. LaBerge continued as a subject with Nagel recording him in the lab. Not only did it soon become clear that his lucid dreams occurred during unequivocal REM sleep rather than in some transitory period of awakening, but follow-up experiments with other subjects who were monitored in the lab demonstrated that thirty-two of their thirty-five reported lucid dreams also occurred during REM. Two others were reported during stage I sleep and another during the transition from stage II to REM. Subjects successfully used eye signals to communicate the onset of thirty lucid dreams. Afterwards, experimenters who were unaware of when subjects reported that lucid dreams began were able to look at the electrophysiological records of eye, brain, and muscle signals and, in 90 percent of the cases, spot exactly where the dreamer had signaled the onset of lucid dreaming. This research using other subjects who had been coached by LaBerge in techniques to facilitate lucid dreaming also indicated that switching on self-awareness during dreaming was a skill that could be learned with practice.

The evidence emerging from LaBerge's experiments was convincing enough to win over Dement and eventually other scientists as well. Dement concluded that by 1980 enough data had been compiled "to prove that in lucid dreaming, the dreamer indeed became conscious of being in the dreamworld, could remain in the dreamworld, and could, from that vantage point, communicate with the outside world." At the 1981 annual meeting of sleep and dream researchers in Hyannis Port, Massachusetts, LaBerge presented four papers on lucid dreaming. Leading the session at which LaBerge presented his data was Robert Van de Castle, who was then head of the sleep lab at the University of Virginia Medical School. "I found his experimental designs carefully conceived and the data from his interrelated studies very impressive," Van de Castle later recalled. "In my remarks to the assembled sleep researchers, I shared these views and said that the only reasonable conclusion was that a firm case had been made for the existence of lucid dreaming under controlled laboratory conditions." Even the most skeptical were convinced that this form of dreaming was a bona fide phenomenon of REM sleep.

Prior to that, researchers essentially had been following a rule of thumb derived from the Marquis de Laplace, an eighteenth-century French mathematician and astronomer who said that "the weight of the evidence must be in proportion to the strangeness of the fact." In essence, a claim that contradicted a substantial body of accepted scientific observations would be accepted only after meeting the most rigorous standards of proof, while a hypothetical finding consistent with previously accepted facts would be accepted with far less evidence. When the results of LaBerge's lucid-dreaming research were presented at that meeting, "the weight of the evidence was finally in proportion to the strangeness of the fact," says LaBerge.

After LaBerge's dissertation on lucid dreaming was published in 1980, he came across the work of Keith Hearne, a graduate student in Liverpool, England. Hearne, who is now a psychologist specializing in hypnotherapy, had run his lucid-dreaming experiments a few years earlier on Alan Worsley, a subject who had been a prolific lucid dreamer since childhood. On eight occasions during the study, the subject signaled the onset of lucid dreaming while being monitored in the lab during REM sleep. Hearne had not publicized his initial results, and LaBerge first learned of them when Hearne wrote a letter to the editor of *Psychology Today* after an article on lucid dreaming by LaBerge appeared. "Had the results of the Liverpool experiments been available to us several years earlier, we could have built on what would have been Hearne's tremendous contribution to the field," says LaBerge.

Dozens of papers on the subject were subsequently published, and the concept of lucid dreaming began to catch on in the popular imagination, spawning a *Lucidity* newsletter, a lucidity association, and eventually Web sites devoted to the subject, including one that currently promotes lucid dreaming as a way for people with spinal cord injuries to enjoy physical experiences denied to them in waking life.

Researchers at universities in the United States, Canada, and Europe have sporadically conducted lucid-dreaming studies, but LaBerge has remained the most visible proponent of research in the field, relying primarily on private donations and income generated by the Lucidity Institute, a business he founded in 1988 to advance research on the subject. He applies the results of his research through workshops (typically held in dreamy locations such as Hawaii) and other means of popularizing lucid dreaming, including devices he developed and markets such as Nova Dreamer—a sleeping mask that detects when dreamers are in REM sleep and then flashes lights in the dreamer's eyes as a cue previously rehearsed to help induce lucidity. LaBerge describes the device as a tool to help people develop habits conducive to lucid dreaming, noting that the Nova Dreamer (at a price tag recently in the $300 range) will not "make people have lucid dreams any more than exercise machines make people develop strong muscles." To dispel any notion that the mask was no better than a placebo, LaBerge conducted a 1995 study of an earlier version of the device. He tested fourteen subjects who used the device nightly but were unaware that it had been programmed to deliver the light cues only on alternate nights—a feature of the study designed to rule out placebo effect and accurately determine how much the light cues specifically contributed to achieving lucidity. The results showed that significantly more people had lucid dreams on nights when they did indeed receive light cues: 73 percent versus 27 percent without the cues.

Despite any New Age trappings lucid dreaming may have acquired in recent years, there's no doubt that the scientific basis on which the phenomenon rests is sound. It's possible to become aware of being in a dreamworld while the dream is still in progress, and some dreamers can also exercise deliberate control over dream actions, including signaling to the outside world and carrying out tasks agreed upon prior to sleeping. In one experiment in Dement's lab, for instance, LaBerge tested whether lucid dreamers could carry out presleep instructions for changing their breathing patterns during a lucid-dreaming period, since respiratory muscles are the only group other than eye muscles that can move during REM sleep as freely as they do in waking. Three lucid dreamers were asked to either breathe rapidly or hold their breath during a lucid dream, using eye movement signals to mark the beginning of each interval of altered respiration. The subjects reported successfully carrying out the agreed-upon shifts in breathing pattern a total of nine times, all of which were detectable later by independent judges' examinations of the printouts from the EEG and other monitoring equipment.

Various surveys about lucid dreaming since the 1980s consistently have found that more than half of those responding (slightly exceeding 80 percent in one survey) report having had at least one dream during their lifetime in which at a minimum they became aware that they were dreaming. In some sleep lab studies, between 1 and 2 percent of awakenings during REM sleep revealed that subjects were having lucid dreams. On average, lucid dreams studied in the lab last only a couple of minutes, though some that have been verified by eye movement signals have lasted as long as fifty minutes.

Frequent lucid dreamers—meaning those having such an experience at least once a month—are in the minority, ranging from less than 10 percent in one survey to slightly more than 20 percent in another. The most powerful predictor of lucidity is having good dream recall in general. Not surprisingly, those who practice meditation also make good lucid dreamers, according to some researchers. Maintaining lucidity for any length of time in a dream requires the delicate balance of remaining a detached, receptive observer of your emotions, actions, and thoughts at the same time that you are actively experiencing them—the same mix that's required for meditation.

Most lucid dreams begin while the dreamer is already in REM sleep, and they most frequently come during the second half of the night. Veteran dream researcher John Antrobus theorizes that lucid dreams tend to occur late in the second half of the night because that's when the heightened cortical activation that automatically accompanies REM sleep is enhanced by the body's also reaching the peak in its diurnal cycle: our internal body clock automatically revs up body temperature and brain activity as morning approaches no matter what sleep stage we're in.

Also, as REM periods become longer in the second half of the night, even nonlucid dreams are intensified and are more storylike, according to Canadian dream researcher Tore Nielsen. "In our studies we found dreams later in the night are longer, more epic, and with more causal coherence," he says.

In fact, LaBerge suggests that one way to increase your odds of lucid dreaming is to awaken an hour or two earlier than usual, stay awake for thirty to sixty minutes, and then return to sleep with the aim of having a lucid dream. LaBerge has found that this "nap technique" increased the likelihood of lucid dreaming by fifteen to twenty times in his subjects. In his studies, however, lucid dreams occur during all REM periods during the night rather than just in the morning, so interrupting sleep with a wakeful period of thirty minutes or more even earlier in the night would work to encourage lucid dreaming, he says.

Lucid dreaming requires high levels of activity in the cortex to trigger self-awareness, and Antrobus has speculated that the left temporal cortex (which is responsible for generating speech and language) would have to be turned on to trigger lucidity. "You need that verbal translation of your state—'I know I'm sleeping'—in order to have a lucid dream," says Antrobus. His belief has been supported by a LaBerge study which demonstrated that in the first thirty seconds of a lucid dream, EEG recordings from twenty-eight electrode placements around the subject's scalp showed a sudden increase in brain activation in exactly that portion of the left hemisphere associated with language. LaBerge concurs that this activation probably coincides with the subject's internal verbal realization that he or she is dreaming.

That realization is often astonishing to the dreamer, especially for those having their first lucid dream. "It is definitely a surprise, especially the first time, to learn that your normally trustworthy senses are reporting to you an absolutely flawless portrayal of a world that doesn't exist outside the dream," he says. "Indeed, one of the most common features of first lucid dreams is a feeling of hyperreality that happens when you take a good look around you in the dream and see the wondrous, elaborate detail your mind can create." That thunderclap moment when a dreamer realizes that nothing he's experiencing comes from current sensory input from the external world is captured perfectly in this report from a lucid dreamer in Everett, Washington, recounted in the *Exploring the World of Lucid Dreaming,* coauthored by LaBerge:

> One night I was dreaming of standing on a hill, looking out over the tops of maples, alders, and other trees. The leaves of the maples were bright red and rustling in the wind. The grass at my feet was lush and vividly green. All the colors about me were more saturated than I have ever seen. Perhaps the awareness that the colors were "brighter than they should be" shocked me into realiz-

> ing that I was in a dream, and that what lay about me was not "real." I remember saying to myself, "If this is a dream, I should be able to fly into the air." I tested my hunch and was enormously pleased that I could effortlessly fly, and fly anywhere I wanted. I skimmed over the tops of the trees and sailed many miles over new territory. I flew upward, far above the landscape, and hovered in the air currents like an eagle. When I awoke, I felt as if the experience of flying had energized me. I felt a sense of well-being that seemed directly related to the experience of being lucid in the dream, of taking control of the flying.

Not everyone who becomes conscious of a dream while it's in progress can manipulate what happens next, but the extent of deliberate control that can be exerted by some lucid dreamers has been demonstrated in studies by LaBerge. Many lucid dreamers have sufficient access to working memory to allow them to carry out presleep plans such as signaling the onset of lucidity to researchers in the lab. Why they have this ability is not known for sure. At least part of the answer may lie in the increased level of cortical activation that occurs in later stages of REM, combined with the greater activation that naturally occurs as part of the body's diurnal rhythm as morning approaches. But LaBerge says that the repertoire of lucid dreaming skills increases also simply with experience, as a dreamer experiments with the operating rules of this different state of consciousness and learns what is within the realm of possibility. In one experiment, subjects were asked to carry out specific tasks in their lucid dreams, including finding a mirror in the lucid-dream setting and looking at the image in the mirror. Twenty-seven lucid dreamers—nearly evenly split between men and women—submitted reports of their attempts to carry out the tasks. Subjects had no difficulty finding a mirror and seeing a reflection, but more often than not, what they saw was somehow different from their usual waking reflection. For more than 40 percent of the participants, however, the image transformed into another image as they watched. So even when lucid dreamers can exert control, it is not quite like waking life. "Self-image is of course a very psychologically loaded thing, probably with very complex internal representations," says LaBerge, who believes this may account for the instability of mirror images in dreams. The transformations that occur are typical of the kinds of setting or character shifts that often characterize nonlucid dreams, but he says it's unclear whether this is due to the absence of anchoring sensory input from the outside world or due to physiological characteristics of the brain in REM sleep.

According to a sampling conducted by Keith Hearne at the University of Liverpool, about a quarter of lucid dreamers never have controlled their dreams but simply have become aware that they are in them. Those who can control what happens in a lucid dream report that the extent of their power can range from manipulating the scenery in a minor way to commanding their own actions and those of other characters, as shown in this dream reported to LaBerge by a lucid dreamer in Chicago:

> In this dream I was at my mother's house and heard voices in another room. When entering the room, I realized without a doubt I was dreaming. My first command was ordering the people in the room to have a more exciting conversation, since this was my dream. At that moment they changed their topic to my favorite hobby. I started commanding things to happen and they did. The more things began to happen, the more I would command. It was a very thrilling experience, one of the most thrilling lucid dreams I've had, probably because I was more in control and more sure of my actions.

Some people claim they use this altered state of consciousness to enjoy the only truly safe sex. For instance, popular psychologist Patricia Garfield has written extensively about her lucid dreams, saying that two-thirds of them are sexual and, of those, half conclude with orgasm. To see whether claims of orgasm in lucid dreaming would be reflected in physiological responses, LaBerge set up a lab experiment for a female subject who frequently reported experiencing lucid sexual dreams. He used sensors to monitor sixteen different channels of data, including respiration, heart rate, vaginal pulse amplitude, and muscle activity, as well as the usual signals for brain electrical activity and eye movements. The dreamer was instructed to use eye movement patterns to signal the beginning of lucidity, as well as the initiation of sexual activity in the dream and the moment of orgasm. She carried out the experimental task exactly as agreed, and there was a significant correlation between what she reported in the dream and the physiological data that was recorded at each step along the way. During the fifteen-second period she signaled as the moment of orgasm, measurements for vaginal muscle and pulse activity and for respiration rate all reached their highest values, underscoring why dream experiences do in fact feel like the real thing. In men, orgasmic experiences were reported during lucid dreams, and they were so vivid that the men were surprised to discover when they awakened that they had not in fact ejaculated.

Since the wet dreams typically experienced by adolescents sometimes occur without any erotic activity occurring in the dream plot, LaBerge speculates that these genuine wet dreams may result from a reflex ejaculation when the penis becomes stimulated during the erections that automatically occur in each REM period. The majority of wet dreams are accompanied by sexual themes, though, so LaBerge suggests that in such dreams, sensory information from the genitals is transmitted to the brain and incorporated into a steamy plot to explain the sensations of physical arousal. In short, the brain spins an erotic story to match the physiological signals it is receiving. In lucid dreams, however, LaBerge suggests that the flow of information is reversed. Since the erotic dream content actually comes first as a result of the dreamer's conscious intent to create that subject matter, the orgasm occurs "in the brain," and the resulting signals that normally would be sent from the brain to the genitals to trigger ejaculation are blocked, as are most motor impulses in REM sleep.

In another study exploring whether actions in dreams are accompanied by the same patterns of brain activity as those actions would be in waking life, four subjects were instructed to sing and then count for an estimated ten seconds during lucid dreams. They used agreed-upon eye signals to indicate when they were beginning each task in the dream. LaBerge was the first subject. When he became lucid, he gave an eye signal and began singing "Row, row, row your boat." He then made another eye movement signal and began to count slowly to ten, after which he gave a final eye signal indicating he had completed the tasks. Measurements of his EEG activity during singing indicated the right hemisphere was more active than the left, just as it would be if singing when awake, while the left hemisphere was more active during the counting task, mirroring what would be expected in waking also. The same results were found when the experiment was repeated with other subjects. And when those dreamers were asked to simply imagine singing or counting while they were awake, EEG measurements did not show the same patterns, again indicating that there is clearly a physiological basis for dream experiences that simulate waking experience in a way that seems much more real than the virtual world we create in our minds if we just close our eyes during waking consciousness and imagine singing or counting.

If we're drawing from the same bank of memories and using the same neural networks in sleep as in waking, why does dreaming simulate waking experience so much more accurately than daydreaming can? When we are driving a car in waking consciousness, our perceptions are being generated by the data we're receiving from the outside world—the feel of the steering wheel in our hands, the cars we see coming toward us, the sound of a fire truck's siren as it passes by. In this bottom-up process, all of the signals from our senses travel up to the appropriate processing centers in the brain and activate the neural networks that generate our perception of reality—"the feeling of what happens," as neuroscientist Antonio Damasio puts it. But when we dream about driving or simply imagine ourselves driving down the road, the resulting images and sensations are generated entirely internally, as the brain relies on memory to activate the appropriate neural networks to create a dreamed or imagined driving experience.

Imagined experience feels less real than either waking experience or dreams for two reasons, argues LaBerge. First, when we're awake, sensory input produces much higher levels of neural activation than imaginary input can. Vivid though our imaginations may be, the disparity in the quality of images and sensations is clearly apparent when they are competing with actual sensory input during waking consciousness. But in dreaming, the only signals the brain has to work with are those internally generated ones, so it's easier to buy them as real. In essence, the bar we have to jump is lower. Second, there is evidence that the brain is deliberately designed to damp down the vividness of images internally generated from memory during waking consciousness because it would be dangerous for any organism to mistake the current perception of a predator about to attack for one conjured up by imagination and memory. Brain cells releasing the neuromodulator serotonin appear to be part of this system that ensures there's no contest between perceptions constructed from sensory input in waking consciousness and the imagery we generate from our imagination. Since these serotonin-releasing neurons are inhibited in REM sleep, however, there's no blocking system to prevent our dreamed images and sensations from appearing and feeling as vividly real as waking experience, especially since there's no competing input from our eyes, ears, and other sensory organs to upstage them.

It's no wonder that we're inclined to mistake our dreams for reality and that we have to devise our own tricks for recognizing during the dream how our brain is conning us. The ability to "think" during a lucid dream varies greatly, but some people have reported high levels of cognitive functioning within that state, such as in this excerpt from a lucid dream report given to LaBerge from a dreamer in Woodland Hills, California:

> I am in a garden and feeling lighthearted and joyous about my ability to fly. . . . I descend then to enjoy the garden at eye level and realize that I am quite alone in this place. At the moment of this realization also comes the awareness that I am in fact asleep in my bed and having a dream. I am fascinated by the seeming solidity of my own body within this dream and find great amusement in the act of "pinching myself to see if I am real." I indeed feel as real to myself as anyone feels to themselves while awake! I become then quite serious in pondering this matter and take a seat on a rock at the edge of the garden to think on this. The thought that comes to me is this: "The degree of awareness one is able to achieve while in a dream is in direct proportion to the degree of awareness one experiences in waking life."
>
> I am startled by the ability to have such a complex and concrete thought within a dream and I begin to examine the condition of my waking life from a perspective that seems impossible to do while living in one's waking life. I am further startled at being able to do such a thing within a dream and begin to experience some apprehension over this entire matter. I decide to get up and inspect my

surroundings. I notice that the garden is a stage set. All the flowers are painted in luminous color and in great detail on freestanding flats. Being an artist, I am quite taken by the skill inherent in the painting of them.

The goal for anyone interested in experimenting with lucid dreaming is to awaken in the dream world and stay there long enough to do a bit of exploring. For instance, a New York design engineer and inventor who had his first lucid-dream experiences in his fifties described a dream in which he suddenly became aware that his brain had created the fabulously detailed Harlem nightclub scene that surrounded him, complete with supplying a catchy original tune that was being performed by a young Louis Armstrong. He was able to sustain lucidity long enough to move around the room, taking in every detail with amazement while being fully aware that it was his own dreamscape. In his next lucid dream, he found himself in a room with a ceiling so low he couldn't stand upright, until he recognized he was dreaming and then immediately stood to his full height, bursting through the ceiling with no adverse effects.

The ability to foster this kind of lucid dreaming begins with what LaBerge calls "reality testing" during waking hours. At least five to ten times throughout the day, he advises asking yourself whether or not you are dreaming so that your brain is conditioned to pose that question during sleep. It's especially helpful to question yourself in this way when you encounter circumstances that are akin to what often happens in your dream life: when something surprising occurs, when you experience a powerful emotion, or when you encounter a vividly dreamy scene or anything that reminds you of something that frequently appears or occurs in your dreams. For instance, if you periodically have anxiety dreams involving elevators, question whether you're asleep or dreaming every time you step into an elevator. This reality testing practice, when combined with visualizing what it's like to be dreaming before going to sleep and repeating to yourself your intention to become lucid, increased lucid dream frequency by more than 150 percent in subjects participating in a 1989 LaBerge study.

Once you're asleep and the suspicion that you're dreaming pops into your mind, LaBerge also suggests quick tests that can help push you into full lucidity, or at least clue you into whether you're awake or not. In your dreamscape, search for writing in any form at all or the face of a clock. In a dream, printed letters nearly always mutate in some way, changing their appearance when you look away and then back again. Similarly clock or watch faces won't display time accurately or maintain a stable appearance. Richard Linklater's intriguing film *Waking Life* depicts the lucid-dreaming phenomenon beautifully and is actually based on an unusual lucid dream he had when he was a teenager. In the film, the protagonist realizes he is dreaming, but his attempts to escape the lucid dream fail. He repeatedly experiences "false awakenings," a common occurrence in which the dreamer believes the dream has ended but is instead merely dreaming that he has awakened. Wavering images on clock faces are the clues he most often uses to test whether he is still dreaming.

The "Aha" moment of first becoming aware that you're in a dream is captured in the following account posted by a dreamer on a lucid-dreaming site for the physically challenged:

> After a few regular non-lucid dreams, I awoke inside a dream. I had been standing in a parking lot searching for my car. After I had found my car, I noticed it had no door handles. This caused me to wonder, it seemed very odd, very dreamlike, but I "knew" I was awake. I thought I would go ahead and do my "reality check" anyway, as practice. I looked at a billboard advertisement, read the words on it, looked away, then tried to read the letters again. I couldn't believe my eyes! The letters were now all scrambled! I then knew I was dreaming.

Sometimes, however, lucidity can come spontaneously. For Piet Hut, an astrophysicist and professor at the Institute for Advanced Study at Princeton University, the onset of lucidity in one of his dreams was announced in a burst of song. As Hut, who has an avid interest in consciousness studies, recorded the dream in his journal:

> I walked into a bar, where I found a group of people sitting, who looked at me when I entered and immediately started singing in unison:

This is Piet's dream,
We are all here,
And that is why
We get free beer.

Some scientists who started out as skeptics about the validity of lucid dreaming, despite the persuasive evidence to the contrary, actually had a change of heart and mind about the phenomenon once they experienced it. As French dream research pioneer Michel Jouvet wrote in 1993, "I must confess that for a long time I did not believe in lucid dreams. However, four times in the last three years I have enjoyed the extraordinary subjective experience of watching the unfolding of dream images that I could not influence but which I knew full well were part of a dream."

Allan Rechtschaffen, the respected sleep and dreaming expert who is now retired from the University of Chicago, is excited by the prospects of what might be discovered through brain-imaging studies of lucid dreamers: "Probably the most distinctive aspect of dreaming is its lack of reflective consciousness. While we are dreaming, we don't realize we are, which is an unusual state of consciousness. The part of the brain that informs us about our state of consciousness is not working during a typical dream, but during a lucid dream it would be. Imaging studies of a subject in a lucid dream should identify the location of the neurons that give us reflective consciousness." Some researchers speculate that this crucial neuronal network will be located in the prefrontal cortex, which normally is not very active during dreaming. A sudden reactivation of neurons in that area—perhaps influenced by an increase in neuromodulators associated with waking consciousness, such as serotonin—may be what transforms a regular dream into a lucid dream.

But LaBerge contends that scans probably won't reveal any major physiological changes. He says that the high level of activation of REM sleep is all that is physiologically needed for lucid dreaming. The other crucial component that is lacking in normal dreaming but present during lucid dreams is not physical. "What is normally missing is a psychological requirement, namely the mindset to recognize that one is dreaming," says LaBerge. The tests he recommends to foster lucid dreaming help supply that psychological component.

I must admit that initially, I had doubts about some of the elaborate accounts of lucid dreaming I'd heard, and I still have not achieved the level of control in dreams described by LaBerge and other "oneironauts," as he refers to accomplished lucid dreamers. But I can personally attest to both the existence of the phenomenon and the reliability of the tests LaBerge recommends for switching on lucidity and intensifying self-reflective awareness in dreaming. On several occasions throughout my life, I'd had dreams in which the appearance of a long-dead relative or friend as a character suddenly struck me as impossible and triggered the realization that I must be dreaming, but that conscious awareness had also triggered the end of the dream. After doing some background reading about lucid dreaming early in my research for this book, however, I spontaneously had my first truly lucid dream—perhaps not surprisingly, on a weekend morning when I was able to sleep later than usual.

In my dream, as I watched my sister approach down a hallway, I suddenly thought that she looked amazingly real considering that I was dreaming. Then it occurred to me that if I touched her face, I wouldn't feel anything and that would prove without a doubt that I was indeed dreaming. When I touched her, however, she did feel real and the scene abruptly shifted to a winding, rickety fire escape that I found myself climbing on the outside of a tall building. As I anxiously made my way ever higher, the realization that I was probably dreaming entered my mind again, and I tested it by saying to myself that if I were dreaming, I would no longer have to keep climbing this scary fire escape. Instead, I could just blink my eyes and instantly fly to the top. I did just that and promptly woke up, feeling the astonishment and exhilaration LaBerge says is characteristic of first-time lucid dreamers, even though the dream itself had been rather mundane.

The fact that I woke up almost immediately is also typical. The onset of lucidity often causes a dreamer to fully awaken, so LaBerge and other lucid dreaming experts offer tips for walking that tightrope to keep the dream going. When a dream begins to fade, visual imagery usually is the first sign that it's going—colors become faded and images are less sharply defined. As soon as you notice that happening, you may prevent the dream from disappearing if you immediately focus on your other senses—rub your hands together in the dream or touch something in the dreamscape. Another technique LaBerge suggests when you're on the verge of waking is to make your dream self begin spinning in circles like a top, which more often than not will be the catalyst for putting you into another dream scene. He says all of the techniques that seem to work have one thing in common: they load up the brain's perceptual system so it can't shift its focus from the dream world to external reality. In tests at the Lucidity Institute, he found that the odds in favor of continuing the dream were about 22 to 1 when using the spinning technique.

When asked why one would bother with any of these tricks to cultivate conscious awareness in dreams, LaBerge has a ready answer: just for the novelty and fun of it. "What's it like to have a world to myself that I'm the creator of? That's what you discover in a lucid dream, and for many people it's an exhilarating, peak experience," says LaBerge. He says some dreamers also use such dreams as a way of overcoming fears and testing new strategies for coping with obstacles in waking life, as shown in this account from a lucid dreamer in Newport News, Virginia:

> Two weeks ago I had a dream of being pursued by a violent tornadic storm. I was on a cliff high above a beach and had been teaching others to fly, telling them that this was a dream and in a dream all you have to do to fly is believe you can. We were having a great time when the storm appeared, coming in from the ocean. Tornadoes and I go way back in dreams. They are some of my pet monsters of the mind.
>
> When this one appeared, it was announced by exceptionally strong winds and lightning and high waves. A young boy, a puppy, and I were together for some time running and seeking shelter, but then we stopped, poised on the very edge of the last great cliff before the open sea. Panic was bringing me close to the point of losing lucidity. But then I thought, Wait! This is a dream. If you choose, you can keep running. Or you can destroy the tornado or transform it. The storm has no power to hurt the boy or the puppy. It is you it wants. Anyway, no more running. See what it is like from within.

> As I thought this, it was as though some exceptional force lifted the three of us, almost blurring our forms as we were pulled toward the tornado. The boy and puppy simply faded out about midway. Inside the storm there was a beautiful translucent whiteness and a feeling of tremendous peace. At the same time it was a living energy that seemed to be waiting to be shaped and at the same time was capable of being infinitely shaped and reshaped, formed and transformed over again. It was something tremendously vital, tremendously alive.

Lucid dreaming can offer powerful insight because "you look around and realize that the whole world that you're seeing is all something that your mind is creating," says LaBerge. "It tells you that you have much more power than you'd ever believed before—or dreamt—for changing the world, starting with yourself." Hearkening back to his interests in spirituality, LaBerge also recalls one of his own lucid dreams that he says illustrates their potential for conveying personal insight:

> I had a dream in which I was going up a mountain path and had been hiking for miles and miles. I came to a very narrow bridge across an immensely deep chasm, and looking down, I was afraid to go across the bridge. My companion said, "Oh you don't have to go that way; you can go back the way you came," and he points back an immense distance to the long way around. And somehow that just seemed the hard way of doing this, and I had the thought, if I were to become lucid, I would have no fear in crossing that bridge. Then I sort of noticed the thought, became lucid, and crossed the bridge to the other side. When I woke up I thought about the meaning of that and saw that it had an application to life in general. Life is, in a sense, a kind of bridge, and what causes us to lose our balance is fear of the unknown, death, the meaninglessness around us, whatever it might be.

LaBerge still feels an affinity with the Buddhist perspective he discovered in the workshop that launched his adult experiences in lucid dreaming: Tibetan Buddhists' use of lucid dreaming as a spiritual practice advocates maintaining conscious control of dream content and viewing reality on an equal footing with dreaming. From the Buddhist viewpoint, to be enlightened is to be aware always of how much of life is illusion in both the dream state and waking. LaBerge believes that lucid dreaming is an effective method of fully comprehending the illusory nature of all experience.

It may seem bizarre to suggest that dreaming and waking reality are both built on illusion or that the two respective states of consciousness may be more alike than they are different, but on close examination, that perspective is grounded in scientific truth. Whether we're awake or asleep, our consciousness operates based on the model of the world the brain constructs from the best available sources of information at any given moment. In waking, the model that guides our actions and feelings comes primarily from sensory input about the external world and secondarily from contextual information stored in the brain—expectations and motivations based on past experience. When the sensory portals to the outside world are shut off during sleep, the model that drives consciousness instead is assembled solely from the contextual information derived from memory. As many of the studies on memory consolidation and learning have demonstrated, dreaming of doing, seeing, or feeling something is not just similar to doing, seeing, or feeling—from the perspective of the neuronal networks that assemble our experiential world, it *is* the same.

Therefore, it's erroneous to conclude that dream experience is unreal and what happens in waking consciousness is the only true reality, argues LaBerge: "Dreaming can be viewed as a special case of perception without the constraints of external sensory input. Conversely, waking perception can be viewed as a special case of dreaming constrained by sensory input. Whichever way one looks at it, understanding dreaming is central to understanding consciousness."

LaBerge and other researchers also suggest that we should not restrict our definitions of states of consciousness to merely "awake" and "asleep." As shown by evidence from various studies of dreaming over the past two decades, our state of mind at any given moment depends on the underlying physiological conditions of the brain. Many of the characteristics of the state of consciousness that produces vivid dreams during REM sleep are dictated by the sudden drop in levels of the neurochemicals serotonin and norepinephrine and the accompanying surge in acetylcholine circulating in the brain, combined with the absence of sensory signals from the outside world. Activation of key attention-directing areas in the prefrontal cortex is probably the added ingredient that produces lucid dreaming. Some neurochemical shifts might also contribute to this altered form of dreaming.

While REM sleep may offer the most dramatic example of the way that consciousness shifts gears, it's only one of many. When you're reading the newspaper and suddenly realize you're halfway through a story without being aware of what you've read, it's likely that your norepinephrine and serotonin levels shifted down and your acetylcholine level jumped up, allowing your mind to wander or drift off into a daydream, according to Harvard neuroscientist Robert Stickgold. "In the end, there is no normal state," he says. "Waking is no more normal than sleeping. Letting your mind wander is no less normal than keeping it on the straight and narrow. Being calm, cool, and collected is no more normal than being impassioned. Our needs change with our environment, and our bodies must be prepared to change states to meet these challenges."

10

Consciousness and Beyond

The brain is the most complex system in the known universe.
—Christof Koch

As he moves from one room to another in the hallways of the California Institute of Technology (Caltech), Christof Koch leaps up and hangs by his fingertips from the top rim of the door frame as he passes underneath. It's an automatic reflex on his part, for one of his great passions in life is climbing—serious climbing. A breathtaking photograph on the home page of Koch's Web site captures the physicist-turned-neuroscientist doing what he loves best: dangling like a spider on a strand of rope 2,800 feet above the floor of Yosemite Valley. When he's not climbing, though, Koch is just as engaged in confronting a daunting intellectual challenge. Since the late 1980s, he has joined with Nobel laureate Francis Crick on a quest to identify the precise set of brain cells that give us consciousness.

Koch's drive to unravel the mysteries of consciousness and his love of scaling sheer rock faces are actually more connected than one might think. Explaining his admitted addiction to the sport, Koch refers to adventure writer Jon Krakauer's description of the experience as "a clear-eyed dream." Koch elaborates: "Climbing is an almost perfect amalgamation of mind and body, with both used to the maximum. When I'm climbing I feel fully alive, fully conscious." He speaks at near-warp speed, as if impatient with the time it takes to communicate his thoughts verbally because life already is too short to cram in everything he wants to accomplish. And an impressive agenda it is. "I'm trying to find out where I came from, where I will go to, and what I am doing here," he says. "I want to find out what make us conscious."

Koch considers dreaming a fascinating piece of the consciousness puzzle. "The hallmark of dreaming for me is how real everything looks and feels," he says. "I once read something that puts it perfectly: 'Dreams are real while they last. Can we say more of life?'" He takes issue with those who contend dreaming is epiphenomenal, having no biological function. To the contrary, he believes dreaming has persisted through various stages of evolution because it serves a genetically determined purpose. What that ultimate purpose is remains to be seen, but Koch is particularly intrigued by studies suggesting the importance of dreaming's role in memory consolidation. "We know that we dream even before we are born, that animals dream, and that the brain basis of their dreaming is not that dissimilar to ours," he explains. "Dreaming looks like a very highly evolved function of the brain, a particularly vivid form of consciousness," he says.

His journey with Francis Crick to identify exactly what gives us that consciousness began when Koch was doing postdoctoral research in MIT's Artificial Intelligence Lab, where he wrote a paper, together with Shimon Ullman, now a professor at the Weizmann Institute outside Tel Aviv in Israel, exploring the cognitive architecture of attention: how the brain manages to select and focus on any one of many competing signals it's receiving at any point in time. For instance, how do you zero in on what the passenger in your car is saying while you're driving in rush-hour traffic with the radio playing, and that mosquito bite on your leg is itching, and a rainstorm is just beginning, complete with booming thunder and flashes of lightning? Crick was so impressed with the paper when it came out in 1984 that he invited Koch and Ullman to spend a week at the Salk Institute, where he was engaged in his own efforts to understand how we direct our attention. His ultimate goal eventually became cracking the mysteries of consciousness, and he hoped to repeat the success he'd had in unlocking the secrets of DNA. The two scientists shared important common bonds: a keen, penetrating intelligence and a passion for the same intellectual quest. Koch became a regular visitor, especially after he moved from MIT to his own lab at Caltech in 1986. The pair began collaborating on research, publishing their first paper together on the biological origins of consciousness in 1989. Since then, Koch typically has traveled to La Jolla once a month to spend two or three days working with Crick, and they are in almost daily e-mail contact regarding their research.

Koch traces his own curiosity about the nature of consciousness to a period in his early thirties when he was lying in bed suffering from a toothache. Though he was fully aware that the pain he was feeling was caused by electrical activity shooting up a nerve into his brain, he began to wonder why that electrical activity could cause him to feel pain, while other types of electrical activity in his brain gave him pleasure or made him smell the odor of onions or hear the sound of a violin. "A computer can be programmed to do all sorts of computations, but it doesn't feel pain. There is something in the brain that gives rise to subjective feeling, and we think we will find a specific set of neurons that share some basic property that created the first subjective feeling in an animal at some point in evolutionary history," Koch says. As brain structures became more complex, the mere awareness of sensation evolved to a more sophisticated level of consciousness in humans, including awareness of our own mortality and the ability to raise the very questions Koch and Crick are hoping to answer. The human brain appears to be uniquely capable of using its computing power to figure out its own operating rules.

The "astonishing hypothesis" about the nature of consciousness that Crick put forward in 1994 now falls in the realm of accepted belief among most scientists. Substantial evidence has accumulated to support Crick's contention that "your joys and your sorrows, your memories and your ambitions, your sense of personal identity and free will, are in fact no more than the behavior of a vast assembly of nerve cells." While many cognitive neuroscientists believe that consciousness emerges from the collective activity of those nerve cells throughout the entire brain and is a function of millions or billions of neurons firing together, Koch and Crick contend it can be narrowed down much more precisely. They believe the secret may lie in the discrete firing of a much smaller group of neurons. "Evolution has created amazing specificity at the level of molecules and individual cells, and Crick and I think this will also be the case for consciousness. We're looking for very specific neuronal properties that give rise to consciousness, rather than assuming it's the collective activity of the entire brain," says Koch.

They call what they are searching for the neuronal correlates of consciousness (NCC)—the minimal set of neurons that not only correlates with but ultimately causes any specific conscious perception. Leaving aside the more slippery question of what gives rise to our sense of being a freely acting self, they are looking for the source of consciousness at its most basic level: which neurons fire to give us our subjective awareness of feeling pain or pleasure, of seeing the color yellow or hearing the whistle of a tea kettle. The task is far from simple. Each molecule within each neuron follows instructions based on genetic programming while under the influence of whatever neurochemicals are predominant at a given point in time. When you consider that a range of activity is constantly being carried out by thousands of molecules within a single neuron, which in turn is acting in concert with a network of tens of thousands of related neurons, all of which figure into a total cast of 100 billion neurons within a single human brain, it's clear why Koch refers to the brain as "the most complex system in the known universe." He is clearly excited by the many questions awaiting answers: "Will there be commonalties between the NCC for a flashing red light, a high C tone, and a dull tooth ache? And what about the NCC generating sensations whilst dreaming, a feeling that can't be distinguished from waking life?"

The most effective way to get the information he and Crick seek at this stage is to study neurons in waking consciousness under circumstances that they can manipulate. Most of their data is based on neuroscientific experiments carried out in animals such as mice and monkeys, because electrodes can be implanted in their brains to record firing patterns of individual neurons—something that would be considered unethical in humans. But a rare opportunity to do exactly that kind of testing in humans recently presented itself, and the results illustrate Koch's point about just how specific the brain's organization is. Neurosurgeon Itzhad Fried at the University of California at Los Angeles (UCLA) allowed Gabriel Kreiman, a researcher from Koch's lab, to conduct experiments with epileptic patients whose brains had been implanted with electrodes to help locate the origin of their seizures as part of their treatment regime.

Koch says that, recording the firing of single neurons in the portion of the brain that is highly active in dreaming and in memory recall, they discovered a small number of individual neurons that fired only in response to very different views of familiar personalities. In one case the patient was shown fifty images of people, known and unknown to the patient, as well as other types of images, such as cars or animals. However, the neurons in question responded only to three images: a line drawing and a photographic portrait of former U.S. president Bill Clinton as well as a group photograph in which he also appeared. The same neuron fired again when the subject was instructed to close her eyes and merely imagine the image of Clinton. Koch suspects the same neuron would fire if the subject dreamed of the former president, though he has no reliable means to test that notion now, because he can't control dream content. But his suspicion is strengthened by the fact that the neurons firing in response to the Clinton images are found in a portion of the limbic system known as the medial temporal lobe—a region that brain-imaging experiments have demonstrated is highly active in dreams. There's nothing magical about Bill Clinton, of course—Koch and his colleagues found that the same neuronal specialization applies to other familiar people or common objects in a test subject's life: specific neurons respond only to a coffee cup or the face of a family member, and those same neurons fire again when the images of the cup or person are called to mind, though the firing rate is stronger for the real thing than for its recalled version. "This helps explain dream imagery, because it tells us we don't need any input from the retina or the primary visual cortex in order to have visual perceptions," says Koch.

In fact, he says, understanding exactly how visual perception works—in both waking and dreaming—may be the best route for understanding consciousness and how it is generated. "We are very visual creatures," says Koch. "One-third of the brain is given over to vision, and we have all sorts of visual experiences that can be analyzed, including vivid dreams." From a practical standpoint, visual perception also works well as a model for investigation because the base of knowledge about the physiology of that form of perception is greater than for any other and it's also comparatively easy to study visual pathways in animals, which expands the repertoire of studies that can be conducted. Experimenters can manipulate what subjects—both animal and human—see on a computer monitor and record how their brains respond to it. Most of Crick's and Koch's theories are based on studies carried out in macaque monkeys, whose visual system is similar to humans'.

On his MacIntosh computer screen Koch shows me "motion-induced blindness," a visual illusion developed at the Weizmann Institute in Israel that works for both monkeys and humans and demonstrates how manipulating visual perception can provide clues about the neuronal basis of consciousness. The black screen displays a cloud of moving blue dots swirling about, along with three vivid and clearly visible yellow disks.

Koch instructs me to focus my eyes on the screen without moving them for a few seconds, and as I do, one, two, or all three yellow disks magically disappear. Or so it seems. The disks themselves never moved, but the blue background creates such a strong perceptual signal competing against the yellow dots that it won out.

My brain focused only on the background while suppressing the image of the yellow dots. All that changed was that one second I was conscious of them and the next second I wasn't. "A set of neurons fires when you 'see' the yellow dots and fails to fire when you don't. Those are neurons that correlate with consciousness," says Koch.

It's fascinating, though a bit disconcerting, to see how thoroughly deceptive my brain can be. But understanding how visual perception really works means accepting the fact that in waking, as in dreaming, we actually see with our brains, not our eyes, and illusion is an integral part of the process. In fact, if our picture of the world exactly matched the information projected from the eye to the brain, the world would seem a strange place indeed. For starters, we move our eyes three times per second on average. If we watched a video filmed with a camera that moved in this herky-jerky way, we'd soon have a nauseating case of motion sickness. Using its own version of auto tracking, the brain automatically adjusts the image for us, creating the illusion of stability.

The manipulation that goes on outside our conscious awareness is on a much grander scale, however. The retina—a thin sheet of neurons at the back of the eye—serves as "evolution's satellite dish" for photons, which are energy particles that bombard the eyes, triggering the electrical signals that set the vision process in motion, explains Thomas B. Czerner, a professor of ophthalmology at the University of California in San Francisco and author of the book *What Makes You Tick?* a lively overview of recent neuroscientific research. But the electrical signals transmitted by the retina don't in and of themselves produce the clear image that you see when you gaze out the window. To the eyes, says Czerner, the world is a senseless, two-dimensional montage of disconnected dots of light, akin to what you would see if you stood too close to a painting by a pointillist, such as Georges Seurat.

To complicate matters further, there's a time lag of about one-twentieth of a second before you see anything at all. "Even then you will not see every point of light striking the retina but only those your brain found interesting and important," says Czerner. "Although the rich visual tapestry of your surroundings seems to be 'out there' and separate from you, this colorful creation is embroidered entirely within your brain."

What the brain selects as important enough to weave into your tapestry is based in part on what is encoded in its DNA—the visual image a bat's brain constructs will be significantly different from the image a human brain assembles from the same raw visual data. Even when two people look at the same street scene, the visual image each person's brain assembles can vary. For instance, about 60 percent of men have a gene that allows them to perceive long-wave-length red photopigment (the basic building block of color) so that the shade they are seeing when they look at a red rose is not quite the same as the color seen by the other 40 percent of men looking at the same flower. And of course two people viewing the same scene will notice different aspects of it, based on their personal history, so how visual attention is focused also affects what is "seen."

"Our perceptual machinery for making use of retinally available information about the disposition of objects in three-dimensional space is deeply entrenched in our nervous system and wholly automatic in its operation," explains Roger Shepard, professor emeritus at Stanford, whose award-winning research career includes many breakthroughs in understanding how visual perception works. "Without our bidding or even our awareness of its existence, this machinery immediately goes to work on any visual input, including the visual input provided by a two-dimensional drawing. As a result, we cannot choose to see a drawing merely as what it is—a pattern of lines on a flat, two-dimensional surface," he says. Our brain is genetically programmed to turn that line pattern into a three-dimensional display, so we should not be surprised that we are powerless to see it any other way. "We have inherited this machinery from individuals who, long before the advent of picture making, interpreted—by virtue of this machinery—what was going on in the three-dimensional world around them with sufficient efficiency to survive and to continue our ancestral line," says Shepard.

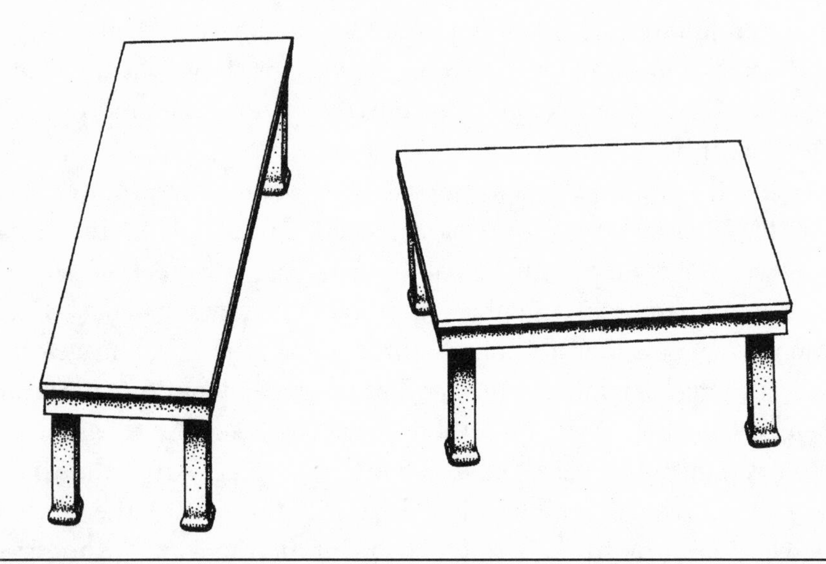

FIGURE 10.1 This drawing, entitled "Turning the Tables," demonstrates that visual perception often involves a fair amount of deception. Contrary to what your first glance may tell you, the tops of the tables actually are of identical size and shape in the plane of the picture, which is one of several visual illusions created by Roger N. Shepard. Shepard holds the copyright to the drawing, which first appeared in his book *Mind Sights* (W. H. Freeman, 1990).

In waking, just as in dreams, how the brain sculpts the visual image you eventually see is also influenced by your unique individual history. As Daniel Dennett, a neurophilosopher at Tufts University expresses it in his book *Consciousness Explained,* "Vision cannot be explained as a bottom-up, data driven process; it requires expectations." Those expectations are built in part on specific memories and predictions instilled in your brain through your experiences from childhood on.

When we're awake, the disconnected dots representing the electrical activity generated by the retina are projected to a relay station in a portion of the brain called the thalamus, which in turn projects to the primary visual cortex. It then passes those signals on to various neuronal systems dedicated to specialized tasks such as face recognition or processing color or motion. Finally, all of that information flows to the highest levels of the visual system, known as the associative cortices, which store memory, direct the most abstract aspects of visual processing, and assemble the final image we see. In dreaming, however, since the retina and primary visual cortex are closed for business, the memory-rich associative cortices are actually both the starting and end points for generating visual imagery in the dreamworld.

"Visual imagery is largely formed by our ideas and feelings about what things ought to look like," according to Czerner. "The eye provides information about light and dark, but it contributes nothing to meaning or perception. In both waking and dreaming, those components are supplied by the associative cortex and—to an even larger extent in dreaming than waking—by the limbic system, which regulates emotionally charged memories."

Illustrating his point, Czerner says that glimpsing a flash of blue among green leaves will activate a diffuse assembly of neurons that have fired previously in response to the sight of blue jays, balloons, or kites in a similar setting. Once your retina signals the presence of enough essential details, the network of activated neurons will become more precise, eventually producing the distinct image of a blue jay. That same assembly of neurons can be reactivated later to recreate that memory or to embellish a dream.

In short, the mass of disconnected dots the retina projects to represent what's "out there" unquestionably reflects a concrete reality in the external world, but the actual visual image that appears in your mind is created the same way a dream image is—and memory plays a crucial role in shaping both. A dramatic example of how much our sense of visual reality is dependent on what we've stored in memory can be found in a novel animal experiment in which cats were prevented from seeing any horizontal lines from the time they were born throughout the early period crucial for development of the brain's visual cortex. Since horizontal lines were not included in the mental model of the world imprinted in their brains, when a horizontal bar later was placed across their path, the cats walked right into it, as if it didn't exist. In a very real way, we see what we expect to see, based on what's happened before.

Another significant characteristic of visual perception is that so much of it goes on outside conscious awareness, as does the vast majority of other brain activity. Therefore, the fact that we are aware of only a small fraction of our dreams either through recall or via lucid dreaming doesn't diminish their value or importance in our lives, especially when you consider that probably no more than 5 percent of all mental activity takes place within the realm of consciousness anyway. According to Dartmouth neuroscientist Michael Gazzaniga, 98 percent of what the brain does is outside of conscious awareness, while a review of scientific evidence on this question published in 1999 concluded that 95 percent of our actions are unconsciously determined.

"Zombie agents" is the term that Koch uses to refer to this preponderance of neural systems that direct our actions without our conscious awareness or control. "I have difficulty explaining what I do to my parents, because from their perspective, there's nothing so complicated about vision—you just open your eyes and see," says Koch. "Now, if you tell people you're building a computer program that plays chess, that sounds like a real challenge, but we think vision is easy because we only see the output. Most people don't see or know about the sophisticated zombie agents within the brain that allow us to move, to talk, to see." He points out that anyone who works in robotics knows how difficult it is to program even a seemingly simple movement. "When I reach out to grab a cup, I have no idea how I'm doing it, no more than I understand how my hand can hang on to a rock I'm climbing or pick up an egg or a feather," he says.

It's also clear that the brain tinkers with other aspects of our sensory perception in waking hours, creating illusions about *when* things happen. A series of experiments performed by cognitive neuroscientist Benjamin Libet in the 1960s and 1970s demonstrated that in order for any sensation to enter our consciousness, it has to first be processed in the appropriate center of the brain and that process takes about a half a second. If someone touches your hand, there should be that amount of time lag before you actually feel anything, but you are never aware of any delay. The brain automatically corrects for its processing time to make it seem as though the feeling of being touched comes exactly at the same time the other person's fingers press against your hand. Libet also used brain-wave recordings to show that 350 milliseconds before you're conscious of making the decision to lift your hand, your brain is already sending signals to your muscles to initiate that process. You're clued in after the fact, so to speak.

Being unaware of these time lags and of all the behind-the-scenes machinations doesn't make us any less effective in terms of how we operate. Why then should consciousness—whether in waking or dreaming form—have emerged at all? "It may be because consciousness allows the system to plan future actions, opening up a potentially infinite behavioral repertoire and making explicit memory possible," says Koch. "Consciousness could involve synchronized firing of neurons at the millisecond level, whereas uncorrelated firing can influence behavior without generating that special buzz in the head that makes us subjectively aware."

Harvard dream researcher Allan Hobson agrees with Koch that visual perception is a good model for understanding the nature of consciousness, for it offers clear proof that any given state of mind is simply a reflection of a physiological process: neuronal activity. In his view, it solves what cognitive scientists call the mind-body problem, which boils down to explaining how the awareness of being uniquely yourself in the world at this very moment in time arises. The question at the heart of the mind-body problem is how does the brain—which is, after all, nothing more than a convoluted mass of tissue—become a thinking, feeling mind? "Once you understand that the visual world is nothing but a sequence of activation patterns of neurons representing images, the ball game is over," Hobson says.

Our sense of consciousness also involves an elaborate process of internal mapmaking in the form of neural networks. The brain "sees" by making internal maps that represent the body and the external world in which we operate. For instance, our awareness of our own body is inextricably linked to the musculoskeletal system that allows us to move around. This system of muscles and bones is in turn represented in the form of a map in the portion of the cortex that directs the body's movements. Even when we aren't actually using our muscles, that map imprinted early in life remains operational, as was demonstrated quite clearly in surprising tests done recently on actor Christopher Reeve, who was almost entirely paralyzed from his shoulders down in a 1995 horseback-riding accident. Though the fall severed most of the nerves in the neural bundle that relays signals between Reeve's brain and the rest of his body, he has worked with physical therapists regularly in hopes of walking again, and his brain has remained surprisingly receptive to signals from his paralyzed body parts.

Seven years after his accident, doctors at Washington University School of Medicine in St. Louis used magnetic resonance imaging (MRI) to survey Reeve's patterns of brain activity in response to touch and movement. They asked Reeve to follow the video image of a tennis ball and indicate the direction in which it was moving either with his tongue or his left index finger, in which he has limited controlled movement. The MRI images detected which parts of the brain were active as Reeve tracked the ball's movements. As Maruizio Corbetta, one of the doctors involved in Reeve's testing, explained it, "There is a picture of your body plotted on the brain with different parts of the brain driving different parts of the body." In Reeve's case, that body map showed that the areas of the brain that normally control motion for the hand had been taken over to some extent by areas that control the face but that, overall, Reeve's results were comparable to those of a healthy twenty-three-year-old who had taken the same test.

Another indication of how important such internal maps are was recently provided by an unusual young man named Tito Mukhopadhyay, who is so severely autistic that he cannot speak but who can communicate via a laptop computer equipped with a voice synthesizer. Tito, who is very articulate and offers a rare window into the autistic mind, is being studied by neuroscientists using imaging to watch his brain in action. What they found is that he seems to lack the internal map that children normally develop in their first few years in brain regions involved in touch and movement. "When I was four or five years old, I hardly realized I had a body except when I was hungry or when I realized I was standing under the shower and my body got wet," Tito wrote. He explained that he spins around and flaps his hands—as many autistic people do—because he needs constant movement just to get the feeling of having a body. Researchers at the University of California at San Diego discovered through other imaging studies that many autistic people have mixed-up brain maps and many can't identify their own body parts in a mirror, which makes it difficult to build other types of mental models of the world to integrate perceptions such as sights, sound, touch, and taste.

Allan Hobson contends that dreaming plays a crucial role in the formation of these vital internal maps of our bodies and the world we must navigate. To be useful, the representations in the brain must match external reality with a high degree of fidelity. "As soon as possible, the brain creates a copy of the world that it uses in all its comparative work so that you can predict what you're going to see without having to reinvent the world in every instant of visual experience," says Hobson. He suggests that the massive amount of REM sleep that we experience in the womb and as infants is part of this mapmaking process. The models must be updated and elaborated in more sophisticated versions as we mature, but the revisions occur at night, off-line, he argues. "I think it all comes together in dreams. This simulacrum of the world in the brain that allows you to dream a fictive reality is used all of the time in waking, even though you're not aware of it. Then at night, the brain takes little bits of today's experience, sticking this or that together with something else in memory you didn't know it was associated with, and on comes the dream."

Each night then, dreaming helps to update our neural networks and refine the internal map of the world that helps guide our behavior. "Waking and dreaming are mirror images of one another which interact throughout our lives to create consciousness in the first place and to endow it with information for purposes of adaptation as we live out our lives," says Hobson in his book *Dreaming*. While cats, monkeys, and even birds appear to refine their neural programming off-line each night just as we do, there's obviously something different about human brain circuitry that allows for our sometimes elaborate dream narratives, which in turn reflect a level of consciousness beyond the simple subjective awareness of sensation that we share with many members of the animal kingdom. Experiments using mirrors have suggested that dolphins, chimps, and gorillas may be able to recognize their own images and thus have some basic sense of visual self-awareness. But the ability to form abstract concepts, to create language, to think about thinking, and to reflect on and plan future experiences rather than simply living them moment-to-moment is what sets humans apart. Locating the neuronal basis for this expanded form of consciousness is part of the longer-term quest that captures the imagination of neuroscientists such as Christof Koch. And while the goal remains elusive, he says at least one clue has appeared in the form of an anomaly in a single type of brain cell.

"If I give you a little grain of human brain and a little grain of monkey brain, very few people on the planet could tell the two apart. They are almost identical," he says. "While there are no major fundamental differences in the hardware itself, there is a type of brain cell called a spindle cell that has recently been found to be nearly unique to humans, though it has been seen in low density in other humanoids such as chimps. So it may be something that is evolutionarily new." Though spindle cells were first described by researchers in 1925, only recently has it become clear that they are unique to humans and great apes. Spindle cells are found exclusively in the anterior cingulate gyrus—the brain region that Francis Crick has speculated is the seat of what we consider free will. And of course, brain-imaging studies have shown that it is also the region that is more highly activated than any other during REM sleep, the peak period for dreaming. Such findings give new meaning to the conclusion reached by children's dreaming expert David Foulkes: "We dream because we have achieved consciousness."

Epilogue

EARLY IN THE PROCESS OF INTERVIEWING neuroscientists for this book, I was discussing dream research with Robert Stickgold in the neurophysiology lab at Massachusetts Mental Health Center. He explained that different researchers' viewpoints about dreaming's function—if they acknowledged that it had any at all—varied based on the type of research each was pursuing. Those conducting psychological research would argue that the dreaming stage of sleep was really centered on regulating emotion, while those studying its role in memory consolidation would disagree, emphasizing instead its importance to learning, and others might argue that while REM sleep is necessary for regulating body temperature and other physiological functions, dreaming itself serves no purpose. When I replied that what he was describing reminded me of a parable I'd recently read to my son, "The Blind Men and the Elephant," Stickgold at first started to disagree but then suddenly broke into an impish smile. "Yes," he said, "that *is* what it's like."

Versions of the tale have come from China, India, and Africa, each with its own variations, but the essence is the same: several blind men encounter an elephant for the first time and must guess its nature solely by touch. The first touches the leg and says it must be something like a tree, the next touches the elephant's tusk and concludes the creature is like a spear, while yet another feels the trunk and insists that what they're confronting is a snake. They are all right in part, of course, but the full truth can be perceived only by viewing the animal as a whole.

Though many questions about the mechanics and functions of dreaming remain to be answered definitively, the research that scientists have amassed to date allows us to step back and take a good look at the elephant in its full splendor. There is considerable evidence that REM sleep evolved in animals as an off-line means of wiring the brain with genetically encoded information in the womb and during infancy. It also became a means of processing survival-related information from each day's experience and integrating it in the brain's internal model for directing future behavior. The studies of rats rerunning their day's work in the maze as they sleep demonstrate that this biological function is still at work in the animal world.

As the human brain evolved—acquiring the capability for language and for subjective awareness of our emotions—dreaming took on added dimensions that reflected the growing complexity of our own brand of consciousness. The mounting evidence from recent studies on learning and memory show that the memory consolidation that characterizes animals' dreaming is also an important part of what the human mind is engaged in at night. The way in which additional layers of complexity are added to make human dreaming unique is demonstrated by the longitudinal studies of children's dreaming, which suggest that the human version of dreaming emerges gradually, tracking our stages of cognitive development. As neural circuitry matures and becomes more sophisticated, human dreams ultimately become narratives, with the dreamer as the key player in a true-as-life reality that our brain constructs anew each night, drawing on both recent and long-term memory.

And because the most highly charged region of the brain during our most fertile dreaming periods is the limbic system—the center for generating emotion-laden action and memories—the type of memory that the brain preferentially selects for incorporation in these narratives tends to be emotionally charged. The predominance of negative emotions in human dreams worldwide probably stems from the genetically programmed component of dreaming that we share with animals—the systematic mental rehearsal of fight-or-flight survival behaviors. But our subjective awareness of emotion also makes humans more psychologically complex, so that for us, dreaming plays a further role in processing emotion and actually influences our mood in waking hours. Emotionally tagged memory has everything to do with our sense of self.

Decades of research by psychologically inclined investigators suggests that the natural cycle of dreaming helps us overcome the emotional traumas we encounter in life. When that cycle goes awry, we get stuck, sinking into depression or disorders such as post-traumatic stress disorder. These findings are supported by brain-imaging studies showing that depressed patients' brain activation cycles during sleep and waking are the reverse of what we see in healthy subjects.

In short, the role of dream-rich REM sleep undergoes an evolution within each individual. While we're in the womb, vast networks of neural circuitry are being established in the brain, and the dreaming stage of sleep apparently facilitates this process and helps install our genetic software. As we mature, dreaming time becomes integral to the brain's process of reorganizing itself nightly, assimilating new information that is important for both our physical and psychological well-being. While cultivating dream recall can sometimes provide insight into which emotional issues are on the front burner, it's also clear that dreams serve their purpose whether we remember them or not, just as much of our necessary mental activity in waking life is effectively accomplished outside our conscious awareness. It appears that by nature's design we were never intended to remember our dreams, so that the fact that most people recall only a miniscule fraction of their dreams doesn't diminish dreaming's importance.

Nevertheless, harnessing that fraction of mental activity over which we do have conscious control in order to improve our recall of dreams can be both fun and useful. The ability to capture a dream or fragment of one in memory can lead to a creative breakthrough or psychological insight. But we also must be aware that some of the dreams we tune into may be rather mundane or little more than phantasmagoric entertainments. In fact, in his book *Lucid Dreaming*, Stephen LaBerge likens dreams to poems: "If you wrote a dozen poems a night every night of your life, what do you suppose you would find among your several hundred thousand poems? All masterpieces? Not likely. All trash? Not likely either. What you would expect is that among great piles of trivial doggerel, there would be a smaller pile of excellent poems, but no more than a handful of perfect masterpieces. It is the same with your dreams, I believe."

Unquestionably, the shifts from waking to deep sleep and then to dreaming offer a wonderful natural laboratory for testing questions about the nature of consciousness. Ever more sophisticated brain-imaging technology makes it possible to actually see how physiological changes correspond to state of mind as these shifts occur. New gene-screening techniques also open the way for understanding what's happening in the brain on a molecular level, which can yield detailed information on how the brain reorganizes itself during sleep and, indeed, why we need to sleep at all.

In the United States, unfortunately, funding for dream research in the past couple of decades has been more difficult to come by than it has been abroad, especially in Canada and Europe, where much innovative dream research has originated in recent years. In this country the main source of funding for such research is the federal government, and during the 1980s and 1990s, those who controlled the purse strings for government-funded research increasingly shifted their focus to studies on sleep disorders such as narcolepsy rather than on dreaming.

William Dement, who shifted from dream research to studying sleep, has long lamented a lack of adequate funding for both dream studies and basic sleep research in this country. "What I have learned during my career is that science is becoming ever more political," Dement has said. "It is my guess that many of our legislators have never heard of REM sleep or, even if they have, certainly don't have a clear idea of what it signifies. Sleep occupies one-third of our lives, and the quality of that third totally determines the quality of the other two-thirds—yet understanding sleep is not a national mandate. Think about it. We spend a third of our lives sleeping and dreaming, and we still do not know why."

That sad state of affairs may be in the process of changing, however, in part because brain-imaging and other technological advances open new avenues of scientific exploration. In a 2003 article in the *New York Times*, David Dinges, a sleep research specialist at the University of Pennsylvania, went so far as to say that a "golden age of sleep research" is dawning, thanks to advances in both neuroscience and sleep medicine. "The field is moving so fast scientifically that few researchers can even take the time to write a book," he said. Similarly, dream content analysis expert Bill Domhoff says he has not been so optimistic about the future of dream research since its heyday in the 1960s. He expects that future neurocognitive research will test current theories and expand what is known about the dreaming brain "so that the late-night movies in the brain can be incorporated into ambitious theories seeking to explain all aspects of the human mind."

Whether greater funding will be forthcoming for research on dreaming, as opposed to sleep per se, remains to be seen, however. The lion's share of funding comes from federal health agencies, and government officials are more interested in funding clinical studies on sleep disorders than they are in providing money for research that focuses solely on dreaming. "If you call what you are studying dreaming, you are sunk as far as grant proposals go," says Ed Pace-Schott, a psychiatric instructor at Harvard and member of the research team in Allan Hobson's neurophysiology lab. For instance, Pace-Schott recently conducted research demonstrating that people taking antidepressants known as serotonin reuptake inhibitors (which include such frequently prescribed brands as Paxil, Zoloft, and Prozac) report that their dreaming is intensified, even though the drugs tend to suppress REM sleep by increasing serotonin levels. More research is needed to understand why this occurs. "Documenting a clinical phenomenon like this is of primary interest to government funding agencies, while dreaming is only a side interest," says Pace-Schott. "But we're hopeful that the renaissance occurring in sleep research will carry dream research along with it, especially because experiments such as Bob Stickgold's Tetris study are demonstrating what a powerful tool dreaming can be in cognitive neuroscience research."

In the meantime, studying sleep disorders remains a hot area of research that can provide valuable insights about dreaming through close examination of what happens when neurological defects derail the normal dreaming process. For instance, Rosalind Cartwright is supplementing her studies of dreaming's role in emotional processing by analyzing what occurs in people who suffer from a form of parasomnia known as arousal disorder. In recent years, she has frequently been called in as a consultant to examine those who have the disorder. Rather than progressing smoothly from slow-wave sleep into dreaming during REM, parasomniacs abort the first dream opportunity by getting out of bed while still in deep sleep and engaging in activities ranging from compulsive eating to violent behavior, including murder—none of which they remember when awakened. It is in essence an extension of the more benign sleepwalking that children and teens often experience. "Like the rest of us, parasomniacs go to sleep with leftover emotional baggage from the day, but rather than dreaming it out, they get up in the first part of the night in deep sleep before entering REM and act on the unfinished business of the day," says Cartwright.

Since the disorder runs in families, she says, it appears to be caused by a genetic flaw. In one case reported in the British medical journal *Lancet* in 2000, a parasomniac was actually captured in the act of getting up while being scanned in a brain-imaging lab. The resulting image showed that compared to normal subjects in deep sleep, the parasomniac had a 25 percent increase in blood flow in the posterior cingulate cortex and anterior cerebellum—brain regions related to sensory input and movement—and a decrease in activity in frontoparietal associative cortices, which indicate that the subject was unquestionably still asleep. These patterns of brain activation are in keeping with the person being able to move around while the brain is technically asleep, and they also account for the lack of recall of the episode, says Cartwright.

Two of the parasomniacs she's examined were charged with committing murder while they were in this bizarre state, and after investigating their cases, she concluded that both were absolutely legitimate. "I've seen a lot that claimed to be and weren't, but in my judgment, these were the real thing," she says. In both cases, the men arose after going to sleep with a resolution to take care of something on their "to do" list, which they then proceeded to act upon when they arose in the midst of deep sleep. When startled by other people while in the midst of their somnambulant activity, they both apparently acted on autopilot, guided by primitive instincts that led them to violently attack anyone who approached them. In the first case, Kenneth Parks of Toronto fell asleep on the couch one night in May of 1987, arose while still in deep sleep, and drove nearly fifteen miles to the house of his in-laws, whom he was planning to visit the next day. When he entered their house in the middle of the night, he fatally stabbed his mother-in-law with the knife she had grabbed to defend herself when she heard what she feared was an intruder in the house. There was no rational motive—Parks was beloved by his in-laws, including the now-widowed father-in-law, who posted bail for him. His attorney successfully defended him on the grounds that he was not responsible for his actions due to the sleep disorder. "When Ken was acquitted, he said he was afraid to go home because he didn't know how he could be sure he wouldn't do something like that again. That's a legitimate concern, unless treated with medication," says Cartwright.

The other case involved Scott Falater, an electrical engineer in Arizona, who killed his wife under similar circumstances. After falling asleep in his bedroom, Falater got up again while most of his brain was still in slow-wave sleep. He went outside to finish repair work he'd started earlier on the family swimming pool filtering system. When he was awakened by the arrival of the police, his wife, who apparently came outside to see why he'd gotten up, was floating in the pool after being stabbed forty-four times. "Scott was sentenced to life without parole, and he told me that what he can't get out of his mind is that he didn't know he was killing her but *she* did," says Cartwright.

By closely examining these cases, it's possible, says Cartwright, to tease out what's working and what's not in this strange state between waking and sleeping. "Parasomniacs with arousal disorder can navigate through space," she says, "but they have no visual recognition of faces, they can't hear screams, nor do they feel pain themselves. Ken Park's hands were badly cut in the struggle with his mother-in-law, yet he didn't awaken. It's also interesting that the drives that are highly activated in these parasomniacs—aggression, anger, appetite, and sex—are exactly the drives that are reduced in my depressed patients. The parasomniacs don't make it into REM to dream at all, while the depressed do get into REM, but they don't have normal dreaming patterns. As we learn more about these two different types of dysfunctions, it will help us to understand the normal functions of dreaming more clearly."

The behavior of parasomniacs underscores the fact that our state of consciousness at any given point in time is a reflection of the physiological state of our brain and that the distinction isn't as simple as awake or asleep. The cases also provide a prime example of Christof

Koch's "zombie agents" in action, for people suffering from the disorder have sufficient activation in the areas of the brain needed to perform complex motor activity, such as driving a car, yet their behavior is outside conscious awareness—the neuronal networks required for subjective self-awareness and for recall are not online.

Yet another recently discovered aberration may shed further light on the mind at night. The syndrome is called REM behavior disorder, and those who suffer from it—primarily middle-aged and elderly men—aren't paralyzed during sleep, as normal sleepers are. Instead, they periodically get up and act out their dreams, much like the cats in Michel Jouvet's experiments leaped up and appeared to stalk prey or attack imaginary enemies while EEG recordings revealed that they were in REM sleep. The cats exhibited this behavior because the part of the brain that inhibits movement during dreaming had been surgically removed, but in humans, the phenomenon occurs as a result of a natural flaw in the brain. When people with REM behavior disorder are awakened after acting out their dream, they usually have vivid recall of the dream that coincided with their actions. "The most common theme is that they're dreaming of being attacked, so they are acting out punching, kicking, or in some other way fighting off an attacker," explains Suzanne Stevens, a neurologist and specialist in sleep disorders at Rush-Presbyterian–St. Luke's Hospital in Chicago. "I had a patient who dreamed he was kicking a dog that was attacking him, and he awakened to find himself violently kicking the nightstand. Unfortunately, though, it's often the spouse who's injured by the dreamer's behavior."

Autopsies of people suffering from REM behavior disorder have shown a common link: all had abnormal cells in the area of the brainstem that is responsible for regulating motor activity during REM sleep. While people as young as twenty-five have had the disorder and women occasionally suffer from it, nearly 90 percent of REM behavior disorder patients are men, so some scientists speculate that male hormones may play a role in triggering the problem. Patients are typically around age sixty when they are diagnosed, but usually begin showing symptoms five to ten years earlier. Medications are available to treat symptoms, but unfortunately for many patients, REM behavior disorder appears to be a precursor of Parkinson's disease and related movement disorders. Recently released results of a study of thirty-eight patients with REM behavior disorder who were followed for twelve years showed that two-thirds ultimately developed Parkinson's.

Currently, parasomnia-related sleep violence of one form or another is reported by slightly more than 2 percent of the population, according to Cartwright. "You don't hear a lot about it unless someone actually murders someone, but there are a lot of cases where wives have to lock husbands in the other bedroom because they don't want to get socked at night," she says. Worrisome signs that the problem may become more widespread have emerged recently as sleep clinics report seeing patients who have developed symptoms associated with REM behavior disorder after taking antidepressants in the selective serotonin reuptake inhibitor category. In addition to intensifying dreaming, as Ed Pace-Schott's research demonstrated, the drugs also appear to disrupt the normal sleep cycle. Sleep disorder clinics report that those on the drugs experience unusual eye movements during non-REM sleep—a phenomenon some doctors have labeled "Prozac eyes"—as well as jerking muscles and movements so extreme that they are thrown out of bed. At least one study found that the unusual eye movements persisted for as long as six months after patients stopped taking the antidepressants. It's not yet clear how common these side effects are or what they portend, but the cases that have been reported to date have prompted one leading sleep disorder specialist to issue a warning against casual prescribing of antidepressants. "The drugs are very effective, but it's the physician's responsibility to make sure the patient's condition is severe enough to warrant prescribing a neuroactive agent," advised Mark Mahowald, a sleep specialist at the Minnesota Regional Sleep Disorders Center who was one of the authors of a study in 1986 that formally identified REM behavior disorder as a new form of parasomnia.

In the years ahead, dream research also could play an important role in the rapidly growing, new field of consciousness studies, according to Finnish cognitive neuroscientist Antti Revonsuo. "The link between dreams and consciousness is very intimate since dreaming is psychological reality at its barest, a subjective virtual reality," he says. One of the core unanswered questions about consciousness is called "the binding problem." All of the sensations that comprise our experience—color, form, sound, touch, and smell—are processed by distinctly different neural mechanisms, and it's unclear how all sensations and emotions are bound together to create the coherent, unified sense of reality we experience. When we have a dream that includes bizarre incongruities and shifts in scene or character, we have a case study of the brain spontaneously failing to bind the phenomenological world together coherently. Understanding what causes that breakdown in dreaming could help elucidate what the brain is actually doing differently in waking life to make experiences feel coherent, suggests Revonsuo.

Studying the bizarre elements in dreams is in fact one of the directions Sophie Schwartz is pursuing in her current post in Switzerland at the University of Geneva's Departments of Physiology and Clinical Neurosciences. "The brain in waking is designed to reject the bizarre and extract what is familiar and expected from experience. In dreaming, though, the brain accepts the bizarre, creating images such as blue bananas. I'm interested in understanding why the neural system begins building the surreal in dreams, because it's not an outcome you would predict based on our neurocognitive models of the waking mind (or brain)," she says.

Schwartz is collaborating with Pierre Maquet, who is setting up a state-of-the-art brain-imaging facility in his lab in Belgium to continue his investigation of how dreaming and other sleep stages contribute to learning and memory consolidation, using a technique called functional magnetic resonance imaging (fMRI). The technique is superior to older technologies such as PET scans because it provides real-time images of the entire brain and can provide more precise images of activation in even very small sections. Another advantage is that no injection of radioactive substances is needed to obtain images, so subjects can be scanned as often as experimenters like. Real-time fMRI provides the most detailed, comprehensive picture now available of the brain in action, across all its different physiological states in waking and sleep cycles, but the technology also has its drawbacks. The imaging equipment is noisy and subjects can't move while being scanned. Lying motionless inside a scanner that is clanking away does not encourage subjects to drift off to sleep, but Maquet is making progress in resolving these problems. "Pierre's lab will be the first in the world using fMRI to concentrate on sleep and dreaming studies," says Schwartz.

They will be using fMRI in conjunction with EEG recordings to study brain activation patterns among both waking and sleeping subjects. One major issue that can be addressed by such brain-imaging methods is whether specific dream contents correlate with activity in brain regions known to be involved in the perception of such content during wakefulness. For instance, Schwartz hopes to be able to see what differences—if any—there might be in brain activation patterns when the brain builds a representation of a face in a dream as compared to recognizing a human face while awake. Mapping brain areas activated by specific content during sleep and wakefulness may help us understand which particular sets of neurons create what we see and feel during dreaming.

State-of-the-art brain-imaging is also central to new research undertaken in South Africa by Mark Solms, whose groundbreaking studies of patients with brain lesions underscored the crucial role played by the forebrain in creating dreams. In collaboration with researchers in Frankfurt, Germany, he is using fMRI studies to pinpoint which brain mechanisms are activated in the subset of non-REM dreams that are considered indistinguishable in quality from REM dreams. "This will enable us to finally isolate those aspects of the brain mechanisms activated during REM sleep that are actually responsible for dreaming, as opposed to those that are responsible for REM," says Solms. Ironically, one of the most amply funded new areas of research on sleep and dreaming is aimed at finding ways to do without both. The Defense Advanced Research Projects Agency (DARPA), which is the U.S. Defense Department's independent research branch, solicited proposals in the summer of 2001 for $100 million in research grants toward the ultimate goal of allowing soldiers to go without sleep for weeks at a time. With what might be considered shades of Dr. Strangelove, DARPA described its goal: "Eliminating the need for sleep while maintaining the high level of both cognitive and physical performance of the individual will create a fundamental change in war-fighting and force employment."

Among the researchers who received one of the grants from DARPA is Jerome Siegel, a leading neurobiological researcher at the

University of California at Los Angeles. Siegel was one of the researchers who recently discovered that narcolepsy is caused by the lack of a specific type of brain cell containing a chemical called hypocretin. He is also an expert in the sleep patterns of various species of animals, and the research he's doing for DARPA is designed to gain more information on dolphins' unusual sleep patterns. Because dolphins must surface periodically to get oxygen and also must remain in motion continuously, only one hemisphere of their brain sleeps at a time. The right hemisphere is in the sleep phase for about a two-hour stretch, and then it shifts to high-level waking activation while the left hemisphere drifts into its sleep period. Throughout all cycles, the dolphin maintains its normal behavior. "We're trying to understand the unihemispheric sleep patterns in dolphins to see whether they can be induced by drugs in humans," says Siegel. While both hemispheres of the brain are never asleep at the same time in dolphins, they can both be in the awake phase at the same time because these marine mammals sometimes go without sleep at all for at least two weeks at a stretch—the time period Siegel says is the military's minimum goal for soldiers to be able to function without sleep. "This is a normal part of dolphin behavior and it has no negative effect for them, so we're investigating that also," he explains. In related research for the military agency, other scientists are studying how some birds are able to migrate over long periods without sleep or to actually sleep while they are flying, he says.

Yet another DARPA-funded project is designed to find the elusive answer to the question of the precise purpose sleep serves in the first place. Chiara Cirelli, a researcher at the University of Wisconsin at Madison, is studying what happens during sleep on a molecular level, identifying which genes are associated with sleep or affected by sleep deprivation. "Only in the last ten years have we had the technology to screen thousands of genes at one time, and that's what makes our studies possible," she explains. The military is funding Cirelli's molecular studies in fruit flies to determine whether mutating genes can affect the organisms' need for sleep. Also, she has been examining the effects of sleep deprivation on rats' brains at the molecular level. Initial results reveal that there is only one gene whose expression is caused by long-term sleep deprivation, and it is one that is involved in balancing levels of neurotransmitters such as dopamine, norepinephrine, and serotonin. Being awake nonstop keeps these brain chemicals circulating in the brain in high concentrations continually rather than being shut off periodically as the brain moves through its various sleep stages. Her research thus far suggests an interesting hypothesis. "It may be that an important part of sleep's function is to give the brain a break from neurotransmitters that are predominant in waking hours. Having them around at high levels all of the time could somehow be toxic to neurons," she says.

It is, of course, the dramatic shift in these neurotransmitter levels that helps create the physiological conditions that make dreaming possible. So developing a drug or some other mechanism that allows us to do without sleep for extended stretches would also wipe out our dreams. It remains to be seen how going without dreaming for any extended period would affect our lives, but given what we now know about its role in our physical, emotional, and cognitive well-being, it's difficult to imagine that our experience of the world would remain as rich.

Future research will undoubtedly fill in the remaining pieces of the puzzle, teasing out exactly how the higher levels of the forebrain participate in dreaming and how the dream scripts are constructed. But the most exciting research frontier ahead will likely use dreaming studies to further understand how the mind works in waking. We know now that we can harness our cognitive powers to become both participants and observers while dreams are still in progress, which lets us eavesdrop on the brain while it's talking to itself. Understanding more about the lucid-dreaming process could help answer questions about the very nature of consciousness.

Thanks to those who are in the forefront of the quest to comprehend those larger questions about how brain becomes mind, we are now seeing that even when we are interacting with the "real" world in waking hours, our experience actually occurs not "out there" but within the brain itself, just as it does in dreams. The ultimate reality show we partake of during waking life is often—like dreaming—a con job beautifully carried out by neural circuitry of astonishing complexity. A half century of dream research has demonstrated that dreaming is a rich form of consciousness that we should prize no less than we do our experience of the world in waking hours. As science shines ever more light on dreaming and the other inner workings of the brain that make us who we are, it can only serve to increase our sense of awe at nature's brilliant design.

Acknowledgments

I COULD NOT HAVE WRITTEN THIS BOOK without the cooperation of many scientists who helped give me a crash course in neuroscience, as well as elucidating their own specific areas of research. Several of them opened their labs to me as either a test subject or an observer, shared wonderful historical material on dream research, or reviewed drafts of chapters for scientific accuracy. Especially generous with their time were John Antrobus, Allen Braun, Rosalind Cartwright, Deirdre Barrett, Bill Domhoff, David Foulkes, Allan Hobson, Christof Koch, Stephen LaBerge, Eric Nofzinger, Al Rechtschaffen, Jerry Siegel, Bob Stickgold, Carlyle Smith, Mark Solms, and Matt Wilson.

Not only has Amanda Cook at Basic Books been incredibly supportive emotionally all along the way, but her intelligent, perceptive contributions in shaping the manuscript epitomize what every writer dreams of but all too rarely finds in an editor. Michael Carlisle deserves full credit for putting the idea of writing a book in my head in the first place and helping me incubate ideas, while Michelle Tessler has been the crucial other half of my agent team, expertly guiding the project from concept to reality.

During stressful times especially, life works because of friends and family. Immeasurable thanks to Fay for providing me with a writing retreat and sustenance in all ways; to Steve for being the writing maestro and spirit booster who's always in my corner; to Joy and Scott for giving invaluable advice and cheerfully sharing child care duties so that I could travel for research; and to my family members in West Virginia and Pennsylvania for their support on all levels. My sons, Adam and Chad, were remarkably patient in giving me uninterrupted hours at the computer night after night. Having to sacrifice time with them made me appreciate even more the joy they bring me when we are together. Finally, deepest appreciation to Anton, who has been my indispensable partner in this project from the outset and who makes waking life more delightful than any dream I could imagine.

Notes

Preface

vii Feynman, from *The Pleasure of Finding Things Out*, pp. 226–227.

ix. Ancient history of dreaming, from Robert Van de Castle's *Our Dreaming Mind*, pp. 47–65; Aristotle's quote from Kramer's "Hall! Like Gaul."

xi. Quote about impressions from earliest years of life from Domhoff, excerpting Freud's *Interpretation of Dreams* (1900); Freudian interpretation of wolves dream, from Gay's *Freud: A Life for Our Time*, pp. 286–290.

xi. Jung, from Domhoff's *The Scientific Study of Dreams*, pp. 144–147, and from Van de Castle's *Our Dreaming Mind*. pp. 147–170.

xiii. Domhoff quote from "The 'Purpose' of Dreams," unpublished article, 1999, available at http://dreamreasearch.net.

xiv. Luce quote from *Current Research on Sleep and Dreams*.

Chapter 1: Rockettes, EEGs, and Banana Cream Pie

1 Opening quote from *The Sleepwatchers*, pp. 104–105.

1 Biographical details on Aserinsky, from Armond Aserinsky interview and from "Memories of Famous Neuropsychologists."

2 Kleitman, first and only man to devote entire career, from Dement's *The Sleepwatchers*, p. 22; in Mammoth Cave, from Luce's *Current Research on Sleep and Dreams*.

3 Description of Kleitman, from Aserinsky's "Memories of Famous Neuropsychologist."

4. Golden manure theory, from Aserinsky's "This Week's Citation Classic"; "What lay ahead," from Aserinsky's "Memories."

5 Belief that brain is turned off, from Dement's *The Sleepwatchers*, pp. 22–23.

6. Crusade led almost single-handedly, from Foulkes's "Sleep and Dreams."

6 Dement-Kleitman meeting from Dement's *The Sleepwatchers*, p. 26.

6. Aserinsky's new job, etc., from Armond Aserinsky interview.

7 Dement on his lab days; Freud and schizophrenic studies, from Dement's *The Sleepwatchers.*

8 Sleep cycle details, from Dement's *The Sleepwatchers,* Rechtschaffen's "Current Perspectives on the Function of Sleep" and Shafton's *Dream Reader.*

8 Female genitals engorged and male erections, from Solms and Turnbull's *The Brain and the Inner World,* p. 183.

8 Dream recall in REM and non-REM, from Rechtschaffen and Siegel's "Sleep and Dreaming."

9 Dement and the Rockettes, from *The Sleepwatchers,* pp. 139–140.

9 Dream research funding in 1960s, from Foulkes's *Sleep and Dreams: Dream Research.*

10 Could dream content be manipulated? from Domhoff's *The Scientific Study of Dreams* and from Rechtschaffen and Siegel's "Sleep and Dreaming"; dream recall and progression of dreams in night, from Luce's *Current Research on Sleep and Dreams,* pp. 96–97.

11 Eye movements not related to dream content, from Foulkes's "Sleep and Dreams: Dream Research."

11 Visual quality more prevalent than other senses and nearly the same as in waking, from Schwartz's "A Historical Loop."

11 Visual experiments with eyes taped open and other details of events in Rechtschaffen lab, from Allan Rechtschaffen interview.

12 Black-and-white versus color dreams, from Schwitzgebel's "Why Did We Think We Dreamed in Black and White?"

13 Sleep deprivation in rats, from Rechtschaffen and Siegel's "Sleep and Dreaming."

13 Fatal familial insomnia, from "To Sleep No More," *New York Times Sunday Magazine,* May 6, 2001.

14 Sleep changes with age, from Dement's *The Sleepwatchers.*

14 Sleep in animals, from Rechtschaffen and Siegel's "Sleep and Dreaming" and from Rechtschaffen interview.

15 Jouvet's study of REM deprivation in cats, from Luce's *Current Research on Sleep and Dreams,* pp. 71–72; cats stalking prey for up to three minutes, from Jouvet's "Paradoxical Sleep."

Chapter 2: The Anti-Freud

17 Hobson biographical information, accounts of research, and quotes, from interviews, as well as from Hobson and McCarley's "The Brain as a Dream State Generator."

19 Jouvet quote, from *The Paradox of Sleep,* p. 5.

28 Foulkes information from interview and from Foulkes's "Dream Reports from Different States of Sleep," Foulkes and Vogel's "Mental Activity at Sleep Onset," Foulkes's *The Psychology of Sleep*, and Foulkes, Spear, and Symonds's "Individual Differences in Mental Activity at Sleep Onset." Non-REM dream reports, more than 50 percent, from Foulkes's "Dream Reports from Different States of Sleep"; sleep onset, up to 70 percent, from Foulkes's *The Psychology of Sleep* and Foulkes and Vogel's "Mental Activity at Sleep Onset";

29 Example of REM and non-REM dreams, from Rechtschaffen, Vogel, and Shaikun's "Interrelatedness of Mental Activity during Sleep" and from David Foulkes's *The Psychology of Sleep*, pp. 129–130.

31 Foulkes on children's dreams and dream reports, from interview.

34 Harvard study on children's dreams, from Resnick, Stickgold, Rittenhouse, and Hobson's "Self-Representation and Bizarreness in Children's Dream Reports."

36 Dreams of the blind, from interviews with David Foulkes and Ray Rainville.

36 Ray Rainville's account of his own dreaming, from interview and "The Role of Dreams in the Rehabilitation of the Adventitiously Blind."

36–40 Domhoff quote, from interview; Antrobus quote, from interview.

Chapter 3: Experiments of Nature

41 Opening quote from Braun's "The New Neuropsychology of Sleep: Commentary," in Nersessian and Solms's *Neuropsychoanalysis*, p. 201.

41 Account of Solms's research, from interview.

46 Dopamine associated with drugs, thrill seeking, from Friedman's "Bored with Drugs, Sex and Rock (Climbing)?"

48 Patient who couldn't distinguish dreams from reality, from Solms's *The Neuropsychology of Dreams*, pp. 185–186.

49 Three states quote and at least 80 percent of awakenings in REM produce dream reports, from Solms and Turnbull's *The Brain and the Inner World*, pp. 183 and 196.

49 Braun-Balkin account, from interview and also from Braun's "New Neuropsychology of Sleep: Commentary."

51. Comparison of dreaming to schizophrenic delusion, from Solms and Turnbull's *The Brain and the Inner World*, p. 213.

52 Maquet reference, from "Functional Neuroanatomy."

51 Hobson's response, from Nersessian and Solms's *Neuropsychoanalysis*, pp. 158–166, and interview.

56 Hobson's stroke etc., from interview and from draft of his unpublished paper on the subject; "dreams are dripping," from Hobson interview.

Chapter 4: The Lesson of the Spiny Anteater

61 Opening quote Winson interview.

61 Domhoff quotes and dream content statistics, from interview and various content analysis studies.

63 Majority of REM dreams have motion, from Porte and Hobson's "Physical Motion in Dreams."

63 95 percent of male college students, from Dement's *The Sleepwatchers*, p. 126.

63 Other studies of dream content, from Rainville, *Dreams across the Lifespan*, p. 101.

65 Dorothea's and Mark's dream accounts, from Domhoff's *The Scientific Study of Dreams*.

65 Other studies of elderly people's dreams, from Barad, Altshuler, and Goldfarb's "A Survey of Dreams in Aged Persons," p. 420.

66 Hall quotes, from "A Cognitive Theory of Dreams."

66 Strauch, from Strauch and Lederbogen's "The Home Dreams and Waking Fantasies."

67 Lakoff, from "How Metaphor Structures Dreams."

67 Canadian students, from Nielsen interview.

68 Winson, from interview; wheelbarrow quote, from Winson's *Brain and Psyche*, p. 204; second quote, from *Brain and Psyche*, p. 209.

69 Spiny anteater has intermediate sleep between REM and non-REM, from J. Siegel's "The Evolution of REM Sleep." Because the platypus, also a monotreme, does experience REM, as do birds, Siegel contends REM may have been present in reptiles, though studies to date have not been able to detect this sleep state in any reptilian form.

70 Material on Jouvet's theory of REM's function, evolution of non-REM sleep and temperature regulation, etc., from LaBerge's *Lucid Dreaming*.

70 Jouvet and amount of REM sleep in womb, from Shafton's *Dream Reader*.

70 Animal and infant REM, from J. Siegel interview and Rechtschaffen and Siegel's "Sleep and Dreaming"; premature infants and elderly REM proportions, from Luce, *Current Research*, p. 92; sleep patterns in prey versus predators, from Jouvet's *The Paradox of Sleep*, p. 45.

71 Revonsuo, from "The Reinterpretation of Dreams."

74 Reading seldom appears, from Hartmann's "We Do Not Dream of the 3R's."

75 Panskepp, from *Affective Neuroscience*, p. 135.

Chapter 5: Rerunning the Maze

77 Opening quote, from States interview.

77 Matthew Wilson information, based on interview and Louie and Wilson's "Temporally Structured Reply of Awake Hippocampal Activity during Rapid Eye Movement Sleep."

80 Crick and Mitchison, from "The Function of Dream Sleep."

80 Description of types of memory, etc., from Peigneux, Laureys, Delbeuck, and Maquet's "Sleeping Brain, Learning Brain."

81 Evidence from patients suffering memory loss, from Solms and Turnbull's *The Brain and the Inner World*, p. 142.

82 LeDoux, from *Synaptic Self*, pp. 117 and 133.

83 Damasio, from *The Feeling of What Happens*, p. 220.

84 "We remember only what we have encoded," from Schacter's *Searching for Memory*, p. 52; subsequent quotes, from p. 5; quote about Proust, from p. 28.

84 Memories that are linked to strong emotions and Joseph LeDoux quote, from LeDoux's *Synaptic Self*, pp. 203 and 222; information on cortisol's effect on memory, pp. 223–224.

85 Flanagan dream, from *Dreaming Souls*, pp. 7–13.

86 Damasio quote, from *The Feeling of What Happens*, p. 196.

87 Schacter quote, from "Memory Consolidation during Sleep," in *Searching for Memory*, p. 88.

87 Red goggles experiment, from Winson's *Brain and Psyche*, p. 210.

88 Stickgold, from interview and "Visual Discrimination Learning" and "Sleep, Learning and Dreams: Off-Line Memory Reprocessing."

92 Episodic memory experiment, from M. Fosse, R. Fosse, Hobson, and Stickgold's "Dreaming and Episodic Memory."

92 Only half contain day residue, from Domhoff's *The Scientific Study of Dreams*, p. 136.

92 Nielsen, from interview.

93 Margoliash, from interview.

95 Smith, from interview.

96 Stage II study at Harvard, from Walker's "Practice, with Sleep, Makes Perfect."

96 Description of SWS and REM sleep stages, from Peigneux et al.'s "Sleeping Brain, Learning Brain," pp. A111–A112.

96 Karni and Sagi study (1994) and replications of it, from Stickgold's "Visual Discrimination Learning Requires Sleep after Training" and from Gais's "Early Sleep Triggers Memory."

97 Pavlides material, from interview and "Induction of Hippocampal Long-Term Potentiation."

97 Napping study, from Walker's "Practice, with Sleep, Makes Perfect"; information on Israeli subject and antidepressants, from Siegel and Smith interviews.

99 Maquet material, from interview.

Chapter 6: Nocturnal Therapy

101 Opening quote and other biographical details, from Cartwright interview.

103 Several studies concur two-thirds of dream emotions negative, from Nielsen, et al.'s "Emotions in Dream and Waking Event Reports."

103 1966 and 1996 study information, from Revonsuo's "The Reinterpretation of Dreams."

103 Joy/elation most prevalent in Norway study, from Fosse, Stickgold, and Hobson's "The Mind in REM Sleep."

104 Maquet concludes that this interplay reflects processing of emotional memory, from Peigneux, Laureys, Delbeuck, and Maquet's "Sleeping Brain, Learning Brain."

105 Other researchers found childhood dreams later in night, from Luce, *Current Research*, p. 97.

106 Results on first twelve subjects—nine recovered and three didn't—from Cartwright interview, citing results of Cartwright, Newell, and Mercer's "Dream Incorporation of a Sentinel Life Event and Its Relation to Waking Adaptation."

107 Cartwright subjects' dream reports, from interview.

107 Recall of drinking dreams, from Schnedl's "Dream Recall."

109 Nofzinger material, from interview.

110 Crick speculates, from *The Astonishing Hypothesis*, pp. 267–268.

112 Joe Griffin quote, from Kiser's "The Dreamcatcher."

112 Hartmann, from his "Outline for a Theory on the Nature and Functions of Dreaming" and Hartmann, Zborowski, and Kunzendorf's "The Emotion Pictured by a Dream."

115 Barrett's air traffic controller example, from interview.

115 Parasol example, from interview.

116 About one-quarter have post-traumatic stress disorder, from Pagel's "Nightmares and Disorders of Dreaming."

116 Vietnam vet's dream, from Hartmann's "Nightmare after Trauma as Paradigm for All Dreams," p. 226.

118 Several studies over the past decade, from Revonsuo's "The Reinterpretation of Dreams."

118 Rehearsing positive ending to nightmares once a day, etc., from Schredl's "Dream Recall."

118 Cartwright on analyzing dreams during waking, from interview.

118 Cartwright on rehearsing new ending, from interview.

119 Dream recall—adults remember less than 1 percent per night—from Domhoff interview. One to two per week and other information on high recallers versus low, from Schredl's "Dream Recall."

119 Suggestions on improving recall, from interviews with Hobson, Stickgold, Barrett, LaBerge, and Cartwright and from Schredl's "Dream Recall."

Chapter 7: The Ultimate Spin Doctor

121 Opening quote from Stickgold interview.

121 Antrobus, from interview.

124 Right/left brain specializations, from "How the Brain and Body Communicate: Specialization of the Two Hemispheres," www.macalester.edu.

124 Gazzaniga information, from *The Mind's Past*, pp. 118–135, 151, and 174.

127 Settings most often incongruous, from Revonsuo's "A Content Analysis of Bizarre Elements in Dreams."

127 Hartmann, from "Outline for a Theory."

128 Restraints on transformations, from Rittenhouse, Stickgold, and Hobson's *Constraint on the Transformation of Characters, Objects, and Settings.*

128 Barb Sanders' dream data from Domhoff interview.

129 Delboeuf and Schwartz, from Schwartz's "A Historical Loop" and Schwartz interview.

130 Artemidorus and statistics on Freudian symbols, from Hall's "A Cognitive Theory of Dreams" and from Van de Castle's *Our Dreaming Mind.*

131 Faraday pun and Kilroe comments on punning, from Kilroe's *The Dream Pun.*

131 Sexual symbols, from Hall's "A Cognitive Theory of Dreams."

131 Solms says Freud may have been wrong, from Solms and Turnbull's *The Brain and the Inner World*, p. 215.

132 Hobson on Freud and record of his Jouvet dream, from Hobson's *Dreaming*, pp. 149–155.

134 LaBerge, from interview.

Chapter 8: Creative Chaos

135 Opening quote from Barrett's *The Committee of Sleep* and other Barrett quotes, from interview.

135 McCartney, Howe, and Horowitz, from Barrett's *The Committee of Sleep.*

136 Chang and allergy drug, from Pollack's "Wrangling May Delay Peanut Allergy Drug."

137 Shepard dream, from Shepard and Hut, "My Experience, Your Experience"; other material from Shepard interview.

139 Newman, from interview.

140 Nicklaus, from *San Francisco Chronicle*, June 27, 1964.

140 Hurxthal, from interview.

141 Dement study results and H_2O example from Barrett's *Committee of Sleep*.

142 Stickgold from interview.

142 Dreams and chaos theory, from Kahn's "Self-Organization Theory of Dreaming."

143Carroll, from "Doctors Look Ahead to 'Pacemakers for the Brain.'"

144 Bert States from interview and *Seeing in the Dark*.

146 Pagel information, from interview.

147 Bunuel's information, from Barrett's *Committee of Sleep*; quotes for Fellini, Cocteau, and Bergman and dream palaces reference, from Pagel, Kwiatkowski, and Bryoles's "Dream Use in Film Making."

Chapter 9: Altered States

149 LaBerge, from interview.

152 Tibetan Buddhists using dream yoga and European history, from LaBerge interview; Aristotle, from Shafton's *Dream Reader*, p. 431.

153 Friday the 13th experiment, from LaBerge's *Lucid Dreaming*, pp.76–70

154 Dement quote and information, from Dement's *The Sleepwatchers*, pp. 127–128.

154 Hyannis Port meeting from Van de Castle's *Our Dreaming Mind*.

155 Keith Hearne, from Foulkes's "Sleep and Dreams" and from LaBerge interview.

156 Effectiveness of Nova Dreamer, from LaBerge and Levitan's "Validity Established of Dreamlight Cues."

156 LaBerge-Dement breathing study, 1982 study, cited in LaBerge's *Lucid Dreaming*.

157 Surveys on how many have lucid dreams, from R. Gruber, Steffen, and Vonderhaar's "Lucid Dreaming, Waking Personality and Cognitive Development."

157 How long LDs last, from LaBerge interview.

157 Characteristics of frequent LDers from Snyder, Thomas, Gacken-

bach, and Jayne's "Individual Differences Associated with Lucid Dreaming, in Gackenback and LaBerge's *Conscious Mind, Sleeping Brain,* and from Shafton's *Dream Reader,* pp. 450–451.

157 Antrobus and Nielsen, from interviews.

158 Lucid dream examples, from LaBerge's *Exploring the World of Lucid Dreaming* (Everett dreamer, pp. 149–150; Chicago dreamer, pp. 154–155).

160 One-quarter don't control dream, from Shafton's *Dream Reader,* p. 447.

160 Lucid dreaming and sexuality, from LaBerge interview.

164 New York design engineer from interview.

165 Parking lot dream, from Lucid Dreaming Guild for the Physically Challenged Web site, http://www.geocites.com/lucidguild.

165 Piet Hut dream from Shepard and Hut's "My Experience, Your Experience."

166 Jouvet, from *The Paradox of Sleep,* p. 75.

167 Hobson and Rechtschaffen, from interviews.

169 LaBerge bridge dream and Buddhist perspective, from LaBerge interview.

Chapter 10: Consciousness and Beyond

173 Opening quote and other Koch material, from interviews.

175 Crick, the The Astonishing Hypothesis, p.3

179 Czerner, from interviews.

181 Dennett, from *Consciousness Explained.*

181 Solms on visual hierarchy, from Solms and Turnbull's *The Brain and the Inner World,* p. 209.

182 Information on cats and horizontal line experiment, from Solms and Turnbull's *The Brain and the Inner World,* p. 154.

183 Percentage of activity outside conscious awareness, from Gazzaniga's *The Mind's Past,* pp. 23–25; 95 percent figure, from Solms and Turnbull's *The Brain and the Inner World,* p. 84.

183 Hobson, from interviews.

183 Libet on half-second delay in sensation, from Winson's *Brain and Psyche,* p. 234; Libet on 350-millisecond time lag, from Gazzaniga's *The Mind's Past,* p. 73–74.

184 Christopher Reeve information from Associated Press, Dec. 10, 2002.

184 Autism information, from Blakeslee's "A Boy, a Mother and a Rare Map."

Epilogue

187 Parable, the Blind Men and the Elephant, in public domain.

189 Dreams like poems, from LaBerge interview.

190 Dement, from *The Sleepwatchers*, pp. 37–38.

190 Dinges quote from Brown's "The Man Who Mistook His Wife for a Deer."

191 Ed Pace-Schott, from interview.

191 Rosalind Cartwright on REM sleep behavior disorder and Suzanne Stevens, from interview; other information on parasomniacs, from Brown's "The Man Who Mistook His Wife for a Deer" and Goode's "When the Brain Disrupts the Night."

195 Link between Parkinson's and use of SSRIs and REM sleep behavior disorder, from Hobson's *Dreaming*, pp. 96–97; eye movements persisting for six months, from Pace-Schott interview; Mahowald, from Goode's "When the Brain Disrupts the Night."

195 Revonsuo, from "A Content Analysis of Bizarre Elements in Dreams."

196 Schwartz on new research, from interview.

197 Solms on new research, from interview.

197 DARPA, from J. Siegel interview and from Groopman's "Eyes Wide Open."

198 Cirelli, from interview.

Bibliography

Aserinsky, E. "Memories of Famous Neuropsychologists: The Discovery of REM Sleep." *Journal of the History of the Neurosciences* 5:3 (1996), pp. 213–227.

Aserinsky, E. "This Week's Citation Classic." *ISI Current Contents* 45 (Nov. 9, 1987).

Barad, M., K. Altshuler, and A. Goldfarb. "A Survey of Dreams in Aged Persons." *Archives of General Psychiatry* 4 (1961), pp. 419–423.

Barrett, D. *The Committee of Sleep: How Artists, Scientists and Athletes Use Dreams for Creative Problem-Solving—And How You Can Too.* Crown Publishers, 2001.

Blakeslee, S. "A Boy, a Mother and a Rare Map of Autism's World." *New York Times,* Nov. 19, 2002.

Brown, C. "The Man Who Mistook His Wife for a Deer." *New York Times,* Feb. 2, 2003.

Buzsaki, G. "The Hippocamp-Neocortical Dialogue." *Cerebral Cortex* 6 (1996), pp. 81–92.

Carroll, L. "Doctors Look Ahead to 'Pacemakers for the Brain.'" *New York Times,* Feb. 18, 2003.

Cartwright, R., P. Newell, and P. Mercer. "Dream Incorporation of a Sentinel Life Event and Its Relation to Walking Adaptation." *Sleep and Hypnosis* 3:1 (2001), pp. 25–32.

Crick, F., *The Astonishing Hypothesis: The Scientific Search for the Soul.* Touchstone, 1994.

Crick, F., and G. Mitchison. "The Function of Dream Sleep." *Nature* 304 (1983), pp. 11–114.

Crick, F., and G. Mitchison. "REM Sleep and Neural Nets." *Journal of Mind and Behavior* 7 (1986), pp. 229–250.

Czerner, T. *What Makes You Tick? The Brain in Plain English.* John Wiley & Sons, 2001.

Damasio, A. *The Feeling of What Happens.* Harcourt, Brace, 1999.

Dement, W. *The Sleepwatchers,* 2nd ed. Nychthemeron Press, 1996.

Dennett, D. C. *Consciousness Explained.* Little Brown, 1991.

Domhoff, G. W. *The Scientific Study of Dreams: Neural Networks, Cognitive Development and Content Analysis.* American Psychological Association, 2003.

Feynman, R. *The Pleasure of Finding Things Out.* Perseus Publishing, Helix Books, 1999.

Flanagan, O. *Dreaming Souls: Sleep, Dreams and the Evolution of the Conscious Mind.* Oxford University Press, 2000.

Fosse, M., R. Fosse, J. A. Hobson, and R. Stickgold. "Dreaming and Episodic Memory: A Functional Dissociation?" *Journal of Cognitive Neuroscience* 15:1 (2003), pp. 1–9.

Fosse, R., R. Stickgold, and J. A. Hobson. "The Mind in REM Sleep: Reports of Emotional Experience." *Sleep* 24:8 (2001), pp. 947–955.

Foulkes, D. *Children's Dreaming and the Development of Consciousness.* Harvard University Press, 1999.

———. "Dream Reports from Different States of Sleep." *Journal of Abnormal and Social Psychology* 65 (1962), pp. 14–25.

———. *The Psychology of Sleep.* Charles Scribner's Sons, 1966.

———. "Sleep and Dreams: Dream Research, 1953–1993." *Sleep* 19:8 (1996), pp. 609–624.

Foulkes, D., P. Spear, and J. Symonds. "Individual Differences in Mental Activity at Sleep Onset." *Journal of Abnormal Psychology* 71 (1966), pp. 280–286.

Foulkes, D., and G. Vogel. "Mental Activity at Sleep Onset." *Journal of Abnormal Psychology* 70 (1965), pp. 231–243.

Friedman, R. A. "Bored with Drugs, Sex and Rock (Climbing)? Try 'Flow.'" *New York Times,* June 3, 2003.

Gackenbach, J., and S. LaBerge, eds. *Conscious Mind, Sleeping Brain: Perspectives on Lucid Dreaming.* Plenum Press, 1988.

Gais, S. "Early Sleep Triggers Memory for Early Visual Discrimination Skills." *Nature Neuroscience* 3:12 (2000), pp. 1335–1339.

Garfield, P. *The Universal Dream Key: The 12 Most Common Dream Themes around the World.* Cliff Street Books, 2001.

Gay, P. *Freud: A Life for Our Time,* W. W. Norton, 1988.

Gazzaniga, M. *The Mind's Past.* University of California Press, 2000.

Goode, E. "When the Brain Disrupts the Night." *New York Times,* Jan. 7, 2003.

Groopman, J. "Eyes Wide Open." *New Yorker,* Dec. 3, 2001.

Gruber, R., J. Steffen, and S. Vonderhaar. "Lucid Dreaming, Waking Personality and Cognitive Development." *Dreaming* 5:1 (1995), pp. 1–11.

Hall, C. S. "A Cognitive Theory of Dreams." *The Journal of General Psychology* 49 (1953), pp. 273–282.

———. *The Individual and His Dreams.* New American Library, 1972.

———. *The Meaning of Dreams*. McGraw-Hill, 1953.

Hall, C. S., G. W. Domhoff, K. A. Blick, and K. E. Weesner. "The Dreams of College Men and Women in 1950 and 1980." *Sleep* 5 (1982), pp. 188–194.

Hall, C. S., and R. L. Van de Castle. *The Content Analysis of Dreams*. Appleton-Century-Crofts, 1966.

Hartmann, E. "Nightmare after Trauma as Paradigm for All Dreams." *Psychiatry* 61 (1998), pp. 223–238.

———. "Outline for a Theory on the Nature and Functions of Dreaming." *Dreaming* 6:2 (1996), pp. 147–170.

———. "We Do Not Dream of the 3 R's: Implications for the Nature of Dreaming Mentation." *Dreaming* 10:2. (2000), pp. 103–110.

Hartmann, E., M. Zborowski, and R. Kunzendorf, R. "The Emotion Pictured by a Dream: An Examination of Emotions Contextualized in Dreams." *Sleep and Hypnosis* 3:1 (2001), pp. 33–43.

Hobson, J. A. *Dreaming: An Introduction to the Science of Sleep*. Oxford University Press, 2002.

Hobson, J. A., and R. McCarley. "The Brain as a Dream State Generator: An Activation-Synthesis Hypothesis." *American Journal of Psychiatry* 134 (1977), pp. 1335–1348.

Jouvet, M. "Paradoxical Sleep and the Nature-Nurture Controversy." *Progress in Brain Research* 53 (1980), pp. 331–346.

———. *The Paradox of Sleep: The Story of Dreaming*. A Bradford Book, MIT Press, 1999.

Kahan, T., S. LaBerge, L. Levitan, and P. Zimbardo. "Similarities and Differences between Dreaming and Waking Cognition: An Exploratory Study." *Consciousness and Cognition* 6 (1997), pp. 132–147.

Kahn, D., and J. A. Hobson. "Self-Organization Theory of Dreaming." *Dreaming* 3:3 (1993), pp. 151–178.

Karni, A., B. Tanne, J. Rubenstin, J. M. Askenasy, and D. Sagi. "Dependence on REM Sleep of Overnight Improvement of a Perceptual Skill." *Science* 265 (1994), pp. 679–682.

Kantrowitz, B. "In Search of Sleep." *Newsweek*, July 15, 2002.

Kilroe, P. A. "The Dream Pun: What Is a Play on Words Without Words?" *Dreaming* 10:4 (2000), pp. 193–209.

Kiser, B. "The Dreamcatcher." *New Scientist*, April 12, 2003.

Kramer, M., "Hall! Like Gaul, Dreams Are Divided into Three Provinces." *Dreaming* 1:1 (1991), pp. 103–105.

LaBerge, S. "Psychophysiological Studies of Consciousness during REM Sleep" in R. R. Bootzen, J. F. Kihlstrom, and D. L. Schacter, eds., *Sleep and Cognition*. American Psychological Association, 1990 (pp. 109–126).

———. *Lucid Dreaming: An Exploratory Study of Consciousness during Sleep*. Doctoral dissertation, Stanford University, 1980 (University Microfilms International No. 80–24,691).

———. "Lucid Dreaming as a Learnable Skill: A Case Study." *Perceptual and Motor Skills* 51 (1980), pp. 1039–1042.

———. "Induction of Lucid Dreams." *Sleep Research* 9 (1980), p. 138.

———. *Lucid Dreaming*. J. P. Tarcher, 1985.

LaBerge, S., and W. C. Dement. "Voluntary Control of Respiration during REM Sleep." *Sleep Research* 11 (1982), p. 107.

LaBerge, S., W. Greenleaf, and B. Kedzierski. "Physiological Responses to Dreamed Sexual Activity during Lucid REM Sleep." *Psychophysiology* 20 (1983), pp. 454–455.

LaBerge, S., L. Levitan, and W. C. Dement. "Lucid Dreaming: Physiological Correlates of Consciousness during REM Sleep." *Journal of Mind and Behavior* 7 (1986), pp. 251–258.

LaBerge, S., and L. Levitan. "Validity Established of Dreamlight Cues for Eliciting Lucid Dreaming." *Dreaming* 5:3 (1995).

LaBerge, S., and H. Rheingold. *Exploring the World of Lucid Dreaming*. Ballantine, 1990.

Lakoff, G. "How Metaphor Structures Dreams: The Theory of Conceptual Metaphor Applied to Dream Analysis." *Dreaming* 3:2 (1993), 77–98.

LeDoux, J. *Synaptic Self: How Our Brains Become Who We Are*. Viking, 2002.

Louie, K., and M. A. Wilson. "Temporally Structured Replay of Awake Hippocampal Ensemble Activity during Rapid Eye Movement Sleep." *Neuron* 29 (2001), pp. 145–156.

Luce, G. G., with J. Segal and D. McGinty. *Current Research on Sleep and Dreams*. U.S. Department of Health Education and Welfare, National Institute of Mental Health, 1965.

Maquet, P., J. Peters, J. Aerts, G. Delfiore, C. Degueldre, A. Luxen, and G. Franck. "Functional Neuroanatomy of Human Rapid-Eye-Movement Sleep and Dreaming." *Nature* 383 (1996), pp. 163–166.

McClelland, J., B. McNaughton, and R. O'Reilly. "Why There Are Complementary Learning Systems in the Hippocampus and Neocortex: Insights from the Successes and Failures of Connectionist Models of Learning and Memory." *Psychological Review* 102:3 (1995), pp. 419–457.

Nersessian, E., and M. Solms, eds. *Neuropsychoanalysis*, vol. 1, no. 2. 1999.

Nielsen, T. A., D. Deslauriers, and G. Baylor. "Emotions in Dream and Waking Event Reports." *Dreaming* 1:4 (1991), pp. 287–300.

Pagel, J. F. *Nightmares and Disorders of Dreaming*. American Academy of Physicians, n.d.

Pagel, J. F., C. Kwiatkowski, and K. E. Bryoles. "Dream Use in Film Making." *Dreaming* 9:4 (1999), pp. 247–256.

Panksepp, J. *Affective Neuroscience: The Foundations of Human and Animal Emotions*. Oxford University Press, 1998.

Peigneux, P., S. Laureys, X. Delbeuck, and P. Maquet. "Sleeping Brain, Learning Brain." *NeuroReport* 12:18 (2001), pp. A111–A124.

Pollack, A. "Wrangling May Delay Peanut Allergy Drug." *New York Times*, March 11, 2003.

Rainville, R. E. "The Role of Dreams in the Rehabilitation of the Adventitiously Blind." *Dreaming* 4:3 (1994), pp. 155–164.

Rechtschaffen, A. "Current Perspectives on the Function of Sleep." *Perspectives in Biology and Medicine* 41:3 (spring 1998).

Rechtschaffen, A., and J. Siegel. "Sleep and Dreaming" in E. R. Kandel, J. H. Scwartz, and T. M. Jessel, eds., *Principles of Neuroscience*. 4th ed. McGraw-Hill, 2000 (pp. 936–947).

Rechtschaffen, A., G. Vogel, and G. Shaikun. "Interrelatedness of Mental Activity during Sleep." *Archives of General Psychiatry* 9 (1963), pp. 536–547.

Resnick, J., R. Stickgold, C. Rittenhouse, J. A. Hobson. "Self-Representation and Bizarreness in Children's Dream Reports Collected in the Home Setting." *Consciousness and Cognition* 3 (1994), pp. 30–45.

Revonsuo, A. "A Content Analysis of Bizarre Elements in Dreams." *Dreaming* 5:3 (1995), pp. 169–186.

———. "The Reinterpretation of Dreams: An Evolutionary Hypothesis of the Function of Dreaming." *Behavioral and Brain Sciences* 23:6 (Dec. 2000), pp. 877-901.

Ribeiro, S., C. Mello, T. Velho, T. Gardner, E. Jarvis, and C. Pavlides. "Induction of Hippocampal Long-Term Potentiation during Waking Leads to Increased Hippocampal zif-268 Expression during Ensuing Rapid Eye-Movement Sleep." *Journal of Neuroscience* 22:24 (2002), pp. 10914–10923.

Rittenhouse, C. D., R. Stickgold, and J. A. Hobson. "Constraint on the Transformation of Characters, Objects, and Settings in Dream Reports." *Consciousness and Cognition* 3 (1994), pp. 100–113.

Schacter, D. *Searching for Memory: The Brain, the Mind and the Past.* Basic Books, 1996.

Schredl, M. "Dream Recall: Research, Clinical Implications and Future Directions." *Sleep and Hypnosis* 1 (1999), pp. 72–81.

Schwartz, S. "A Historical Loop of One Hundred Years: Similarities between 19th Century and Contemporary Dream Research." *Dreaming* 10 (2000), pp. 55–60.

Schwitzgebel, E. "Why Did We Think We Dreamed in Black and White?" *Studies in the History and Philosophy of Science* 33 (April 2002), pp. 649–660.

Shafton, A. *Dream Reader: Contemporary Approaches to the Understanding of Dreams.* SUNY series in Dream Studies, edited by Robert L. Van de Castle. State University of New York Press, 1995.

Shepard, R. N., and P. Hut. "My Experience, Your Experience, and the World We Experience: Turning the Hard Problem Upside Down." In *To-*

ward a Science of Consciousness II: The Second Tucson Discussions and Debates. A Bradford Book, MIT Press, 1998 (pp. 143–148).

Siegel, B. "Applications of Dreams and Drawings." *Association for the Study of Dreams Newsletter* 1:2 (1984), pp. 1–2.

Siegel, J. M. "The Evolution of REM Sleep." In *Handbook of Behavioral State Control.* CRC Press, 1999 (pp. 87–100).

Snyder, T., and J. Gackenbach. "Individual Differences Associated with Lucid Dreaming." In J. Gackenback and S. LaBerge, eds., *Conscious Mind, Sleeping Brain: Perspectives on Lucid Dreaming.* Plenum Press, 1988.

Solms, M. *The Neuropsychology of Dreams: A Clinico-Anatomical Study.* Lawrence Erlbaum Associates, 1997.

Solms, M., and O. Turnbull. *The Brain and the Inner World: An Introduction to the Neuroscience of Subjective Experience.* Other Press, 2002.

States, B. *Seeing in the Dark: Reflections on Dreams and Dreaming.* Yale University Press, 1997.

Stickgold, R., J. A. Hobson, R. Fosse, and M. Fosse. "Sleep, Learning and Dreams: Off-Line Memory Reprocessing." *Science* 294 (2001), pp. 1052–1057.

Stickgold, R., L. James, and J. A. Hobson. "Visual Discrimination Learning Requires Sleep after Training." *Nature Neuroscience* 3:12 (2002), pp. 1235–1236.

Stickgold, R., A. Malia, D. Maguire, D. Roddenberry, and M. O'Connor. "Replaying the Game: Hypnagogic Images in Normals and Amnesics." *Science* 290 (2000), pp. 350–353.

Strauch, I., and S. Lederbogen. "The Home Dreams and Waking Fantasies of Boys and Girls between Ages 9 and 15: A Longitudinal Study." *Dreaming* 9:2–3 (1999), pp. 153–161.

Tuller, D. "A Quiet Revolution for Those Prone to Nodding Off." *New York Times*, Jan. 8, 2002.

Van de Castle, R. *Our Dreaming Mind.* Ballantine, 1994.

Walker, M. P., T. Brakefield, A. Morgan, J. A. Hobson, and R. Stickgold. "Practice, with Sleep, Makes Perfect." *Neuron* 35 (2002), pp. 205–211.

Winson, J. *Brain and Psyche.* Anchor Press, 1985.

Index